Leisure Studies in a Global Era

Series Editors
Karl Spracklen, Leeds Beckett University, Leeds, UK
Karen Fox, University of Alberta, Edmonton, AB, Canada

In this book series, we defend leisure as a meaningful, theoretical, framing concept; and critical studies of leisure as a worthwhile intellectual and pedagogical activity. This is what makes this book series distinctive: we want to enhance the discipline of leisure studies and open it up to a richer range of ideas; and, conversely, we want sociology, cultural geographies and other social sciences and humanities to open up to engaging with critical and rigorous arguments from leisure studies. Getting beyond concerns about the grand project of leisure, we will use the series to demonstrate that leisure theory is central to understanding wider debates about identity, postmodernity and globalisation in contemporary societies across the world. The series combines the search for local, qualitatively rich accounts of everyday leisure with the international reach of debates in politics, leisure and social and cultural theory. In doing this, we will show that critical studies of leisure can and should continue to play a central role in understanding society. The scope will be global, striving to be truly international and truly diverse in the range of authors and topics.

Editorial Board
John Connell, Professor of Geography, University of Sydney, USA
Yoshitaka Mori, Associate Professor, Tokyo University of the Arts, Japan
Smitha Radhakrishnan, Assistant Professor, Wellesley College, USA
Diane M. Samdahl, Professor of Recreation and Leisure Studies, University of Georgia, USA
Chiung-Tzu Lucetta Tsai, Associate Professor, National Taipei University, Taiwan
Walter van Beek, Professor of Anthropology and Religion, Tilburg University, The Netherlands
Sharon D. Welch, Professor of Religion and Society, Meadville Theological School, Chicago, USA
Leslie Witz, Professor of History, University of the Western Cape, South Africa.

More information about this series at
http://www.palgrave.com/gp/series/14823

Tania Wiseman

Leisure in Later Life

palgrave
macmillan

Tania Wiseman
Robert Dodd Building
School of Health Sciences
Eastbourne, UK

Leisure Studies in a Global Era
ISBN 978-3-030-71671-4   ISBN 978-3-030-71672-1   (eBook)
https://doi.org/10.1007/978-3-030-71672-1

Cover image: © Maciej Bledowski/Alamy Stock Photo

This Palgrave Macmillan imprint is published by the registered company Springer Nature Switzerland AG
The registered company address is: Gewerbestrasse 11, 6330 Cham, Switzerland

Dedicated to John, who loved tea and biscuits, and Gavin, Katie and James, who I love with all of my heart, and with whom I hope to grow very, very old.

Preface: Clearing the Ground

I have always been curious about later life and what might be waiting for me if I live a very long time. In my early twenties I trained as an occupational therapist in order to help people with illness and disadvantages to be more engaged in their lives. I worked as a therapist with older people, once their basic needs were met I ensured that hobbies were not neglected so that there was a reason to get up and dressed when it was difficult. Cooking and gardening were the main activities that I adapted and adjusted to help people engage in their lives. Gardening took more effort but gave more reward. There were clinical settings where people never normally went outside, I rearranged them to accommodate mobility or other safety concerns so that people could feel the rain on their faces and get their hands in the soil. Chair gardening, palliative gardening and allotment gardening all increased people's motivation and improved clinical outcomes. I secured a part-time teaching post and soon I was modelling therapeutic use of gardening to occupational therapy students. Research in partnership with those students focused on the benefits of therapeutic gardening.

I took an additional part-time temporary research post, evaluating residents' experience of gardening in sheltered housing. This was my first experience of working with independent older people. It challenged the things I was reading and teaching about later life, my experience of older people was conditioned by illness, disability and power relations that led to compliant participation. My new experience of older people opened my eyes to a more enticing prospect of what might be waiting for me when I grow old.

An opportunity to lead a second gardening group presented. An Age UK programme leader approached me offering £500 funding to introduce a gardening group to a sheltered housing unit. My employer gave me scholarly activity time, so I used that to plan and implement a participatory project. My research students carried out literature reviews and evaluations, and we found that gardening and the outdoors were becoming hot topics.

My success in encouraging later life leisure gardening inspired this thesis, informed my role as a lecturer in occupational therapy, and directed my occupational therapy research students' work. At the beginning of my research journey, I focused on creating gardening groups with older people who lived in sheltered housing. What follows is a story about leisure transition in sheltered housing, this story highlights a research problem that became the focus of this book. In this preface to the main research, I draw on direct quotations and field notes from the gardens to present a coherent story from composite places (Mair, 2009). Real places, real people, real context, but blurred in order to provide anonymity for the people involved.

This story raises questions about how leisure is constrained in sheltered housing, and what this means for research on leisure in later life.

Week 1: 'What are you up to?'

Sick with nerves, I was finally preparing to meet with the residents, take a chance to repeat my gardening magic and get them gardening together. I had already visited on-site, secured funding from a national charity, ensured formal support from the landlords and assistance from the warden. I was walking into the unknown on my active ageing mission. Prior experience had taught me that I could expect just about anything, hence the nerves.

I had allowed myself to get too excited and invested, fighting down feelings of enthusiasm, imagining awesome success, writing papers and books, becoming a grand advisor on such matters. On that first late winter morning I was too nervous to eat breakfast, wondering how on earth I had got myself into this situation.

I drove to the house early, parked up and waited in my cosy camper van for half an hour. Then it was time to go and see what was waiting for me inside the house. The warden greeted me at the door with the funders and we walked into the lounge to meet the assembled group of twelve residents. Before we had settled into our seats the interrogation began on three fronts;

"Have the council sent you?.... What?? (Exaggerated surprise/horror) The lottery funded you? – they fund all those druggies - Are you going to grow cannabis? We know what you students are like!...What are you up to? No-one ever does anything nice for folk like us, not without wanting something in return".

I was not offended, I've heard worse. They spent an hour grilling me about my intentions, the other 'organisational' people were pinned back in their allocated parker knoll chairs, eyes wide, mouths neutral, wondering what they had walked into. Very early in the discussion, I told the group that there was a £500 budget and they would be able to choose how that was spent. At some point, tea and biscuits were provided and we started to imagine as a group what it would be like to do a little bit of gardening, spend some of that money. They were very wary, but I seemed harmless, so when I offered to provide some plants and suggested a small temporary project of herb planters, they agreed that might be OK. It was decided that I would plan, choose, buy, bring and organise it all. Then if there were any problems, with the other residents, or managers, that I would deal with that, and take it all away again. We established that Monday mornings would be a good time for all of us, I waved a cheery goodbye and told them I was looking forward to seeing them the following week. I had one loud flat reply from one of the residents.

"I probably won't be here."

The warden tried to lighten the moment, said she was really looking forward to doing some lovely gardening. We all paused and looked at each other in awkward silence. I left. All the way home in the van I was shaking my head, asking myself what on earth I was doing. I wasn't at all sure that there would be anyone there the following week. I was also concerned that it was early spring and the weather could be cruel. That difficult beginning balanced some of the power dynamics, but with time and distance, I now realise that it let me know how vulnerable they felt. They wanted me to feel some of their anxieties. I really did, every Sunday was a sleepless night, every Monday was an anxiety-fuelled breakfast-less start to the week.

Week 3: Business as usual

I sat with the group laughing, as usual, waiting for my cup of tea, talking about what we would do today, very much queen of the castle. I noticed it all, the slight bristling between a couple of the ladies, the overemphasis of certain words conveying the subversive nature of our mission. The way 'garden' was said in a quieter tone, almost inhaled, but with big mouth movements, mouthing the inappropriate words, as if garden was a naughty one. I sat deliberately with my back to the wall, encircled by my group. I could see the poster 'gardening group— all welcome', and the 'gardening update newsletter' was dotted around, inviting anyone in the housing complex to try a few of the herbs we had planted, or join us to do some gardening. Tea came, the chatter continued, what had happened since last week, the surprise that no one had complained, in fact everyone had been saying how nice it all looked. Then I saw her, standing a few feet away, halfway behind the pillar, in a blue checked housecoat, the kind that 1950s housewives wore. She was new, but clutching a pair of secateurs to her chest, ready uniformed and armed for some outdoors housework. When she caught my eye she stepped forward a pace and said quite loudly;

"I want to join your group"

I smiled and invited her to sit with us. I had saved a couple of seats with my bags and coat, and swiftly moved these into one, creating a space for her that meant she was directly in my line of sight, eye contact was continually refreshed until she was sitting, I smiled warmly and offered a hot drink, someone else provided it, asking all the questions that a stranger must answer—tea or coffee, how much milk? Sugar? Biscuits?— go on then, just one, the conventional restraint around eating biscuits. I deliberately took a second one and gave them a cheeky smile. Someone said, *"we'll work it all off in the garden anyway"*. Everyone dove for the biscuit tin, there was some confusion before it was passed in an orderly way around the circle. I noticed the lack of introductions, I paused to think. If I asked if they all knew each other, it may mean that neighbours of many years may have to admit to not knowing each other's names—so I went the informal route *"It's lovely to meet you – I'm Tania – I'm going to be coming for the next ten weeks to help set up the gardening group"*, *"Alice"* she said by way of return, the chatter continued and we decided to go out to the garden and decide what to do. The group slowly arranged the dirty cups and headed into the garden; I hung back with the new girl. The doors slid open and we were out in the spring sunshine. Alice was right beside me, as we crossed the threshold she paused, then muttered

"I've waited ten years to get into this garden".

She shot me a sideways glance—I smiled and raised my eyebrows to show her that I fully appreciated what she had said. She smiled a timid smile and we marched on into the garden together.

Week 4: Strength in numbers

We had been making great plans, the housing management had given us permission to cultivate the overgrown garden that used to be attached to the old wardens flat. We finished up our tea and wondered out together. In the corner of the garden was a gate and behind the gate was the most overgrown mess of a courtyard garden I have ever seen. We crammed into the small space that was left and tried to get an idea of what we were in for. We were about eight people, me, a caseworker from the funding charity, the warden and a handful of residents. We started to work, we chopped and pulled, carried and cleared. We piled it all out in the main garden. Half an hour in, we found the buried rotary washing line and that came out too. We moved 'the garden' out. There was enough to fill a large skip, it was gently chaotic, but we all just kept pulling and chopping and it started to shape up. Within an hour we were down to the last big tree, a couple of the men were fighting, hacking, digging, sawing. It was going nowhere. Then we all took it in turns to pull. We could see the roots, but they were so firmly stuck into the ground, we were all sweating, the sun was out and the tree was winning. Then Iris had an idea. She drove up to the tree, wrapped the branch around her good arm, put her chair in reverse and sped away. Everyone roared with laughter as the tree tore out of the ground, there was cheering and clapping, and even a whoop. She dragged it out and threw it onto the skip pile. There were many times in the garden where Iris was the strongest person. She was the only one that could carry compost over uneven ground, she could balance large pots, and trays of seedlings, no spillage, no strain, no problem!

When we had cleared up, I lifted the heavy patio slabs, and piled them up, we dug and hoed, and I relaid them in a way that would accommodate Iris' powered chair and settled them in. We added compost and dug it in. The morning was incredible; we were our own little ground-force, with me as the muscles, Iris as the power and the rest as the crew. Together we made sure the turning circle would work so she could reach every corner.

In the later discussions, the clearing of the garden was described as the most satisfying part of the gardening group, turning a wild overgrown area into a pretty and productive fruit and vegetable garden. It was physically challenging, but fun too with lots of laughter.

'everybody here is much more able than I am, … I've been in a chair for many years, you know and I haven't really done much, I did in the early days, with lectures … and stuff like that, but this was more of an achievement in my world than anything else.…When I got back upstairs I thought …excuse my language…that was bloody fantastic' (Iris)

Week 4 in detail: 'The shush in the garden'
The amazing day where we cleared the garden was so raucous and exciting, so vibrant and loud. The sun was beaming down at us and we were full of fun. We were all grinning at the antics and the progress, cheering as the big things fell. It was full of laughter, then suddenly Jenny

stood stock still, drawing everyone's attention and said in a very loud whisper;

"SHUSH, stop laughing, there's supposed to be old folk living here! What will the neighbours think? They'll get us thrown out."

The sudden stillness was broken as half of the group roared with laughter and the other half made them laugh even more by looking so perturbed at the idea of being expelled from the housing for having too much fun. Someone made a quip about ASGO's—anti social gardening orders, a play on the antisocial behaviour orders (ASBO's) associated with badly behaved teenagers. This really didn't help us to quieten down, *"you can get 5 years for that!"* Lottie quipped—*"I've already had 10"* said Alice. *"Count yourself lucky"* said Sam, the warden, *"I've been inside for 15 years – twenty to go!"*. *"20 years"* echoed Jenny, *"can you imagine?"* There was a pause as everyone imagined, then Ella jumped in with *"I'll be lucky if I make it through the night after all this digging"* and laughter was restored, but more subdued, more appropriate. Nothing that the neighbours would be complaining about.

Jenny was a very keen participant, but only while I was there. She didn't really like gardening, she enjoyed the fun, but it worried her. When she shushed us, she did actually want us to quieten down. She was genuinely expressing concern. It was swept away in a wave of jokes and laughter. I really didn't understand it at the time.

Two years after the first group meetings I visited after an invitation to see how well the garden was doing. While we sat drinking tea in the lounge people buzzed in and out of the garden. At first, my hosts began to name all the people that now used the garden, but eventually they realised that everyone that lived there regularly accessed the garden. Before we started only two residents used the garden regularly. The municipal space was claimed, new habits and routines developed. The garden was now a part of their home.

A meeting was arranged to share a book chapter with the gardening group. It was five years on, all of the main gardeners were there. It was amazing that after only twelve gardening mornings and a couple of follow up meetings, five years on, we fell into the same routine. Sit and establish purpose, relax and share tea and biscuits, tell me how it is. Jenny said she hadn't done any gardening except for when I was there. I thought often about Jenny's fear of being accused of not deserving the housing and support and how we had created the garden in a hidden part of the housing complex which allowed us privacy. No one seemed any older, not even me. I was at an impasse in my research and wanted to know if they would be interested in resurrecting the gardening group, the response was confusing:

> *"They've knocked down the wall now and flattened the garden – the council did it."*

I asked how they felt about that and they laughed,

> *"Relieved, I've got other things to be getting on with, travel and stuff. NOOOO don't make us do the gardening again, we did it for years, bloody garden!"*

They had let the garden go, expressing bluntly the idea of leisure as burden. Like Blackshaw's postmodern consumptive leisure butterflies (2010), they had moved on. Out into the garden, then out into the world, doing things that the neighbours would certainly have things to say about, but no longer so concerned.

Those explicit concerns about being seen to participate in fun active leisure in later life created a lot of questions. It was unclear if this was a function of living with strangers, negotiating this kind of tenancy, or part of leisure in later life more generally. This situation had so many confounding characteristics; the residents receiving social and financial support, the spatial politics of gardening, the intensive social nature of shared living space, the therapist-researcher intervention, novelty and entertainment in a static environment. In order to more fully understand leisure in later life, a study needed to be designed that radically simplified things.

I developed a sociological and leisure studies perspective during doctoral studies which enabled a deeper understanding of the nature of social pressures that can constrain leisure participation for some people.

In the work with people in sheltered housing to develop leisure gardening groups, the social pressures were very significant, they expressed feeling multiply disadvantaged and therefore felt they needed professional help to negotiate perceived constraints to leisure. My contribution was confusing for me because there is a strong active ageing metanarrative that supported my participation and theirs in this wholesome activity. This idea of active ageing led me to believe that the best thing people can do is be physically active and improve the environment of their home in a very inclusive and sociable way. Yet the anxieties about being heard having fun complicated it. Imagining other people watching, self-regulation, and fear of regulation by others frames the whole story of the gardening group and highlights the complexity of negotiating leisure in later life.

It transpired that they had physical capacity, educational capital and the motivation to do the gardening among themselves. My help was not educational, physical or motivational, it was more about professional negotiation of the spatial and social politics. Despite the professional support I provided they still expressed concerns about being observed enjoying themselves by neighbours and doubted their capacity to carry on gardening independently when my help stopped.

We do not know if fear of being viewed as hedonistic overshadowed the virtuous elements of the activity. We do not know if the fear was that laughter would attract attention and judgement and highlight that being old and ill does not mean being unable to enjoy participation. Or worse still, that they were old and not ill and in some sense, a fraud may be on display. Ideas about being old and being ill are joined together here because they are joined together in the culture of the housing complex, but we do not know if this is a sound couplet and if it exists elsewhere in relation to ageing. We really do not know very much about how leisure in later life is conditioned, but illness confuses it. Teasing these two things apart may enable a clearer picture of leisure in later life to be constructed. It is a problem that we may be applying ill and vulnerable roles to people, and they to themselves because they are old.

These small groups of gardeners expressed an explicit awareness of the social contract that they were engaged with in relation to their housing and other benefits, which meant that they could not admit to, or encourage, empowered views of themselves at leisure. They could not be frivolous in their leisure, they had a responsibility to participate in health and community promoting activities, so long as they were not fun. There is a huge gap in our understanding of leisure in later life.

The consequence of this for potential research was that the gardeners were cautious and concerned to be represented as recipients of therapy, rather than having fun doing something different. This limited the exploration of leisure with this group to its instrumental functions. I presented the work at conferences; audiences were astonished that the visibly aged participants in the pictures had created the gardens in the pictures; the gardener's capacities and my academic peers' perceptions of their capacities were unrelated. They would ask again and again who had actually made the garden, unable to perceive that the grey-haired participants had the physical capacities to uproot trees and plant and tend potatoes. I enjoyed telling them that the strongest person in the group was the lady in the powered wheelchair, not only had she pulled a tree from the ground with her reverse gear, but she could transport 40-litre bags of compost across uneven ground.

The shocking thing for me was that people either disbelieved me or wanted to know my 'secret' to motivating 'these people'. After conducting a literature review into leisure in sheltered housing I realised that my 'secret' was that I did not identify as middle class. My class, age, professional status and purpose, were all ambiguous; on one visit a staff member was shocked to hear that I, a student, had children, she demanded to know how old I was. The whole group stopped to listen, *my age* was a matter of public concern.

I conducted further research with people that visit gardens as part of the National Gardens Scheme and people that enjoy rambling, both highlighted a sense of duty and noble pursuit, and some muted enjoyment. That new work focused on outdoors 'active ageing' pursuits that people participated in independently of therapists, it was this combination of work with supported and independent leisure that led to my questioning concepts that underpin how we research leisure in later life.

A different kind of reductionism …

I had previously studied natural sciences and occupational therapy. Human geography, sociology and leisure studies came into the work. It became ungainly and confused, then I was asked:

"what if – and go with me on this – what if, we took out gardening and housing, re-write it without them?"

I took out therapy, gardening, housing, later life research, Rousseau's social contract, Bourdieu's markers of distinction, until there was a danger of there being nothing left. What remained was leisure, as freedom and choice and constraint and commodification (Spracklen, 2013), despite the concerns that leisure theory is contradictory and the concept of leisure is nebulous, the theoretical focus was leisure. The research transformed, it was no longer a local action research enquiry because the research that needed to be done was much further up the conceptual stream. The focus of the research went from the politics of negotiating gardening participation in shared housing to a much bolder investigation into the negotiation of leisure in later life. It was apparent in the gardens, in the conference rooms, in the written research and the media; that what we think is a suitable way to see leisure in later life, and the empirical day-to-day leisure lives of older adults, are very far apart.

Eastbourne, UK   Tania Wiseman

References

Blackshaw, T. (2010). *Leisure*. Abingdon: Routledge.
Mair, H. (2009). Club life: Third place and shared leisure in rural Canada. *Leisure Sciences, 31*(5), 450–465.
Spracklen, K. (2013). *Leisure at the end of modernity*. In T. Blackshaw (Ed.), Routledge Handbook of Leisure Studies (pp. 141–149). London: Routledge.

Acknowledgements

Sincerest thanks go to the Mass Observation Archivists, and the Trustees of the Mass Observation Archive, University of Sussex for the incredible work they do in nurturing a rich and sustainable research resource, and enabling those that choose to do so, to make their mark. To Neil Ravenscroft, Andrew Church and Paul Gilchrist, who gave me space to grow and provided a sturdy structure onto which I could cling. To the many occupational therapy students who made me think and joined me in my quest. To my colleagues, my gardening groups and the University of Brighton for supporting my precarious journey. To Gavin, Katie and James for their love and support. And to the Mass Observation Archive Correspondents who have taught me, my family and my students that we should look forward to later life and start practising for it yesterday.

Quotations Reproduced with permission of Curtis Brown Group Ltd, London on behalf of The Trustees of the Mass Observation Archive © The Trustees of the Mass Observation Archive.

Archive Materials

Directive full name	Year	Short name/code
http://www.massobs.org.uk/mass-observation-project-directives Use this link to view full directives as sent to correspondents.		
73: Autumn 2004 Directive Part 1: Being part of research	2004	research
81: Summer 2007 part two: You and gardens	2007	loss
82: Spring 2008 part two: Your lifeline	2008	lifeline[1]
88: Spring 2010. Part I. A working day. Day Diary for Wednesday, May 19, 2010	2010	Working day
89: Summer 2010 part one: Families and holidays	2010	holidays
91: Spring 2011 part two: Gambling and household	2011	Gambling

92: Summer 2011 part two: Ageing and care	2011	Ageing and care
95: Summer 2012 part three: The Diamond Jubilee 2nd – 5th June 2012	2012	Jubilee
98: Winter 2013 Part two: What makes you happy?	2013	Happy
99: Spring 2014 Part Three: Eurovision Evening Diary, May 10	2014	Eurovision
101: Autumn 2014 part one: The First World War	2014	Remembrance Sunday
102: Spring 2015 part two: The General Election	2015	Election day
104: Autumn 2015 part two: Bonfire Night	2015	Bonfire night

---

[1] The main directives are shaded in grey. The remainder are supplemental.

Contents

List of Figures

List of Tables

1

Introduction to a New Ageing Population

I suggested in the preface that the practice of treating old age as problematic has implications for leisure studies and may obscure our understanding of leisure in later life. This means that there may be some benefit in seeing leisure in later life from different perspectives. The apparent cause of the shush in the garden was a form of self-imposed sick role. If we attempt to untangle old age and illness and vulnerability, we may gain a different understanding of how people in later life negotiate leisure. It may not be possible to study later life leisure without the shush, but if the shush inhibits and inhabits leisure, it is worth trying.

We know that older people are not homogenous, and life moves at different paces for different individuals. A view of ageing that presumes that ill health is the destination, often considerably before death is not sound now, and may never have been. This view leads us to only one possibility, and therefore leads the research agenda towards fulfilling its presupposition that ageing is the inevitable progress toward infirmity and poverty. This is the image of later life that the shush in the garden was responding to, despite the gardeners' capabilities and comfortable lifestyles. There is huge variation in the onset and experience of old age.

© The Author(s), under exclusive license to Springer Nature Switzerland AG 2021
T. Wiseman, *Leisure in Later Life*, Leisure Studies in a Global Era,
https://doi.org/10.1007/978-3-030-71672-1_1

It is important to state here that I am aware that as people age they move closer to death, but the age of death is so variable that I believe age does not warrant its powerful influence as an organising factor in society, or the impact that this idea of being closer to death has on views of later life. I am also aware that many people develop age-related disabilities, or accumulate accidental damage, but it is not the case that most people in later life are frail or vulnerable, this is expanded upon in the background chapter. A central concern of this book is that a view of later life as problematic informs much leisure in later life research.

New ageing populations are emerging all over the world (United Nations, 2011). People are surviving into later life in greater numbers than ever before (ONS, 2015b), many of those people are healthy (Office for National Statistics, 2014a), which is a new phenomenon. The cultural context of a booming older generation in the twenty-first century has made later life leisure a hot research topic. Lifestyles are transforming, with active leisure very much a part of contemporary later life representation. We do not have much information about the lives and lifestyles of this new population.

When Lewis Carroll wrote his jovial poem:

You are old father William the young man said, and your hair has become very white, and yet you incessantly stand on your head, do you think at your age this is right? (Lewis Carroll, 1865)

'Old' meant something very different, but it was still a matter of concern. When Carrol was writing during the mid-Victorian period, life expectancy in England was under 45, with some very privileged people living into their seventies and eighties but this has changed. Life expectancy has risen, by 1900 it was 50, by the 1930s it was 60, by the 1950s it was 65 and by the time I was born in 1970 I could expect 72 years. Baby girls born in 2014 can look forward to 83 years, but many of them are predicted to reach the grand age of 120 (Office for National Statistics, 2015a). So the number of years has increased, and the proportion of those years in good health has also increased (Office for National Statistics, 2014a). This means that most people in England can look forward to confounding youth with their white-haired antics. This research recognises that the age of 'the old' has changed, and therefore the role of age as an organising factor in society should also be impacted. The idea of the vulnerable ager that underpins the shush in the garden is still operational, but there are alternative ideas that engage with conceptualisations of later life as a time of growth and self-development. Successful Ageing and Active Ageing are the most dominant, and their evolution and impact will be considered in the introduction chapter that follows.

It is a problem that we may be applying ill and vulnerable roles to people, and they to themselves because they are older. This may be constraining leisure in later life, causing inhibitions, and taking the fun out of leisure. This book explains an in-depth qualitative study that exposes and illustrates alternative stories about leisure in later life, in order to present a counter-narrative to challenge the current ideas of leisure in later life being useful only for instrumental purposes.

This chapter considers the shush in the garden and looks in more detail at some of the ideas that may help to explain it. The older population in the UK is considered in order to get a fuller picture of whether the shush extends beyond the garden of this supported housing complex. To do this it starts with an exploration of what most people in later life do and considers ideas about active ageing.

1.1   New Ageing Population

A new ageing population was noted at the beginning of this chapter, here the details of this are explored. In 2013, 19.6 million people in the UK were over 60, and this was predicted to increase to 31.1 million by 2037 (Office for National Statistics, 2013). Healthy life expectancy has increased at a greater rate than overall life expectancy in the UK which means that people are living longer healthier lives (Office for National Statistics, 2014a). It is very difficult to understand lifestyle with mean averages; cross-sectional studies can lack cultural and temporal detail. They also smooth out inequalities, unable to accommodate details such as men in the most deprived areas of the UK can expect 52 years in good health, compared with 71 years in more affluent areas (Office for National Statistics, 2014a). With more than six older people dying from the cold every hour in the winter in England and Wales (calculated by author from Office for National Statistics, 2014b) poverty in later life has an undeniable impact; one of the consequences of this is that poor people are likely to be disabled and die younger and therefore not be included in much later life research.

Poverty is not the final destination of old age; poverty and ill health come together, and the poorest members of British society are experiencing life expectancies well below the average. To add further to this argument, life expectancy in the UK has not increased since 2011, it has levelled in England, but in both Wales and Scotland it has fallen (Office for National Statistics, 2018). This decrease in life expectancy is not occurring in other European countries. Although life expectancy is starting to decline in the UK, the actual number of older people will continue to increase due to the large cohort of people born in the post-World War 2 period, that constitute the Baby Boomer generation.

Quality of life from the perspectives of older people in the UK was studied using mixed methods (Gabriel & Bowling, 2004). A research team surveyed 999 people, and 80 respondents were interviewed in-depth. Themes that emerged in support of quality of later life were brought forward by Horwitz (2014). These include sufficient income, staying well or as well as possible, being connected with meaningful participation, and feeling 'in control, happy, secure, at home, valued by others and that life has a purpose.' (Horwitz, 2014, p. 5). There are varied experiences of ageing even within small geographical areas, but most research focuses on frailty and vulnerability in later life (Humberstone, 2019).

Frailty of mind and body form part of a stereotypical image of later life. Of those that live into an extended later life the Alzheimer's Society states that one in six people over 80 have dementia (Alzheimer's Society, 2019), the estimates of projected increases work with the questionable assumption that people will live longer, but still become ill with the same frequency at the same ages as earlier cohorts. A robust systematic review contradicts this assumption and asserts that the incidence of dementia in the UK, and right across Europe is reducing, despite population ageing (Wu et al., 2016). Physical frailty, defined as "*a consequence of age-related decline in multiple physiological systems, which collectively results in a vulnerability to sudden health status changes triggered by relatively minor stressor events.*" (Clegg et al., 2013, p. 752) increases steadily with age, the rates of frailty are: 65–69 years: 4%; 70–74 years: 7%; 75–79 years: 9% 80–84 years: 16%; > 85 years: 26%. Dementia and frailty data combined suggest that most older people, even aged over 85, are not frail in body or mind. Some researchers measure later life from the age of 50, which is appropriate in socioeconomically disadvantaged areas, others from 65, from a traditional male retirement age in the UK, some focus on the '4th age' from 75 onwards. They are searching for a point at which most people will be reliably old, and if by this they mean infirm and poor, then the age increases as the group gets smaller because the heathiest and wealthiest are robust well past 85 years old. Ill health is not the final destination for all, and certainly not for an extended period of life for many people.

Feeling lonely is often associated with later life due to the correlation of age and death, and as a consequence of this perception it is a focus of research about the ageing population (Thomas, 2015). However, when it is considered in relation to the life course it becomes clear that loneliness can be a feature of all stages of life and is not a direct hazard of growing old. Middle-aged people perceived reduced social contact and increased loneliness, and this appears to make sense, reduced social contact correlates with loneliness. However, in the over 75 age group people report more social contact than all age groups apart from the under 24s but felt more lonely than all but the middle-aged group (Siegler et al., 2015). Joseph and Southcott (2019) studied line dancers with an average age of 65 and were surprised to find that loneliness was not reported, but many health benefits were, including brain training. Other studies relating to recent transitions did find that loneliness was a factor for recently retired or widowed Spanish participants reported taking up new activities to alleviate loneliness (Jaumot-Pascual et al., 2015), and loneliness was a driver of participation of men in coffee groups following retirement (Broughton et al., 2017). Reported loneliness may then relate to a recent loss. The average age of divorce is 43, death (of spouse) peaks at age

80, the loneliness peaks could be explained by this. It may be that what counts as meeting socially in middle age is interpreted differently in later life. It may be that the way that socialising and loneliness is measured needs to be adjusted according to life stage. It may be that the two constructs of socialising and loneliness are not on the same continuum. This idea is explored further next.

A cross-sectional study was carried out in order to explore the cultural participation of older adults (Toepoel, 2011). It used data from responses to an online panel of 5910 Dutch speaking respondents from the Netherlands. Social integration and leisure time were investigated in order to discover if social isolation and feelings of loneliness were higher for adults over 55. The measure of social contact was made using subjective and objective questions; people over 55 did report less social gatherings and less close relationships from age 65 onwards. They also reported more feelings of loneliness but felt more socially integrated. The objective questions were far more detailed than those in the European Social Survey represented in the graph above, and one conclusion drawn from this research was that "*Subjective measures of social integration (loneliness and feelings of social integration) were better explanatory variables for satisfaction with life than objective measures of social integration (number of social gatherings and number of close contacts)*" (Toepoel, 2011, p. 127). This suggests that quality of social interaction is more important than quantity. Mair (2009) explains the importance of intergenerational social integration and lifelong belonging to rural Canadian curling clubs as a way to address loneliness. The quantity of socialising does not correlate with feelings of loneliness. Throughout this research, attention will be paid to treating quantity and quality of social interaction as different constructs.

1.2   They Do Not Really Plan Old Age, but It Happens Anyway

In order to explore how people look forward to later life 1,867 people of all ages were surveyed by the National Centre for Social Research in face-to-face interviews in the summer of 2010, and many of them reported having no hopes or ambitions for life after 60, or for those already over 60 when surveyed, for the future (Humphrey et al., 2011). Drawing on the idea that work is key to social legitimacy in US society, cross-sectional research with 423, 55–75-year-old midwestern Americans showed that leisure attitudes and leisure self-efficacy are significant resources in shaping a sense of coherence on transition to retirement, and positive attitudes towards leisure help them to manage the increased free time, attitudes towards retirement were mediated by access to resources (Lee et al., 2020). The UK study found that many people had no hopes or ambitions for life after 60 (Humphrey et al., 2011).

On first inspection, this appears a rather bleak comment on how people view life after 60 in the UK. On closer examination, among those people aged 50–59 who report not having any hopes or ambitions for life over 60, 22% reported that they did not think they would be able to afford to do what they wanted, so their attitudes towards retirement are also mediated by access to resources. However more than half explain that they do not tend to plan out their lives in advance, reducing the usefulness of bodies of work that aim to assist in this planning process (such as Stebbins, 2013) and a further 22% said they see it as a chance to relax and do nothing (Humphrey et al., 2011), consistent with studies that note relaxation in leisure (Broughton et al., 2017; Choi et al., 2018; Gibson et al., 2003; Ryu & Heo, 2016). Multivariate analysis using logistical regression found that age, income, occupation and education were significant predictors of hopes and ambitions for later life (Humphrey et al., 2011). For those people that did report having some plans, travel, income planning, and deciding when to retire were most common, followed by plans about moving house or area (Humphrey et al., 2011). Given the relationships between increased age, income, occupation, education and having plans. Unsurprisingly, those with more money, make more plans around travel, income planning, choosing when to retire and perhaps moving home.

People that do indicate hopes and ambitions for an active life beyond 60 describe wanting to travel and enjoy leisure pursuits (Humphrey et al., 2011). This subset was the 'planners', and this included people who tend to have more money, so the data was narrowed down to mainly middle-class respondents reporting a middle-class range of activities. Details of what people of any age believe they might be interested in doing when they are over 60 were collated; the dataset excluded everyone that indicated that they felt too young to be thinking about life after 60. Their aspirations for their leisure life over 60 are noted in Table 1.1 (Humphrey et al., 2011). This middle-class focus of how active ageing is visually represented is noted by Martin (2011) who reports on flash images of fit older people driving sports cars on weekend mini-breaks and visiting galleries.

When this aspiration was broken down by age group of respondents there were big disparities. Travel and holidays slipped down from a peak of 88% of 35–49-year-olds dreaming of a retirement that involves holidays and travel, to a still substantial, 65% of the 65+ age group. Perhaps holidays lose their appeal, or financial constraints make them less important or possible. Despite this drop in interest, there is an active research agenda around later life leisure travel in the UK (Fox et al., 2017). Holidays are the most commonly expressed leisure aspiration (Humphrey et al., 2011), however in a study of actual participation in leisure activities watching television, socialising, reading, listening to music, shopping, eating out, gardening, and days out are the most popular free-time activities actually participated in by over 65's in the UK (Seddon, 2011). Although the leisure activity categories are not exactly the same, it is interesting to compare the aspirations of one study, with the actual participation reported in another from the same time. The following table is initially confusing, it helps to focus the literature that follows to explore how particular sets of activities have become a focus for researchers interested in the leisure lives of people in later life. The Humphrey et al. dataset offers activities congruent with a focus on active ageing, with culturally condoned activities for 'old people', the Seddon report had a broader focus, including more passive, relaxing leisure activities, so there are not many categories that overlap.

Where there is overlap of aspirations for leisure in later life and actual participation in leisure activities, only those who are already over 65 are reporting similar aspirations and actions. Those under 60 appear to be reporting their current activity as aspirations for later life, and willing it to continue, rather than choosing stereotypical later life activity profiles. It is worth noting that people anticipate their interests staying the same,

Table 1.1 Leisure: aspiration and actual participation in later life

Popular categories across both studies	What leisure activities/hobbies people aged 16–65 + aspired to, for when they are over 60 years old (Humphrey et al., 2011)	What leisure activities/hobbies people aged 65 + aspire to do when they are over 60 years old (Humphrey et al., 2011)	what aged 65 + report doing in their leisure time (Seddon, 2011)
Watching television			92%
Spending time with friends/family			82%
Reading	57%	66%	73%
Listening to music			69%
Shopping			69%
Eating out			65%
Travel/holidays	82%	65%	
Gardening	50%	58%	62%
Days out			59%
Visiting art galleries and museums and theatres	52%	51%	
Physical activity such as walking, cycling, swimming, dancing etc. Sports/exercise	69%	49%	35%
Going to pubs/bars/clubs			33%
Hobbies—painting cooking craft playing an instrument etc.	49%	41%	
Computing Internet/emailing	39%	40%	24%
Attending community/social groups	24%	22%	
Going to cinema			21%
Going to sporting events	35%	20%	

but they change, an example of this is well researched in relation to sports in later life where older adults consistently transition from team sports to individual sports (Murtagh et al., 2014). Although what people do changes, their habits do partly track into later life (Hamer et al., 2012). It is important to note that leisure activities, apart from computing and gardening were linked to income, education and occupation (Humphrey et al., 2011). For each additional indicator of adverse socioeconomic position, physical activity reduces further (Hillsdon et al., 2008).

There is a broad spread of leisure activities that people report doing, including watching television. The full study reports age-related differences in listening to music, sport/exercise, attending cinema, going to pubs and clubs, all decreasing with age. Watching TV and reading increased slightly with increased age, supporting ideas of more time spent at home in later life, in home-based leisure (Seddon, 2011). Overall, holidays are the most popular leisure aspiration, and gardening and reading are the most popular home-based leisure activities chosen by the over sixties, for the over sixties (Humphrey et al., 2011), and are even more popular than predicted. Activities including sports and computing are much less popular than anticipated.

There is a disparity between the aspirations for active leisure and the actual participation in active leisure. Home-based passive activities such as watching television and reading increase slightly with increased age, and sport/exercise and going out decrease dramatically (Seddon, 2011). It is recommended that people participate in 150 minutes of physical activity a week (Hillsdon et al., 2008), but research demonstrates that only two-thirds of older people report participating in any active leisure at all, with just 10% reporting any physical exercise, and the influence of cultural and material disadvantage is powerful (Chatzitheochari & Arber, 2011). Aspirations and actual participation in physical activities are so far apart that a deeper consideration of what is happening in people's leisure lives is warranted. Systematic reviews examining the health impact of leisure in later life are critical of how leisure is conceptualised in the research to date (Adams et al., 2011; Fallahpour et al., 2016). Leisure researchers present a range of different perspectives on leisure that help to explore the gap between active leisure aspirations and participation which will be explored in the literature review, but it is important to first consider how satisfied people are with their later leisure lives and what people actually do in later life. The Taking Part Survey from the Department for Culture, Media and Sport aims to capture trends in participation, and consistently finds that passive pastimes are most popular with all age groups (Department Culture Media and Sport, 2014). More than half of people, aged over 50, reported that they were generally satisfied with the amount of leisure time that they have (Joloza, 2013). The proportion of satisfied people increases with age, up to and past normal retirement age. Joloza (2013) also found that 91% of people that were satisfied with the amount of leisure time, were satisfied with life overall.

Although people are more likely to live alone in later life (Age UK, 2014), and not go out as much (Brownsell et al., 2008), and therefore participate in home-based leisure activities, people aged between 65–79 are more likely to report higher levels of life satisfaction, worthwhile activities and happiness, and lower levels of anxiety than working age people (Thomas, 2015). Well-being begins to reduce again over the age of 80, but is still higher than that of working-age people (Thomas, 2015).

An open-access data source, The English Longitudinal Study of Ageing (ELSA) established a panel of 11, 391 representative men and women between the ages of 50–100 living in England in 2001. It has collected economic, social, psychological, cognitive, health data every two years since 2002, using self-completion questionnaires, computer-assisted personal interviews and nurse visits for biological and genetic biomarker assessment every 4 years. ELSA is linked to financial and health registry data. The dataset is openly available and had resulted in over 130 studies by 2012 (Steptoe et al., 2013). This is a powerful resource for exploring relationships between quantifiable items. This dataset has been used to explore the relationship between happiness and the quality and length of later life. Even after health and loneliness and socioeconomic factors are controlled for, greater enjoyment of life is associated with a 28% lower mortality risk (Steptoe & Wardle, 2012), this has led to a suggestion that "*The link between enjoyment and survival at older ages is not fully accounted for by demographic factors or major pre-existing illnesses… efforts to improve enjoyment of life, as well to manage and prevent disease, could have beneficial effects on life expectancy.*" (Steptoe & Wardle, 2012, p. 273).

A six-year longitudinal study of activity and successful ageing found that levels of activity related to happiness, but not life satisfaction (Menec, 2003). Menec (2003) further suggests that life satisfaction found in prior cross-sectional studies is a precursor rather than a consequence of activity. An acknowledged weakness of this study is that it did not measure the frequency or intensity of activities (Menec, 2003), despite this it is reported here because the one activity that did show a correlation with life satisfaction was sports participation. By chance, this was inadvertently more quantifiable, in that it was the only activity that was measured by Menec that also has culturally agreed parameters that mean it was likely that people participated actively for more than a few minutes. This may in part explain the focus on these minority sports focused activities in leisure studies in later life. This raises the question of whether better measures of participation in the other activities might also show increased life satisfaction in a range of leisure activities. However, the link between happiness and activity is clear in all of the studies discussed, with or without feelings of satisfaction. Adding life to years (Havighurst, 1961) requires enjoyment (Steptoe & Wardle, 2012).

1.3   Good and Bad Leisure in Later Life

Some research findings challenge conventional wisdom; such as drinking alcohol increases life expectancy for regular drinkers aged over 65 (Ronksley et al., 2011). There is also research that evaluates cultural participation in passive physiologically identical activities having different health benefits, a good example is the strange categorizations noted in a systematic review that is found with reading, with reading books being categorised as active and health promoting; and reading magazines being categorised as passive and therefore health reducing (Fallahpour et al., 2016). This kind of positivist research with no critical explanation of how this can work requires a review. If positivist is the paradigm then it should be followed through. How can a rational researcher separate these two activities? If anything, magazines are bigger and require larger movements, and more frequent page-turning, potentially resulting in more activity. There is much more new material, ideas, connection with the world and other people in gossip magazines than in books. Much more potential to discuss and debate the latest gossip, share intergenerational concerns, thus building social bonds and group identity. Or it may be that there is a common cause with reading books being a mark of distinction.

Quantitative research has limits in this area of study. The research that supports this enquiry and is cited in the introduction and this background chapter leads to the conclusion that being born lucky is the best thing a person can do for their health in later life. After that, it appears that being happy and not smoking are important. So a focus on happiness is warranted, the past cannot be changed, but happiness has some potential. A synthesis of these studies suggests that satisfaction with leisure time is linked to satisfaction with life (Joloza, 2013), but the intensity of the activities may play a part (Menec, 2003). Enjoyment of life is linked with longer healthier lives (Steptoe & Wardle, 2012). So leisure may be important for the enjoyment that it brings, or it because people are feeling good about themselves for 'doing the right thing' thus experiencing 'cultural consonance' as a result (Dressler, 2012). However, cultural consonance is problematic as an explanation, because we know that the 'right thing' is physically active leisure, and this is not what people are actually doing (Nimrod & Shrira, 2016). People are happy and living longer healthier lives and they are generally passive in their lifestyles, and the people in my gardening group worried about being judged for enjoying an active, fun leisure pastime.

1.4 Active Ageing

It is worth spending a little time here unpacking the idea that being active is good for people. Successful ageing is widely discussed in gerontology (Cooney & Curl, 2019), initially introduced into gerontology in 1960s, to balance ideas about withdrawal from society being a natural part of ageing (Havighurst, 1961; Katz, 2013). *'a theory of successful aging is a statement of the conditions of individual and social life under which the individual person gets a maximum of satisfactions for the various groups that make it up…the greatest good for the greatest number.'* (Havinghurst 1961, p. 8). There were two competing forms of successful ageing in support of this definition, The Activity Theory which meant the *'maintenance as far and as long as possible of the activities and attitudes of middle age* (1961, p. 8) And Disengagement Theory, where successful aging meant *'acceptance and the desire for a process of disengagement from active life'* (1961, p. 8). Activity Theory influenced leisure studies in the 1980s (Godbey et al., 2010), and USA policy by the late 1990s. A concept of 'adding life to the years' survived, but where it is being carried forward in policy the focus is on studying specific behaviours of people who have lived long, and the main behaviour is that of being 'active', and the ambition is to 'add years to life'. Successful ageing focused on activity theory, and morphed into Active Ageing, although both terms continue to be used, they are used in the individualistic sense, not the original societal sense. The increase in the proportion of people reaching later life internationally has led to the adoption of the principles of active ageing by the World Health Organisation (World Health Organization, 2002). Later life is approached in research as if trying to prevent, postpone, or repair illness or disability, with this comes social responsibility to take care of an ageing self, and being active is the focus of this self-care (Higgs et al., 2009). The United Nations principles of independence, participation, dignity, care and self-fulfilment reflect the relatively recent move from a passive to an active conceptualisation of later life (United Nations, 2011). Social policy and health concerns are the primary routes of enquiry in later life research (Leontowitsch, 2012). Variations on a theme of successful ageing have been under academic scrutiny since the 1960s (see for example; Boudiny, 2013; Havighurst, 1961; Jolanki, 2004, 2008; Katz, 2000, 2013, 2018; Lassen, 2014). All through life there are structural drivers to control the leisure pursuits of people and many of these are health-related, and in this way, people are subject to the active ageing ideas throughout their lives. Of course, people wish to maintain good health, but the idea of active ageing has become a meta-narrative and overplays the control that an individual has over their own health (Gard et al., 2017). There is an alternative view to this, but it is not comfortable to read about because it appears deterministic, it is supported by demographic studies and is considered next.

1.5   Life Course Perspective

This broader perspective, beyond self-care responsibility, considers social context as essential to understanding lives through time and is called the 'life course perspective' (Ferraro, 2016). This fits well with studies of leisure in later life that lean towards a more universalist view of leisure (Roberts, 2013). Cain's (1964) seminal work explored and set the scene for life course research, the timeline of the 'life course lens' runs alongside that of 'active ageing'. Cain's work was developed by Elder throughout the 1970s (Elder, 1999), and the resulting body of work has produced extensive evidence about the ways that context shapes lives. The long arm of childhood, some of the effects of which reach from before conception, appears to have an enormous influence on the life course (Kemp et al., 2018). Specifically, childhood socioeconomic circumstances are closely related to mortality and morbidity (Warren, 2016), and cognitive ability in later life (Foverskov et al., 2019). Childhood socioeconomic conditions have a lasting influence on adult health which may be independent of adult health and socioeconomic status (Hayward & Gorman, 2004; Henretta & McCrory, 2016; Pavela & Latham, 2016; Warren, 2016; Whitley et al., 2018). Poverty in earlier life carries through into later life and shortens it (Tampubolon, 2015). Engagement in outdoor active leisure pastimes is researched in relation to the life course (Hickman et al., 2018; Wheaton, 2017). The powerful influence of genetics and socioeconomic disadvantage or advantage are compounded throughout life (Cooney & Curl, 2019; Tampubolon, 2015), and it can appear that much of morbidity and mortality is pre-determined (Henretta & McCrory, 2016), but just because it is this way, it does not mean that it has to be this way, and although the remainder of this book will focus on the more privileged survivors, it is with hope of informing researchers to ask better questions for all.

Laslett is credited with naming a 'third age' of the life course (1989), in effect bringing these two ideas of successful ageing and the life course perspective together. He described a cohort of people who benefitted from collective advantages of the United Kingdom's post-war economy and social and health care system (Richards et al., 2012). Laslett was a historian with a keen interest in improving later life, and co-founder of the University of the Third Age in the UK (Manley, 2003). The third age focused on a new stage of healthy leisured life, which worked well with the idea of active ageing because it grew up in that context, as did the researchers and the people entering later life at that time. But the idea of the third age was so set in the individualistic active ageing ideals that it ignored some of the implications of the life course perspective, particularly those that identify structural contributors to healthy ageing inequalities. Despite clear demographic information that people 'age' at different rates the third age was set at 65–74. In the years that followed research considering the third age in leisure studies was rich and diverse, but overshadowed by medical research that pathologised ageing (Humberstone, 2010). The 'fourth age', 75+, has become the focus of 'traditional' later life research into infirmity and poverty (Gilleard et al., 2005). Dannefer et al. (2016) suggest that this body of work still relies on functional assumptions about the individuals' control of an ageing body which inhibit the deep exploration of how social forces influence lives. There is an emerging literature that supports a fuller consideration of the life course approach within ageing research. It questions some of the underpinning constructs of an active ageing approach, but it is nevertheless situated in a paradigm of loss of function that is related to ageing (Cooney & Curl, 2019; Mejía et al., 2017). At a recent conference presentation, a world-leading critic of the concept of active ageing suggested, perhaps ironically, the idea of introducing the fifth age, because fourth agers did not appear to be sufficiently conforming to their stage (Katz, 2018). 'Fourth agers' are getting 'too good', like my gardeners, they are not playing their roles cautiously, and this is confusing onlookers.

It is not clear if it was specifically the activity that my gardeners were concerned about, but the fun in it was certainly a threat. The life course lens could have an impact, we could consider the implications of the residents' status as council tenants in receipt of supported housing that relates to their reduced-health status. It may be entirely reasonable that these gardeners could not engage publicly with productive activities, demonstrating strength and fitness, and having fun doing so may even be a danger to their tenancy. A simple explanation could be had here, but how could these 'poor sick people' be passive agers for, in some cases, over 10 years, then shake that off after a few mornings of gardening? This explanation is too simple, there must be a richer story to tell about leisure in later life than one about how perceived stereotyping takes the fun out of leisure. The majority of people in later life are fit and happy and own their own homes, and are relatively inactive. Does the spectre of 'vulnerable old people' impact on how they negotiate the complexity of metanarratives of ageing, what engagement with these ideas or concern about how they are portrayed can be anticipated from older people who do not identify with this stereotype?

Leisure scholars do not simplify leisure participation as wholesome and healthy, they highlight that there is confusion about what is meant by 'activity' in the active ageing that it is recommended but not done by most people (Genoe et al., 2018; Liechty et al., 2017). There are more nuanced understandings about the part that leisure can play in lives. Veblen's ideas of 'exploit and drudgery' (2007) and Critcher's explanation of 'moral regulation' concepts (Yeomans & Critcher, 2013) support understanding of human flourishing through leisure as a complex negotiation between self and others. Leisure participation is not a straightforward combination of opportunity and interest. Historical perspectives explained by Spracklen are essential to understanding leisure, where people have always tried to find comfort and self-expression in the time and spaces they are able to save for themselves, but are always finding stronger forces in tradition, religion, government, or economic inequality that try to keep them in their place (Spracklen, 2011). In this way, people have always been subject to social and cultural pressures to perform culturally consonant leisure lives. The pressure to perform as an 'old person' is not unique to this time, the pressure to turn leisure to instrumental purposes is also not new but this large population of relatively healthy, happy older people living a retirement lifestyle is new, and they appear to be feeling in control, and enjoying their lives, and that is worth a closer look. Crouch adds a call for more contextualised research in a variety of settings '*there remains significant complementary progress to be made in terms of more dispersed, nuanced happenings in the gentle space and politics of everyday life'* (2016, p. 3). Leisure theory is rich and complex and leisure is a contested concept, the comparatively simple approach to leisure is taken in active ageing research does not engage fully with the complexity of leisure practices (Clarke & Warren, 2007) or theory (Adams et al., 2011; Fallahpour et al., 2016). The concept of leisure as 'freely chosen activities' that have fortunate instrumental health outcomes is widely used in active ageing research and this is reasonable; but the idea that a 'freely chosen activity' can be legislated for, that is inherent in active ageing approaches to later life, is contradictory. Leisure is about choice and freedom, and yet it is being legislated for, with instrumental drivers supporting this. This is further complicated by ability and disability, and resources in the form of finance and social relationships, which are both further complicated by a negative age association.

The idea behind active ageing of 'adding life to the years' links with Glyptis' (1989) tentative assertion that leisure for the sake of enjoyment should be an adequate rationale for public support. Her ideas were developed around another economically inactive group; unemployed people; but now appear more current than ever in appealing against the political incoherence in leisure policy that can support leisure only if other instrumental reasons, such as health, are the primary motivation (Glyptis, 1989). This instrumental approach to leisure raises fundamental questions about the nature of leisure, and particularly leisure in later life. If taking Blackshaw's (2010) self-development freely chosen approach, such 'active ageing' activities cease to be leisure. Even Rojek (2010) in his structuralist approach accepts that there is at least perceived freedom in leisure choices. This raises the questions of whether activity is still leisure if it is appropriated by 'active ageing' drivers. These concerns mean that when research about twenty-first-century later life leisure in the UK focuses on instrumental outcomes, it presupposes too much, about both leisure and later life, and suitable leisure for later life. It presupposes that health is a primary constraint, and that prevention of ill health is a primary driver. These presuppositions create a knowledge gap that stop researchers from finding out how leisure is negotiated.

Leisure studies and gerontology share the idea that poor motivation to participate in health enhancing activities is due to a limited understanding of what is good for us (Godbey et al., 2010). This idea has supported the case for public health education on active ageing (United Nations Economic Commission for Europe, 2012; World Health Organization, 2002). Active ageing education encourages participation in a wide range of activities by explaining the health and well-being gains that can be achieved through mainly leisure-based activities. In the UK volunteering (Department for Work and Pensions, 2012) was a key focus, but research demonstrating the lifelong nature of volunteering has turned the focus to young people (Cooney, 2017; Lindsey et al., 2016). Current strategies include active sports participation (Sport England, 2016) and continued work (Department for Business Energy and Industrial Strategy, 2019; Department for Work and Pensions, 2012) to support healthy ageing. Health guidelines promote the benefits of leisure-linked interventions such as walking groups and balance training (Sherrington et al., 2019; NICE, 2015), and social prescribing of leisurely activities is core to the new long-term NHS plan (Alderwick & Dixon, 2019). Content analysis I conducted of the most recent guidance on 'living well for longer' from the Department of Health and Social Care, UK (Department of Health and Social Care, 2018) reveals it features the words 'volunteering' twice, 'exercise' twice, 'leisure' twice and 'work' 108 times. This may indicate shifting priorities as work starts to take a leading role in discussions around living well. Leisure focused research projects have explored morbidity, mortality and quality of life in support of the idea that active ageing is health-promoting, and it does appear that people with active ageing lifestyles have better outcomes in all of these measures (Menec, 2003). There is debate about whether the association between health and activities is causal or has a common cause.

Is the shush the echo of withdrawal theory haunting the garden? Are active ageing initiatives battling it? To complicate this simple battle of the metanarratives, we could consider that active ageing is dependent upon ideas of disability and vulnerability being associated with later life, people are active to delay withdrawal. The story of withdrawal only makes sense in relation to it following on from an active life, they define each other, like life and death, and they can come to take on those meanings. There are public health messages generated in the drive for additional exercise, healthy eating and civic and educational engagement, but it is not clear how it is received and managed, only that it is not much acted upon by most people in later life. There is a partial explanation for the people in my sheltered housing gardening group, and their social situation obscures understanding much more about it with them as informants. However, it is known that most people in later life are not engaged with physical activity, so the general population of healthy people in later life would make good informants about how active ageing ideas play out in everyday later life. These inhibitions are not unique to my gardeners, leisure theorists suggest that leisure has always been influenced by powerful external forces. There are many healthy but 'inactive' people in later life, further investigation is needed to understand if and how the shush could be impacting other leisure lives. There are two paradoxes in later life leisure studies. The big one is that these 'old people' that 'need help' to be 'more active', report feeling happier than the majority of younger people in many countries (Kusumastuti et al., 2016). The second one is that despite more and more research evidence about 'what is good for them', active leisure; people do more and more of what is 'bad for them', passive leisure (Phoenix & Bell, 2019), and yet they are living longer and healthier lives than ever. Enjoyment is linked with longer healthier lives, independently of other more tangible health-promoting elements, such as exercise (Steptoe et al., 2013). There needs to be space to ask if the instrumental components of leisure activities that tend to get the most credit for improving quality of life are as important as they appear to be. There needs to be space for people who enjoy hanging out with friends and family, listening to music and watching television (Seddon, 2011) to speak and be heard.

In order to better understand the paradoxes in leisure in later life, the literature review that follows examines what research about leisure constraints brings to understanding the impact of active ageing on leisure in later life. With complex drivers in the background, and so much research responding to a problematised ageing population, the following literature review addresses what is known about constraints to leisure in healthy later life.

References

Adams, K. B., Leibbrandt, S., & Moon, H. (2011). A critical review of the literature on social and leisure activity and wellbeing in later life. *Ageing & Society, 31*(04), 683–712.

Age UK. (2014). Later life in the United Kingdom. Retrieved from http://www.ageuk.org.uk/Documents/EN-GB/Factsheets/Later_Life_UK_factsheet.pdf?dtrk=true.

Alderwick, H., & Dixon, J. (2019). The NHS long term plan. *BMJ (Online), 364*.

Alzheimer's Society. (2019). *Facts for the media.* Retrieved February 3, 2019, from https://www.alzheimers.org.uk/about-us/news-and-media/facts-media?documentID=535&pageNumber=2.

Blackshaw, T. (2010). *Leisure.* Routledge.

Boudiny, K. (2013). "Active ageing": From empty rhetoric to effective policy tool. *Ageing & Society, 33*(6), 1077–1098.

Broughton, K. A., Payne, L., & Liechty, T. (2017). An exploration of older men's social lives and well-being in the context of a coffee group. *Leisure Sciences, 39*(3), 261–276.

Brownsell, S., Blackburn, S., & Hawley, M. S. (2008). Evaluating the impact of 2nd and 3rd generation telecare services in older people's housing. *Journal of Telemedicine and Telecare, 14,* 8–12.

Cain, L. (1964). Life course and social structure. In R. E. L. Faris (Ed.), *Handbook of modern sociology* (pp. 272–309). Chicago: Rand McNally.

Carroll, L. (1865). *Alices adventures in wonderland.* London: Macmillan.

Chatzitheochari, S., & Arber, S. (2011). Identifying the third agers: An analysis of British retirees' leisure pursuits. *Sociological Research Online, 16*(4), 1–12. Retrieved from http://www.socresonline.org.uk/16/4/3.html.

Choi, W., Liechty, T., Naar, J. J., West, S., Wong, J. D., & Son, J. (2018). "We're a family and that gives me joy": Exploring interpersonal relationships in older women's softball using socio-emotional selectivity theory. *Leisure Sciences, 0*(0), 1–18.

Clarke, A., & Warren, L. (2007). Hopes, fears and expectations about the future: What do older people's stories tell us about active ageing? *Ageing and Society, 27*(04), 465–488.

Clegg, A., Young, J., Iliffe, S., Olde Rikkert, M. G. M., & Rockwood, K. (2013). Frailty in older people summary. *Lancet, 381*(9868), 752–762. https://doi.org/10.1016/S0140-6736(12)62167-9.Frailty.

Cooney, R. (2017). *Government begins consultation on volunteering and young people | Third Sector*. Retrieved February 3, 2019, from https://www.thirds ector.co.uk/government-begins-consultation-volunteering-young-people/vol unteering/article/1443960.

Cooney, T. M., & Curl, A. L. (2019). Transitioning from successful aging: A life course approach. *Journal of Aging and Health, 31*(3), 528–551.

Crouch, D. (2016). *Flirting with Space: Journeys and creativity*. London: Routledge.

Dannefer, D., Kelley-Moore, J., & Huang, W. (2016). Handbook of the life course. In M. J. Shanahan & E. Al. (Eds.) (paperback, p. 23). Springer International Publishing.

Department Culture Media and Sport. (2014). Taking Part 2014 / 15 Quarter 2 (December).

Department for Business Energy and Industrial Strategy. (2019). *The grand challenge missions—GOV.UK*. Retrieved February 3, 2019, from https:// www.gov.uk/government/publications/industrial-strategy-the-grand-challe nges/missions#healthy-lives.

Department for Work and Pensions. (2012). *Preparing for an ageing society: Evaluating the ageing well programme parts 1 and 2*. London: DWP.

Department of Health and Social Care. (2018). *Prevention is better than cure: our vision to help you live well for longer—GOV.UK*. Retrieved February 3, 2019 from https://www.gov.uk/government/publications/prevention-is-better-than-cure-our-vision-to-help-you-live-well-for-longer.

Dressler, W. W. (2012). Cultural consonance: Linking culture, the individual and health. *Preventive Medicine, 55*(5), 390–393.

Elder, G. H. (1999). *Children of the great depression: Social change in life experience*. Boulder: Westview Press.

Fallahpour, M., Borell, L., Luborsky, M., & Nygård, L. (2016). Leisure-activity participation to prevent later-life cognitive decline: A systematic review. *Scandinavian Journal of Occupational Therapy, 23*(3), 162–197.

Ferraro, K. F. (2016). Life course lens on aging and health. In *Handbook of the life course* (pp. 389–406). Springer International Publishing.

Foverskov, E., Mortensen, E. L., Holm, A., Pedersen, J. L. M., Osler, M., & Lund, R. (2019). Socioeconomic position across the life course and cognitive ability later in life: The importance of considering early cognitive ability. *Journal of Aging and Health, 31*(6), 947–966.

Fox, E., Hitchings, R., Day, R., & Venn, S. (2017). Demanding distances in later life leisure travel. *Geoforum, 82*(March), 102–111.

Gabriel, Z., & Bowling, A. (2004). Quality of life from the perspectives of older people. *Ageing & Society, 24*(5), 675–691.

Gard, M., Dionigi, R. A., Horton, S., Baker, J., Weir, P., & Dionigi, C. (2017). The normalization of sport for older people? *Annals of Leisure Research, 20*(3), 253–272.

Genoe, R., Kulczycki, C., Marston, H., Freeman, S., Musselwhite, C., & Rutherford, H. (2018). E-Leisure and older adults: Findings from an international exploratory study. *Therapeutic Recreation Journal, 52*(1), 1–18.

Gibson, H., Ashton-Shaeffer, C., Green, J., & Autry, C. (2003). Leisure in the lives of retirement-aged women: Conversations about leisure and life. *Leisure/Loisir, 28*(3–4), 203–230.

Gilleard, C., Higgs, P., Hyde, M., Wiggins, R., & Blane, D. (2005). Class, cohort, and consumption: The British experience of the third age. *The Journals of Gerontology. Series B, Psychological Sciences and Social Sciences, 60*(6), S305–S310. Retrieved from http://www.ncbi.nlm.nih.gov/pubmed/16260712.

Glyptis, S. (1989). *Leisure and unemployment.* Open University Press.

Godbey, G., Crawford, D., & Shen, X. S. (2010). Assessing heirachical leisure constraints theory after two decades. *Journal of Leisure Research, 42*(1), 111–134.

Hamer, M., Kivimaki, M., & Steptoe, A. (2012). Longitudinal patterns in physical activity and sedentary behaviour from mid-life to early old age: A substudy of the Whitehall II cohort. *Journal of Epidemiology and Community Health, 66*(12), 1110–1115.

Havighurst, R. J. (1961). Successful aging. *The Gerontologist, 1*(1), 8–13.

Hayward, M. D., & Gorman, B. K. (2004). The long arm of childhood: The influence of early-life social conditions on men's mortality. *Source: Demography, 41*(1), 87–107.

Henretta, J. C., & McCrory, C. (2016). Childhood circumstances and mid-life functional mobility. *Journal of Aging Health, 28*(3), 440–459.

Hickman, M., Stokes, P., Gammon, S., Beard, C., & Inkster, A. (2018). Moments like diamonds in space: Savoring the ageing process through positive engagement with adventure sports. *Annals of Leisure Research, 21*(5), 612–630.

Higgs, P., Leontowitsch, M., Stevenson, F., & Jones, I. R. (2009). Not just old and sick—The 'will to health' in later life. *Ageing & Society, 29*(05), 687.

Hillsdon, M., Lawlor, D. A., Ebrahim, S., & Morris, J. N. (2008). Physical activity in older women: Associations with area deprivation and with socioeconomic position over the life course: Observations in the British Women's

Heart and Health Study. *Journal of Epidemiology and Community Health,* *62*(4), 344–350.

Horwitz, W. (2014). *Looking forward to later life.* London.

Humberstone, B. (2010). *Third age and leisure research : Principles and practice* (B. Humberstone, Ed.). Leisure Studies Association.

Humberstone, B. (2019). Embodied life-long learning in nature, narratives and older bodies -'quit or crash'. *Journal of Adventure Education and Outdoor Learning, 19*(2), 101–110.

Humphrey, A., Lee, L., & Green, R. (2011). Aspirations for later life: A report of research carried out by the National Centre for Social Research on behalf of the Department for Work and Pensions (Research Report No. 737). *(Research Report No 737),* (737). Retrieved from http://dera.ioe.ac.uk/3563/1/rrep737.pdf.

Jaumot-Pascual, N., Monteagudo, M. J., Kleiber, D. A., & Cuenca, J. (2015). Gender differences in meaningful leisure following major later life events. *Journal of Leisure Research, 8*(1), 83–103.

Jolanki, O. (2004). Moral argumentation in talk about health and old age. *Health: An Interdisciplinary Journal for the Social Study of Health, Illness and Medicine, 8*(4), 483–503.

Jolanki, O. (2008). Discussing responsibility and ways of influencing health. *International Journal of Ageing and Later Life Introduction, 3*(1), 45–76.

Joloza, T. (2013). *Measuring national well-being : Older people's leisure time and volunteering.*

Joseph, D., & Southcott, J. (2019). Meanings of leisure for older people: An Australian study of line dancing. *Leisure Studies, 38*(1), 74–87.

Katz, S. (2000). Busy bodies: Activity, aging, and the management of everyday life. *Journal of Aging Studies, 14*(2), 135–152.

Katz, S. (2013). Active and successful aging: Lifestyle as a gerontological idea. *Recherches Sociologiques et Anthropologiques [En Ligne], 44*(1), retrieved online 7/2/14 URL http://rsa.revues.or.

Katz, S. (2018). Livable longevity: Remaking survivorship in old age. In *XIX ISA World Congress of Sociology* (p. Paper presentation 21st July 2018). Retrieved from https://isaconf.confex.com/isaconf/wc2018/webprogram/Paper90209.html.

Kemp, B. R., Ferraro, K. F., Morton, P. M., & Mustillo, S. A. (2018). Early origins of adult cancer risk among men and women: Influence of childhood misfortune?. *Journal of Aging and Health, 30*(1), 140–163.

Kusumastuti, S., Derks, M. G. M., Tellier, S., Di Nucci, E., Lund, R., Mortensen, E. L., et al. (2016). Successful ageing: A study of the literature using citation network analysis. *Maturitas, 93*, 4–12.

Laslett, P. (1989). *A fresh map of life*. Macmillan Press.

Lassen, A. J. (2014). *Active ageing and the unmaking of old age*. University of Copenhagen.

Lee, C., Payne, L. L., & Berdychevsky, L. (2020). The roles of leisure attitudes and self-efficacy on attitudes toward retirement among retirees: A sense of coherence theory approach. *Leisure Sciences, 42*(2), 152–169.

Leontowitsch, M. (2012). *Researching later life and ageing: Expanding qualitative research horizons*. Palgrave Macmillan.

Liechty, T., Genoe, M. R., & Marston, H. R. (2017). Physically active leisure and the transition to retirement: The value of context. *Annals of Leisure Research, 20*(1), 23–38.

Lindsey, R., Bulloch, S., & Metcalfe, L. (2016). *Volunteering 1981–2012*. Retrieved from https://longitudinalvolunteering.wordpress.com/.

Mair, H. (2009). Club life: Third place and shared leisure in rural Canada. *Leisure Sciences, 31*(5), 450–465.

Manley, I. (2003). *The UK/U3A approach to life long learning*. Retrieved from http://www.worldu3a.org/resources/UKlearning.pdf.

Martin, W. (2011). Visualizing risk: Health, gender and the ageing body. *Critical Social Policy, 32*(1), 51–68.

Mejía, S. T., Ryan, L. H., Gonzalez, R., & Smith, J. (2017). Successful aging as the intersection of individual resources, age, environment, and experiences of well-being in daily activities. *Journals of Gerontology—Series B Psychological Sciences and Social Sciences, 72*(2), 279–289.

Menec, V. H. (2003). The relation between everyday activities and successful aging: A 6-year longitudinal study. *Social Sciences, 58*(2), 74–82.

Murtagh, E., Murphy, M., Murphy, N., Woods, C., & Lane, A. (2014). *Stay Active—The physical activity, ageing and health study*. Retrieved from www.CARDI.ie.

National Institute for Health and Clinical Excellence. (2015). *Older people with social care needs and multiple long-term conditions (NG22)*. London: NICE.

Nimrod, G., & Shrira, A. (2016). The paradox of leisure in later life. *The Journals of Gerontology Series B: Psychological Sciences and Social Sciences, 71*(1), 106–111.

Office for National Statistics. (2013). Statistical Bulletin national population projections, 2012-based statistical Bulletin (November), 1–19.

Office for National Statistics. (2014a). *Healthy life expectancy at birth and at age 65: Clinical commissioning groups (2010–12)*. Retrieved from http://www.ons.gov.uk/ons/rel/census/2011-census-analysis/healthy-life-expectancy-at-birth-and-at-age-65–clinical-commissioning-groups–ccgs–2010-12/rpt-hle.html.

Office for National Statistics. (2014b). Statistical Bulletin excess winter mortality in England and Wales, 2012/13 (Provisional), *13*, 1–23.

Office for National Statistics. (2015a). *Statistical Bulletin national life tables, United Kingdom 2012–2014*. Retrieved from http://www.ons.gov.uk/ons/dcp171778_416983.pdf.

Office for National Statistics. (2015b). *Statistical Bulletin national population projections, 2012-based statistical Bulletin*. Retrieved from http://www.ons.gov.uk/ons/dcp171778_420462.pdf.

Office for National Statistics. (2018). *National life tables, UK: 2015 to 2017. Statistical bulletin*. Retrieved from https://doi.org/10.1016/j.chroma.2004.09.049.

Pavela, G., & Latham, K. (2016). Childhood conditions and multimorbidity among older adults. *Journals of Gerontology—Series B Psychological Sciences and Social Sciences, 71*(5), 889–901.

Phoenix, C., & Bell, S. L. (2019). Beyond "move more": Feeling the rhythms of physical activity in mid and later-life. *Social Science & Medicine, 231*, 47–54.

Richards, N., Warren, L., & Gott, M. (2012). The challenge of creating 'alternative' images of ageing: Lessons from a project with older women. *Journal of Aging Studies, 26*(1), 65–78.

Roberts, K. (2013). Leisure and the life course. In T. Blackshaw (Ed.), *Routledge handbook of leisure studies* (pp. 257–265). Routledge.

Rojek, C. (2010). The labour of leisure. In *The labour of leisure*. Sage.

Ronksley, P. E., Brien, S. E., Turner, B. J., Mukamal, K. J., & Ghali, W. A. (2011). Association of alcohol consumption with selected cardiovascular disease outcomes: a systematic review and meta-analysis. *Bmj, 342*(feb22 1), d671–d671.

Ryu, J., & Heo, J. (2016). Relaxation and watching televised sports among older adults. *Educational Gerontology, 42*(2), 71–78.

Seddon, C. (2011). Lifestyles and social participation. *Social Trends, 41*(1), 3.

Sherrington, C., Fairhall, N., Wallbank, G., Tiedemann, A., Michaleff, Z., Howard, K., … Sherrington. (2019). Interventions for preventing falls in older people living in the community. *Cochrane Database of Systematic Reviews* (Vol. 9).

Siegler, V., Njeru, R., & Thomas, J. (2015, July). *Inequalities in social capital by age and sex* (July), 1–25. Retrieved from http://www.ons.gov.uk/ons/dcp 171766_410190.pdf.

Sport England. (2016). *Tackling inactivity-active ageing prospectus.* Retrieved from https://www.sportengland.org/media/11410/active-ageing-prospectus. pdf.

Spracklen, K. (2011). *Constructing leisure: Historical and philosophical debates.* Basingstoke: Palgrave Macmillan.

Stebbins, R. A. (2013). *Planning your time in retirement: How to cultivate a leisure lifestyle to suit your needs and interests.* Rowman & Littlefield.

Steptoe, A., Breeze, E., Banks, J., & Nazroo, J. (2013). Cohort profile: The English longitudinal study of ageing. *International Journal of Epidemiology, 42*(6), 1640–1648.

Steptoe, A., & Wardle, J. (2012). Enjoying life and living longer. *Archives of International Medicine., 172*(3), 273–275.

Tampubolon, G. (2015). Growing up in poverty, growing old in infirmity: The long arm of childhood conditions in Great Britain. *PLoS ONE, 10*(12), 1–16.

Thomas, J. (2015). *Insights into loneliness, older people and wellbeing.* Retrieved from http://www.ons.gov.uk/ons/dcp171766_418058.pdf.

Toepoel, V. (2011). Cultural participation of older adults: Investigating the contribution of lowbrow and highbrow activities to social integration and satisfaction with life. *International Journal Disability and Human Development, 10*(2), 123–129.

United Nations. (2011). *Follow-up to the Second World Assembly on Ageing: Report of the Secretary-General. General Assembly Resolution A/66/173* (Vol. 42883). Retrieved from http://www.ohchr.org/Documents/Issues/SForum/ SForum2014/A.66.173_en.pdf.

United Nations Economic Commission for Europe. (2012). *Active ageing. UNECE Policy Brief on Ageing* (Vol. 13). Retrieved from http://ci.nii.ac. jp/naid/80016084632/.

Veblen, T. (2007). *Theory of the leisure class.* Transaction Publishers.

Warren, J. R. (2016). Does growing childhood socioeconomic inequality mean future inequality in adult health? *The ANNALS of the American Academy of Political and Social Science, 663*(1), 292–330.

Wheaton, B. (2017). Surfing through the life-course: Silver surfers' negotiation of ageing. *Annals of Leisure Research, 20*(1), 96–116.

Whitley, E., Benzeval, M., & Popham, F. (2018). Associations of successful aging with socioeconomic position across the life-course: The West of Scotland twenty-07 prospective cohort study. *Journal of Aging and Health, 30*(1), 52–74.

World Health Organization. (2002). *Active Ageing, a policy framework (No. WHO/NMH/NPH/02.8).* Geneva.

Wu, Y.-T., Fratiglioni, L., Matthews, F. E., Lobo, A., Breteler, M. M., Skoog, I., et al. (2016). Dementia occurrence in Europe: Epidemiological evidence and implications for current policy making Yu-Tzu. *The Lancet Neurology, 15*(1), 116–124.

Yeomans, H., & Critcher, C. (2013). The demon drink. In T. Blackshaw (Ed.), *Routledge handbook of leisure studies* (pp. 305–315). London: Routledge.

2

Constraints to Leisure in a Healthy Later Life

This literature review provides a critical position from which to evaluate research about how leisure constraints affects the new ageing population. It considers what is known about constraints to pleasures found in active and passive leisure in later life. This literature review engages with a range of leisure in later life research that does not focus on illness and vulnerability. It starts with the history of the development of leisure constraints research to demonstrate the shifts in focus and development of the constraint's literature, then focuses on the last 10 years of empirical work.

Leisure studies, leisure science and critical gerontology are the three main disciplinary fields that will be synthesised and evaluated, with a focus on research that engages with leisure constraints theory and later life. This literature review will not include research that focuses on managing big noisy constraints such as a specific illness or recent bereavement or recent major role loss. This is to avoid overwhelming knowledge about ageing with knowledge about disability, bereavement and loss. These experiences are defining periods of change and adjustment but they can happen at any time of life. I am concerned with how

© The Author(s), under exclusive license to Springer Nature
Switzerland AG 2021
T. Wiseman, *Leisure in Later Life*, Leisure Studies in a Global Era,
https://doi.org/10.1007/978-3-030-71672-1_2

people manage constraints in everyday life and these things are exceptional. They may come to define the everyday for some people, but they do not happen every day, and the everyday continues despite them.

2.1 Development of Leisure Constraints Research

Leisure constraints literature has been in development formally since the early 1980s, but with roots in 1960s studies in outdoor recreation, and the North American parks and recreation movement (Jackson, 2005). Knowledge about leisure constraints in relation to age, gender and structural inequalities has co-evolved, but this literature review mainly focuses on the ageing research. Age emerged as a significant concern for leisure constraints research in the 1980s, during this phase research in leisure constraints focused on later life as a time of increasing constraints and non-participation. This was considered an opportunity as latent demand for leisure services could potentially provide custom for recreation services. From 1981 to 1986 research into constraints focused on outdoor recreation across the lifespan (Mcguire & Norman, 2005). Mcguire (1984) identified 'approval' as one of five constraints, in a factor analytic study of constraints in advanced adulthood.[1] The full set was developed, and approval became part of interpersonal constraints, where it was mainly related to a partner, and structural constraints where it related to *"reference group attitudes concerning the appropriateness of certain activities"* (Crawford & Godbey, 1987, p. 124).

Meanwhile, Glyptis and colleagues in the United Kingdom (UK) used time space diaries in a leisure and time study and found that older people spent more time at home than other age groups (Glyptis et al., 1987). The idea of leisure time at home was problematic in the context of research that mainly focused on outdoor recreation. Glyptis' and

---

[1] 1984 is the year James Fixx died of a heart attack, aged 52. He started the jogging craze in 1967, following the early death of his father who died of a heart attack at age 43. His jogging was inspired by a will to improve his own odds, which he did, but the irony of his famous death was widely reported. https://www.nytimes.com/1984/07/22/obituaries/james-f-fixx-dies-jogging-author-on-running-was-52.html.

Kay's studies of the leisure of unemployed people, another problematised group, found that location and privacy were important factors in leisure participation and enjoyment (Glyptis, 1989; Kay, 1987).[2]

In 1988 Jackson provided a review of leisure constraints research (1988). The initial research papers focused on non-participation, which is still a focus of concern in current literature. By 1991 Jackson proposed the idea of a field of leisure constraints research.

> *there is a sense among many leisure scholars that constraints research represents a distinct focus of investigation in leisure studies…there is also a danger that the research, and those who contribute to it, will become inward-looking and thus isolated from the broader field of leisure studies.* (Jackson, 1991, p. 276)

An important development was the description of negotiation of constraints and perceived constraints (Kay & Jackson, 1991) by the research team in the UK, it was suggested that people managed constraints and perceived constraints, and participated despite them, sometimes these constraints did not impact on participation at all. Initially, there was a lack of clarity between constraints that were observable by others and perceived constraints that only the participant could experience (Jackson, 1988). The development of ideas around internal and external constraints was hampered in the early stages by different understandings of how one constraint may precede another. A model of leisure constraints that included intrapersonal, interpersonal and structural constraints to leisure was proposed. An approach to assessing the order of importance from internal to most external constraints was taken and the Hierarchical Model of Leisure Constraints was named (Crawford et al., 1991).

A hierarchy is perhaps not so useful to understanding the shush that triggered this research, as it is not possible to know which came first. The three forms/locations of constraint combine in the shush in the garden;

---

[2]At this time in the UK, unemployment had been over 10% since 1981, but fell rapidly in the early 1990s, rose again briefly, but by then the researchers had moved onto other research. https://www.ons.gov.uk/employmentandlabourmarket/peoplenotinwork/unempl oyment/timeseries/mgsx/lms. Unemployment in the USA had already fallen by the mid-80s, so the audience for this research was reduced. https://data.bls.gov/timeseries/LNS14000000, despite another peak in the 1990s.

from the person producing it, to their perception of critical others behind the garden wall, to the understanding of the social contract and their place in receipt of welfare. This idea of constraints is complicated by interplay, but the shush in the garden did not stop participation, just the overt demonstration of enjoyment. It was produced by a gardener based on a perceived threat, so the idea of negotiating perceived constraints, (Kay & Jackson, 1991) could be helpful here, in terms of understanding participating in activities despite constraints, and how that may impact enjoyment.

From 1993 to 1998 healthy later life constraints was a focus (Mcguire & Norman, 2005), and by 1999 a clear understanding of the complexity and interplay of different forms of constraint was being discussed.

> *constraints influence far more than the choice to participate or not, but many other aspects of leisure, including the formation of preferences, the derivation of enjoyment.* (Jackson & Scott, 1999, p. 2)

By 1999 Jackson and Scott were already expressing concern that the term 'constraints' was being so widely used that it was in danger of swallowing up the whole field of leisure studies (1999). From 2002 to 2005 more time use studies were conducted (Mcguire & Norman, 2005). Twenty years into the study of constraints to later life leisure it was identified that there was not sufficient interaction between the fields of gerontology and leisure. Mcguire and Norman (2005) highlighted gerontological theories of ageing expressing concern that there was a disconnection between the fields of later life leisure studies and geron-tology. They took a critical stance on active ageing, citing Katz (2000) who challenged and continues to challenge a view of hyperactive old age as essential to well-being (Katz, 2013, 2018). The active ageing stance is prevalent in leisure and ageing research.

The hierarchical model of leisure constraints does not help us to know what the constraints are, which ones are most important or which order we should negotiate the constraints in, but knowing that it is complex, negotiable and multi-layered is useful. Godbey et al. suggested future research should focus on how these constraints interact, and explained that cultural heterogeneity creates diversity in how people perceive and experience leisure constraints, so culturally conscious research is needed (2010). How and when constraints interact remained complicated (Godbey et al., 2010).

2.2   Leisure Constraints in Later Life Research

Leisure researchers have looked closely at the lifecourse and well-being, given an ageing population. The significance of leisure to well-being increases throughout life, providing more benefits in later life than earlier (Nimrod & Shrira, 2016). Both quantitative and qualitative studies express concerns that later life is subject to more leisure constraints (Nimrod et al., 2015; Nimrod & Shrira, 2016). The constraints that are reported are still referred to as age-induced limitations, such as physical changes, health conditions, finance, mobility and access, weather, moving home, friends and loved ones becoming ill or dying and ageism (Meisner et al., 2019). A different view rejects the pathological approach to ageing, emphasising the positive experience of leisure in later life (Hickman et al., 2018). Most leisure in later life research has an activity, or 'little leisures' (Roberts, 2011) focus, and therefore activity type is the organising factor of the next section of this literature review.

At the active ageing end of the spectrum the disapproval of the inactive/passive ager is clearest in the sports literature. Very active agers tell us that 'other (passive) old people' are lazy and ignorant (Gard et al., 2017). There is research about constraints to leisure-time physical activity that focuses on inactivity due to disability, moderate activity and Masters athletes research (Meisner et al., 2019). Findings include the power of participating in physical activity to overcome doubts about their potential to participate and ageist ideas (Massie & Meisner, 2019), and the physical and emotional health benefits of sports are so entrenched in policy and social discourse that they are taken as facts, the idea that anyone can be active ignores the luck and geography of 'ageing well'. But despite clear policy and practice of active ageing (Higgs et al., 2009), there is still an idea of the 'exceptional older person' created in opposition to the norm of a frail ill older person, there is a hierarchy of sorts in the experience of being treated as exceptional, Masters athletes embrace the status (Dionigi, 2006; Gard et al., 2017), the active people in the Massie and Meisner study are a little annoyed by it and try to hide their age, so as not to surprise other, often younger, people with their high levels of activity (2019).

Recent exploration of the perspectives of a relatively privileged group of Masters sports participants in 2017 recognised how people misattributed their 'successful ageing' to their own efforts, whilst blaming less healthy older adults for their immoral inactivity, and the potential costs to health services and burden to society in general (Gard et al., 2017).

> one reason might be that the sample came from industrialized/Western countries that share similar neoliberal views of healthy, active ageing and Sport for All that are evident in current social policy… attributing a negative internal cause, such as laziness or lack of motivation, to what may be societal (e.g. lack of access, opportunity), uncontrollable (e.g. disability, disease) and/or personal (e.g. they do see the value of sport) reasons why there are older adults who are inactive. (Gard et al., 2017, p. 265)

It is a reflection on the way that sports participation is considered as a gold standard of leisure in later life, that the article was printed with an error, it was clearly meant to say that some people 'do _not_ see the value of sport', but it was published as 'they do see the value of sport', and it was not picked up in proofreading.[3] The idea of people not seeing the value of sport, as a valid reason for non-participation is also raised by Godbey et al. who explain (2010) that lack of interest is not an intrapersonal constraint.

The participants speak for themselves and the researchers speak up for the missing voice, the othered 'passive ager'. Lifestyle activities, which are non-competitive, flexible and fitness-oriented are carried on for longer than competitive sports. *"In general, participation [in sport] declines with age and this decline becomes more marked after the age of 45 years"* (Thurston & Green, 2004, p. 383). A preference for lifestyle activities fits well with Roberts ideas about leisure as part of life in the round (1999).

---

[3]This is something I noticed myself, it is still an error in the online article.

Notable examples of sport participation through lifestyle activities are bowls (Heuser, 2005), 'veteran' games (Dionigi, 2006) and curling (Mair, 2009), yoga (Humberstone, 2010) and windsurfing (Humberstone, 2011), cycling (Minello & Nixon, 2017) and surfing (Wheaton, 2017). Dionigi (2006) suggests that what is really important to the participants in their sports participation is a sense of fun, sociability and vitality that Heuser (2005) and Mair (2009) also highlight. There is a focus on pleasure and competency of participation in the less competitive activities of yoga, windsurfing and surfing (Humberstone, 2010, 2011; Wheaton, 2017). Mair's work in rural Canadian curling clubs comes close to doing what Crouch describes as 'studying the character of ordinary life' (Crouch, 2012, p. 255). Minello and Nixon highlight concerns about the internalisation of individual responsibility for ageing successfully, as their cyclists negotiated ideas of resistance to ageing, expressed empowerment, and shared the identity of successful agers through enjoyable sports participation (2017). In all of these studies, constraints are apparent, the way that older people in society are viewed is the main one, changes in capacities and adaptation another. It tells a different story to the usual one of decline and vulnerability, but it raises concerns too about what may happen to a person who values this level of activity so highly, in a culture that focuses on personal responsibility for managing an ageing body. If bad luck intervenes, it asks how they may adjust or adapt to being more like their negative view of 'other old people' (Gard et al., 2017). This othering of old people, particularly those who are ill is not the ideological othering of an abject class, it is the othering of risk (Higgs & Gilleard, 2014). In taking responsibility for the luck associated with health of the future self, a different risk is taken, that of failure to appreciate other possibilities that life has to offer.

There are other elements to successful ageing beyond being active, which are not so well understood. The heritage of the constraints literature means researchers are focused on physical outdoors activity, and this may alienate researchers with alternative viewpoints, even within the sports leisure field, who call for a more nuanced and embodied understanding of leisure (Humberstone, 2011, 2019; Humberstone & Cutler-Riddick, 2015). Indeed some of the research that sheds light on problems participating in satisfying leisure does not mention constraints, even in passing, suggesting that 40 years of leisure constraints research has not, as Jackson and Scott predicted (1999), enveloped leisure research.

Gardening is promoted as a physical work out activity by active ageing literature (Hawkins et al., 2015; Park & Shoemaker, 2009; Park, 2007; Park et al., 2008; Wang & MacMillan, 2013), but leisure gardening is just as much about being in the garden, as it is doing the gardening (Hawkins et al., 2013). It's an escape, a retreat (Bhatti & Church, 2000; Bhatti et al., 2009), and the work can be a burden (Bhatti, 2006). Gardening as a leisure activity enhances well-being (Kingsley et al., 2009; Leaver & Wiseman, 2016; Van den Berg et al., 2010; York & Wiseman, 2012). But the experience of negotiating constraints to gardening in later life is not well understood (Okvat & Zautra, 2011). Some constraints may appear obvious such as physical barriers or lack of space, others are more subtle, such as identity conflict, with people preferring to be seen as lazy, to being seen as incapable (Jun & Kyle, 2011). Despite the constraints focus of the research, gardening is found to be a popular leisure choice in later life (Freeman et al., 2012), the idea of negotiation of constraints is useful here, but also the idea of outdoors housework, as gardening is not always leisure. Coming back to Godbey et al.'s wry observation that a lack of interest is not a constraint (2010), with gardening, participation does not necessarily indicate a valued leisure pastime. The garden is an extension of home (Bhatti & Church, 2004), and as such must be maintained to an acceptable standard. However research focuses on those people that enjoy gardening, Cheng found that people *"…obtained high levels of leisure satisfaction specifically from the relaxation, psychological and physiological aspects of gardening"* (2010, p. 395). However despite this research considering leisure and life satisfaction of people that are in healthy later life, with only 4 of 433 participants noting a disability, the author still suggests reducing constraints to gardening in order to include those with less ability. Advocating for more gardening help for old people, not from the data, but from the cultural knowledge of the researcher that gardening becomes more difficult as people age, this is a clear example of the impact of disability on ageing being introduced into research despite the data. This is usual, the benefits and attractions are evaluated, people that hate gardening are not included in these studies, any more than anti-cycling participants are included in cycling research, or people that leave groups are not included in group research. Of course this is the case, but it means that we are trying to find out why 'people do not do what is good for them' by asking people that do, and they are unlikely to know that any better than the researchers. The missing are reluctant gardeners, lazy TV viewers, people who do not like organised groups. If the large scale activity studies are to be believed most old people are in this missing group (Department Culture Media and Sport, 2014). Perhaps they are not interesting, they are not ill, so they cost society little; they are not doing anything odd so we cannot marvel at them; they are not participating in our favourite leisure activity, so we cannot hang out with older practitioners and be comforted and inspired toward our own later leisure life exploits. But they are there, and they are participating in leisure, and that alternative to being frail and dependant or hyperactive should be interesting to the study of constraints, because they are very possibly leading the resistance to the neoliberal appropriation of all of our leisure lives, and they must be skilfully negotiating cultural constraints in order to do so.

Overall, those who exercise, play sport and work in the garden are more satisfied with life, and their satisfaction is partly influenced by the social elements of the activities (Donovan & Halpern, 2002). The activities themselves are complex and embedded in a lifestyle and time and place that are important to consider. If the aim is to understand participation in leisure in later life it may be better to focus more research resources on understanding personal satisfaction with leisure lifestyle rather than the impact on health or relationships of a specific activity. Chilvers et al. (2010) asked ninety healthy Australian people in later life to record the activities they participated in over twenty-four hours; their leisure time was spent in enjoyable activities. An examination of less active, more popular leisure pursuits that are less commonly associated with later life research, because their health outcomes are less apparent is needed.

Holidays at their best in later life are a luxury, an adventure, and enjoyed when all else is under control. *"Satisfaction with family, health, emotional state, and leisure life positively influences satisfaction with overall quality of life. Overall quality of life is positively related to travel motivation in the elderly"* (Kim & Woo, 2014, p. 629). Travel is difficult in varied societies, for example, Chinese women are subject to multiple constraints to travel, and it is important to consider age, gender, race and cultural norms and environments when trying to understand how people manage constraints to taking holidays (Gao & Kerstetter, 2016). Benson and O'Reilly researched migration lifestyles, their study focused on affluent migrants who re-negotiated their work-life balance (2009), people preferred to see themselves as having serious reasons for migrating, relating to well-being, and their part in society, rather than view themselves as affluent consumers (Benson & O'Reilly, 2009). Others embark on a later life sports tourism career, as in the case of Japanese Masters Games participants (Ito & Hikoji, 2018). There is evidence that these privileged forms of mobility and migration have recently increased worldwide (Casado-Diaz, 2012; Janoschka & Haas, 2014), this increase coincides with an increasing number of people in later life. The concepts and ideas developed in lifestyle migration work supports the research of Kordel (2016) who explored German retirement communities in Spain where the idea of healthy later life being one long holiday is acted upon by many people. This idea is further explored in relation to Canadian 'snowbirds' moving south for the winter to be temporarily free from family caring commitments (Wood & Kulczycki, 2018). In China, lifestyle seasonal migration of older people is largely dependent on the financial support of adult children (Kou et al., 2018). The idea of holiday is very extended here, with it lasting up to six months each year, but the level of freedom and active leisure participation are discussed as one. The active choice for an active winter in a warmer climate is firmly explained as a healthy ageing strategy (Kordel, 2016; Kou et al., 2018; Wood & Kulczycki, 2018). Here there are ideas around healthy ageing and work–life balance invoked to explain taking extended holidays. It is interesting to see healthy ageing used in justifying choices that are not immediately obviously health-promoting. There are clearly fewer weather constraints to enjoying leisure in the warmer destination than the cold home, but there are also fewer constraints on other levels too, fewer responsibilities for family care, more opportunities to join in with organised activities, a holiday from everyday life. Why then is that not a justification for these participants, why is there a need to make it moral?

There is little attention in the leisure constraints literature to the most common leisure pastimes in later life, media consumption. When it is discussed it is in relation to its displacement of more appropriate activities, or as a result of enforced immobility. As one cycling enthusiast states *"I think they're just lazy. They just don't have the wherewithal to get out and do it. Anyone can go for a walk, it doesn't cost you anything. Some people just prefer to sit on the couch and watch tv and eat chips"* (Minello & Nixon, 2017, p. 89).

This passive, sometimes dangerous, television watching is appreciated in other spheres of leisure studies as an important mass-mediated experience that enables sharing of a variety of narratives and communication of shared and different shifting identities with viewers (Stevenson, 2013). Van Der Goot et al. (2012) interviewed 86 people in later life in the Netherlands and found that for most people television habits did not change in response to ageing. For some people viewing habits changed after the loss of a loved one, television provided company, emotional uplift, distraction and structure in a changed life. Other people avoided it, and the emotions and memories it stirred up. Some reported a new time freedom, they could choose what and when to watch, this freedom of choice to watch more or less television was important. The changes were most marked in relation to recent retirement or confinement due to illness. Some of the changes included more current affairs programmes to engage with society, and quizzes and foreign language films to stimulate the brain, and participants reported beliefs about this stimulating television content preserving cognitive abilities (Van Der Goot et al., 2012). In this way, the participants are reporting the health benefits of their television watching. Not all of the participants approved, one person reported that *"he and his family had always looked down on television viewing. Even though he spent most of the time at home, he only watched a few particular programmes that he thought were valuable and focused on things that he appreciated more, such as reading"* (Van Der Goot et al., 2012, p. 16). In this way, the disapproval of television watching affects participation in, and enjoyment of television watching for some people, but many report enjoying the freedom of choice. A study of people over 50 in Korea illustrates an interactive and exciting time watching televised sports with family, and the pleasure of relaxation. In this way passive leisure activities may also contribute to well-being; and entertainment was the strongest predictor of relaxation and the social aspect of television watching was valued (Ryu & Heo, 2016). This raises the questions of how values are placed upon particular pastimes, and what impact might this have on participation and enjoyment.

A cross-sectional one day sample of the variety and duration of media use across seven European countries and Israel was analysed. It was found that media use in later life was varied, and some of the things that influenced this were education, income, retirement status and country (Nimrod, 2017). There was a tendency to stay with traditional media use reported by older people, and some people had extensive media time. Maladaptation to retirement is suggested as an explanation for very heavy mass media use of traditional media, such as television and radio, there is concern raised by the researcher of the negative impact of this very passive lifestyle, relating to all health domains, physical, social and psychological (Nimrod, 2017), it is suggested that high media consumption results from constraints to more beneficial, active activities. Disapproval of media consumption is added to the research by the researcher. This position is informed by knowing that a greater leisure repertoire, beyond media consumption, is linked with life satisfaction in retirement (Nimrod, 2016).

Along with eating and drinking habits, gardening, and shopping, reading assists people to remain socially active in later life and acts to reduce loneliness (Pettigrew & Roberts, 2008). Reading books or doing crosswords is treated differently in the literature to other passive activity, it is privileged, with some suggestion that keeping mentally active produces benefits for people's well-being (Guell et al., 2016), this is consistent with beliefs about some of the other consumptive media, such as brain training games (Millington, 2012). It is also suggested that "While reading books is not a successful predictor for social gatherings, it is one of the most important predictors for the number of close relationships an individual has" (Toepoel, 2013, p. 362). The habit of reading has parental influence, and reading with children features in the discussion of this finding, with the implication that lifelong readers have stronger connections with their adult children, due to shared reading in childhood (Toepoel, 2013). Here the social connections are presented as desirable, to avoid the threat of loneliness in later life, and a warning is given against TV, radio or computer use as passive activities that were not associated with social connectedness (Toepoel, 2013). However in other research computer use was valued, particularly in relation to online communities, and only TV and radio were considered passive (Khvorostianov et al., 2011; Nimrod, 2014, 2016). There is a lack of agreement about what constitutes active and passive activities and their potential for enhancing or endangering later lives.

Alcohol and well-being research focuses on 'problem drinking', and until recently ignored later life (Mortimer, 2011). Statistics on alcohol consumption in England (Office for National Statistics, 2013) suggest that people over 65 have the highest rates of regular drinking of all age groups, but the drinking is moderate, and unproblematic (Paganini-Hill et al., 2007). The benefits of social drinking in later life are recognized in this culturally normal practice (Ward et al., 2011). The importance of drinking alcohol as a pleasurable leisure activity is highlighted, but alcohol consumption has an ambivalent status in leisure studies (Yeomans & Critcher, 2013). Prevention and management of problem drinking with youth is the main focus in constraints research. There is intergenerational research that mentions alcohol (Duarte Alonso et al., 2018; Mair, 2009) and perhaps for these reasons, despite being a very popular pastime in later life, much like shopping, it did not emerge in the literature search. A related ethnographic study of drinking practices of older Caribbean Canadian male cricket spectators and players proposes an explanation of the functions it serves (Joseph, 2012). It is suggested that 'heavy drinking' masks "the effects of old age (limping, forgetfulness and declining physical strength)" (Joseph, 2012, p. 147), and helps the men to avoid family responsibilities, both embracing and challenging dominant gender stereotypes. *"Players refer to their drinks as 'blood-thinners', 'medicine', and 'tonic', and advocate that alcohol is strength-giving and nerve-calming, which are essential for skilful batting"* (Joseph, 2012, p. 154) drinking alcohol is expected of all cricket players and being able to drink heavily gives an enhanced identity of being better able to cope with drink than the younger men. The function of alcohol for the younger men in this context was not addressed. Although this research is not discussing constraints it is reinforcing a theme that runs through this literature review of participants appropriating health messages to justify their favoured pastime.

In the US, gambling is one of the most popular commercial leisure pastimes (Waller & Martin, 2017), and much research focuses on problem gambling (El-Guebalay et al., 2015; Lister & Nower, 2014; Loo et al., 2008; Subramaniam et al., 2015; Walker et al., 2006). Hope and Havir (2002) argue that casino visits in later life are fun and the view of older people as vulnerable is simply ageist, their study which included mainly highly educated participants supports the idea that this is a group of gambling consumers that have the experience to recognise if a problem is developing and enjoy it for the fun that it is. Fantasies, feelings and fun, are three essential elements of hedonic consumption which gambling for leisure satisfies (Loroz, 2004). Gambling has long been incorporated into leisure lives in the UK (Downs, 2011), and across the world (Bedford et al., 2016) from the football pools to the national lottery, and more recently online gambling, much of the research focuses on problem gamblers, rather than the leisurely aspects. Bingo, like lottery playing, has an interesting position as so often it is associated with charitable fundraising, where gambling vice meets the virtue of community participation and local charity (Bedford et al., 2016). Much of the research focuses on problem gamblers, rather than the leisurely aspects. Although not specifically about later life, Casey's exploration of the every-dayness, pleasure and agency of working-class women's national lottery gambling experience creates space for alternative views (Casey, 2006). In considering these less noble pastimes we can start to consider if there is agency in people not, to paraphrase Godbey et al. (2010), 'doing what is good for them'.

There is critique of the medicalization of heteronormative sexual function in later life (Katz & Marshall, 2003) and the resulting commercialization of sexual expression in later life. Katz and Marshall assert that *"Sexual function, like physical fitness more generally, has become central to contemporary conceptions of the good life"* (2003, p. 13). Berdychevsky and Nimrod conclude that sexual expression is a meaningful leisure activity in later life. The happiness and vitality of sexual expression promoted physical, psychological, social and spiritual well-being. Intimacy and familiar and new forms of pleasure were discussed (Berdychevsky & Nimrod, 2015). The idea of 'familiar and new' resonates with the ideas of continuity and constant contingent state (Blackshaw, 2010) in leisure theory.

2.3   Culture in Leisure Constraints Research

There is constraints research from many different countries, and the hierarchical leisure constraints model was intended to be a universal framework for explaining all of leisure behaviour, not free-will, injustice or enjoyment, just leisure behaviour (Godbey et al., 2010). The constraint categories are conceived in relation to individuals but they are profoundly shaped by culture, and further research with people in later life, and in specific cultural contexts is suggested (Godbey et al., 2010). *"The social psychological processes involved in the constraint negotiation process, including the costs reflected in compromise behavior, are yet to be examined in depth by future research efforts"* (Godbey et al., 2010, p. 125).

Leisure constraints are broadly considered in leisure research, particularly in relation to culture, but also still gender and age within that work. Earlier work, from the wider field of leisure studies is not always included, particularly disconfirming research. For example, Humberstone and Kirby (2003) found that some younger women no longer thought that gender was a problem for their sports participation, and Son, Kerstetter and Mowen (2008) found motivation to be the most important factor in physical activity participation, and age was not significantly related by active participants to overall constraint levels. The building of knowledge is disrupted by specialisation and possibly entrenched beliefs about later life or gender. A recent tetrad analysis of the categories in quantitative leisure constraints research suggest *"an alternative agenda for constraints research to find powerfully constraining factors in particular contexts"* (Kono et al., 2018, p. 18). The shush in the garden was very specific and may have kept one participant out of her garden for 10 years, there are more to be found in ordinary later lives. There are ordinary older people, their leisure lives explored in context then left behind in the literature (Gibson et al., 2003). This research recommended a life course perspective for further research, in keeping with the developments with gerontology, embedded in culture, in line with leisure theory.

In 2005, McGuire felt the need to explain gerontology theories, and I felt that need in the background chapter because it is part of the landscape of constraints research and also the social context within which the leisure research is conducted, and lives are lived. Active ageing and successful ageing underpin much later life leisure research. Waves in leisure scholarship followed gerontology but leisure constraints scholarship did not really follow, it continued to focus on activity, it continues to look at participation. The leisure as experience research creates a better understanding of bodies in leisure and a more diverse appreciation of leisure. The leisure and well-being research tells us that people can articulate the health benefits of doing things that they like doing.

The life course perspective advocated in conversations about everyday life in retirement in Florida by Gibson and colleagues (2003) has not taken prominence in constraints research. The move towards intersectionality may bring more ideas together than previous moves towards specialisation have (Gao & Kerstetter, 2016). More often now researchers merge the big concepts, for example, digital leisure studies bring together the big conceptualisations of leisure, time in digital spaces and practices in a leisurely state of mind under the concept of digital leisure cultures (Redhead, 2016). This complexity and sometimes fragmentation of leisure studies, also reflected on by Redhead, is described by some as a field in flux, others as vibrant (Silk et al., 2017).

The idea of how people negotiate perceived disapproval in later life warrants further investigation, in the context of an emerging new cohort of people in later life. Constraints research has its roots in increasing activity, and knowledge about structural constraints has produced more inclusive environments for women, people with disabilities and older people. But we do not yet understand the interplay between the intra/inter/cultural and how constraints, as reducing or enhancing forces, work (Godbey et al., 2010). True to its roots in travel to visit national parks for outdoor recreation, tourism and sport are the most cited areas of studies of constraint. But constraints are present in everyday leisure, and there is not yet a study of the perspectives of people in the new cohort in later life in the UK who are not usually selected for leisure research, a study of their everyday lives is needed.

2.4   Conclusions

Waves in research and theory in leisure and gerontology are important to consider, because the general constraints to leisure in later life literature is working with both, but not always in the same time frame. Activity Theory is hard to get away from, as constraints to participation focus on activities, mainly sports (Samdahl, 2005; Samdahl & Jekubovich, 1997) the field mainly focuses on restrictive constraints to participation in socially sanctioned leisure activities, which confuses me and my shush in the garden, because the gardening was socially sanctioned, yet constrained. It largely ignores people who are deviant or criminal in their behaviour, which in the context of active ageing would be wilfully sedentary. It individualises responsibility and it works in congress with active ageing to constrain leisure. It means that it works very well for research into things like sports and tourism participation and gardening groups, particularly at the therapeutic and commercial end (Samdahl, 2005). A more subjective state of mind view, in a specific cultural context, may offer more, and looking for that shush in the reports of later life leisure is difficult when so much research into constraints that has been done focuses on motivation, and opportunity, placing undue responsibility on people for things that they cannot control such physical capacities (Gard et al., 2017), and overlooking things that they have a chance of managing, such as enjoyment. All the time that the research focuses essentially on health and well-being, over which people have very little actual control, an opportunity is missed to engage with and understand how culture influences leisure in later life.

In 2000 McGuire wrote a critique of the state of leisure in later life research, he suggested we were not asking the right questions, that the field was underfunded, that concepts from other fields were used over developing concepts of our own, we lacked a critical mass of scholars, time to carry out research, and a coordinating body. He also suggested that there was a gulf between theory and practice. He concluded that there was not much known at that point about ageing and leisure (Mcguire, 2000), Eight years later there was considerable literature about constraints to participation or enjoyment and the suggestion of a positive role of constraints (Kleiber et al., 2008). Exponential growth in research output about later life leisure occurred between 2000 and 2015 (Nimrod et al., 2015). However, this idea that not much is still known is still relevant because there is a lot of research, but it does not come together to form bodies of knowledge that can offer explanations for example about why, when we know more and more about diet and exercise, that people are increasingly sedentary and obese. When active ageing has been a dominant metanarrative throughout the lifetime of the currently retired, why are they mainly sedentary? In my gardening story it is suggested that disengagement is still present as a metanarrative and inhibiting enjoyment in active leisure, but we do not know a great deal about how this new generation of people in healthy later life negotiate their later leisure lives in this complex cultural environment. The hierarchical leisure constraints model may not be effective in helping us to understand leisure constraints, and we need to go back and examine the categorisation in more depth, and in specific contexts.

> *…to value diversity and difference in the ageing experience, there is a need to understand what ageing well means to older people and to respect the individual variability (or heterogeneity) of older adults.* (Dionigi & Son, 2017, p. 2)

Liechty et al. warn that *"findings suggest that scholars and leisure professionals need to take care in assuming that leisure constraints simply increase with age"* (2016, p. 308). This selection of everyday leisure research suggests that some people are successfully negotiating all kinds of leisure in later life. There is a new cohort of healthy people in an extended later life in the twenty-first century in the UK who have grown up and grown older with 'active ageing'. The changing demographics have ramped up the active ageing rhetoric, but it is not clear how they negotiate between the promises of affluent fun and the threat of illness and vulnerability.

There is a lack of agreement about what constitutes active and passive activities and their potential for enhancing or endangering later lives.

Many studies of later life presuppose decline and disability as people age, including active ageing and leisure constraints research. The focus on health and well-being means that there is a knowledge gap in research and theory for more leisurely pastimes in later life for those that are ageing well. My research asks what happens if we disconnect declining ability and later life and look instead at what people are reporting about their leisure lives. In order to better understand the shush in the garden that triggered the enquiry, we first need to know what older people are doing in their private leisure lives, then we can ask if and how they negotiate the impact of metanarratives about ageing. The research questions of how people negotiate leisure in the context of everyday later life, and how they interact with metanarratives about ageing will be addressed in this book.

References

Bedford, K., Alvarez-Macotela, O., Casey, D., Jobim Kurban, M. L., & Williams, T. (2016). *The bingo project: Rethinking gambling regulation.* University of Kent. Retrieved October 28, 2020, from https://kar.kent.ac.uk/58505/1/BT_121718_Bingo_v5.pdf.

Benson, M., & O'Reilly, K. (2009). Migration and the search for a better way of life: A critical exploration of lifestyle migration. *Sociological Review, 57*(4), 608–625.

Berdychevsky, L., & Nimrod, G. (2015). "Sexual until we drop": Sex as leisure in later life. In *Leisure studies association conference* (p. 1).

Bhatti, M. (2006). "When I'm in the garden I can create my own paradise": Homes and gardens in later life. *Sociological Review, 54*(2), 318–341.

Bhatti, M., & Church, A. (2000). 'I never promised you a rose garden': Gender, leisure and home-making. *Leisure Studies, 19*(3), 183–197.

Bhatti, M., & Church, A. (2004). Home, the culture of nature and meanings of gardens in late modernity. *Housing Studies, 19*(1), 37–51.

Bhatti, M., Church, A., Claremont, A., & Stenner, P. (2009). 'I love being in the garden': Enchanting encounters in everyday life. *Social and Cultural Geography, 10*(1), 61–76.

Blackshaw, T. (2010). *Leisure*. Routledge.

Casado-Diaz, M. (2012). Exploring the geographies of lifestyle mobility: Current and future fields of enquiry. In J. Wilson (Ed.), *The Routledge handbook of tourism geographies* (pp. 120–125). Routledge.

Casey, E. (2006). Domesticating gambling: Gender, caring and the UK National Lottery. *Leisure Studies, 25*(1), 3–16.

Cheng, E., Patterson, I., Packer, J., & Pegg, S. (2010). Identifying the leisure satisfactions derived from leisure gardening by older adults. *Annals of Leisure Research, 13*(3), 395–419.

Chilvers, R., Corr, S., & Singlehurst, H. (2010). Investigation into the occupational lives of healthy older people through their use of time. *Australian Occupational Therapy Journal, 57,* 24–33.

Crawford, D. W., & Godbey, G. (1987). Reconceptualizing barriers to family leisure. *Leisure Sciences, 9*(2), 119–127.

Crawford, D. W., Jackson, E. L., & Godbey, G. (1991). A hierarchical model of leisure constraints. *Leisure Sciences, 13*(4), 309–320.

Crouch, D. (2012). Ordinary lives: Studies in the everyday. *Leisure Studies, 31*(2), 255–256.

Department Culture Media and Sport. (2014). Taking Part 2014/15 Quarter 2 (December).

Dionigi, R. (2006). Competitive sport as leisure in later life: Negotiations, discourse, and aging. *Leisure Sciences, 28,* 181–196.

Dionigi, R. A., & Son, J. S. (2017). Introduction to critical perspectives on physical activity, sport, play and leisure in later life. *Annals of Leisure Research, 20*(1), 1–6.

Donovan, N., & Halpern, D. (2002). Life satisfaction: The state of knowledge and implications for government. *Strategy Unit* (December), 1–64.

Downs, C. (2011). Two fat ladies at the seaside: Gambling in working class holidays 1920–1970. *Recording Leisure Lives: Holidays and Tourism in 20th Century Britain, 112*(112), 51–73.

Duarte Alonso, A., Alexander, N., & O'Brien, S. (2018). 'Every brew is a challenge and every glass of a good beer is an achievement': Home brewing and serious leisure. *Leisure/Loisir, 42*(1), 93–113.

El-Guebalay, N., Casey, D. M., Currie, S. R., Hodgins, D. C., Schopflocher, D. P., Smith, G. J., & Williams, R. J. (2015). The Leisure, Lifestyle, & Lifecycle Project (LLLP): A longitudinal study of gambling in Alberta, 1–161.

Freeman, C., Dickinson, K. J. M., Porter, S., & van Heezik, Y. (2012). "My garden is an expression of me": Exploring householders' relationships with their gardens. *Journal of Environmental Psychology, 32*(2), 135–143.

Gao, J., & Kerstetter, D. L. (2016). Using an intersectionality perspective to uncover older Chinese female's perceived travel constraints and negotiation strategies. *Tourism Management, 57*, 128–138.

Gard, M., Dionigi, R. A., Horton, S., Baker, J., Weir, P., & Dionigi, C. (2017). The normalization of sport for older people? *Annals of Leisure Research, 20*(3), 253–272.

Gibson, H., Ashton-Shaeffer, C., Green, J., & Autry, C. (2003). Leisure in the lives of retirement-aged women: Conversations about leisure and life. *Leisure/Loisir, 28*(3–4), 203–230.

Glyptis, S. (1989). *Leisure and unemployment*. Open University Press.

Glyptis, S., McInnes, H., & Patmore, J. A. (1987). *Leisure and the home*. Sports Council and Economic and Social Research Council.

Godbey, G., Crawford, D., & Shen, X. S. (2010). Assessing hierarchical leisure constraints theory after two decades. *Journal of Leisure Research, 42*(1), 111–134.

Guell, C., Shefer, G., Griffin, S., & Ogilvie, D. (2016). "Keeping your body and mind active": An ethnographic study of aspirations for healthy ageing. *British Medical Journal Open, 6*(1), 1–10.

Hawkins, J. L., Mercer, J., Thirlaway, K. J., & Clayton, D. A. (2013). "Doing" gardening and "being" at the allotment site: Exploring the benefits of allotment gardening for stress reduction and healthy aging. *Ecopsychology, 5*(2), 110–125.

Hawkins, J. L., Smith, A., Backx, K., & Clayton, D. A. (2015). Exercise intensities of gardening tasks within older adult allotment gardeners in Wales. *Journal of Aging and Physical Activity, 23*(2), 161–168.

Heuser, L. (2005). We're not too old to play sports: The career of women lawn bowlers. *Leisure Studies, 24*(1), 45–60.

Hickman, M., Stokes, P., Gammon, S., Beard, C., & Inkster, A. (2018). Moments like diamonds in space: Savoring the ageing process through positive engagement with adventure sports. *Annals of Leisure Research, 21*(5), 612–630.

Higgs, P., & Gilleard, C. (2014). Frailty, abjection and the 'othering' of the fourth age. *Health Sociology Review, 23*(1), 10–19.

Higgs, P., Leontowitsch, M., Stevenson, F., & Jones, I. R. (2009). Not just old and sick—The 'will to health' in later life. *Ageing & Society, 29*(5), 687.

Hope, J., & Havir, L. (2002). You bet they're having fun! Older Americans and casino gambling. *Journal of Aging Studies, 16*(2), 177–197.

Humberstone, B. (2010). *Third age and leisure research: Principles and practice* (B. Humberstone, Ed.). Leisure Studies Association.

Humberstone, B. (2011). Engagements with nature: Ageing and windsurfing. In B. Watson & J. Harpin (Eds.), *Identities, cultures and voices in leisure and sport LSA Publication No. 116* (pp. 159–169). Leisure Studies Association.

Humberstone, B. (2019). Embodied life-long learning in nature, narratives and older bodies -'quit or crash'. *Journal of Adventure Education and Outdoor Learning, 19*(2), 101–110.

Humberstone, B., & Cutler-Riddick, C. (2015). Older women, embodiment and yoga practice. *Ageing & Society, 35*(6), 1221–1241.

Humberstone, B., & Kirby, L. (2003). "Contested knowledges" and leisure studies provision. *Leisure Studies, 22*(1), 51–64.

Ito, E., & Hikoji, K. (2018). Constraints and constraint negotiation when participating in domestic and international masters games. *International Journal of Sport and Health Science, 16*, 120–127.

Jackson, E. L. (1988). Leisure constraints: A survey of past research. *Leisure Sciences, 10*(3), 203–215.

Jackson, E. L. (1991). Special issue introduction leisure constraints constrained leisure. *Leisure Sciences, 13*(4), 273–278.

Jackson, E. L. (2005). *Constraints to leisure*. Venture Publishing, Inc.

Jackson, E. L., & Scott, D. (1999). Constraints to leisure. In E. L. Jackson & T. L. Burton (Eds.), *Leisure studies: Prospects for the 21st century* (pp. 299–321). Venture Publishing, Inc.

Janoschka, M., & Haas, H. (2014). *Contested spatialities of lifestyle migration: Contested spatialities, lifestyle migration and residential tourism*. Routledge.

Joseph, J. (2012). Around the boundary: Alcohol and older Caribbean-Canadian men. *Leisure Studies, 31*(2), 147–163.

Jun, J., & Kyle, G. (2011). The effect of identity conflict/facilitation on the experience of constraints to leisure and constraint negotiating. *Journal of Leisure Research, 43*(2), 176–204.

Katz, S. (2000). Busy bodies: Activity, aging, and the management of everyday life. *Journal of Aging Studies, 14*(2), 135–152.

Katz, S. (2013). Active and successful aging: Lifestyle as a gerontological idea. *Recherches Sociologiques et Anthropologiques [En Ligne], 44*(1), retrieved online 7/2/14. http://rsa.revues.or.

Katz, S. (2018). Livable longevity: Remaking survivorship in old age. In *XIX ISA world congress of sociology* (p. Paper presentation 21st July 2018). Retrieved from https://isaconf.confex.com/isaconf/wc2018/webprogram/Paper90209.html.

Katz, S., & Marshall, B. (2003). New sex for old: Lifestyle, consumerism, and the ethics of aging well. *Journal of Aging Studies, 17*, 3–16.

Kay, T. (1987). *Leisure in the lifestyles of unemployed people: A case study in leicester*. Loughborough University. Retrieved from https://dspace.lboro. ac.uk/ and was harvested from the British Library's EThOS service. http:// www.ethos.bl.uk/.

Khvorostianov, N., Elias, N., & Nimrod, G. (2011). "Without it I am nothing": The internet in the lives of older immigrants. *New Media & Society, 14*(4), 583–599.

Kim, H., & Woo, E. (2014). Research note an examination of missing links between quality of life and tourist motivation. *Tourism Analysis, 19,* 629–636.

Kingsley, J. 'Yotti,' Townsend, M., & Henderson-Wilson, C. (2009). Cultivating health and wellbeing: Members' perceptions of the health benefits of a Port Melbourne community garden. *Leisure Studies, 28*(2), 207–219.

Kleiber, D., Mcguire, F., Aybar-Damali, B., & Norman, W. (2008). Having more by doing less: The paradox of leisure constraints in later life. *Journal of Leisure Research, 40*(3), 343–359.

Kono, S., Ito, E., & Loucks-Atkinson, A. (2018). Are leisure constraints models reflective or formative? Evidence from confirmatory Tetrad Analyses. *Leisure Sciences, 0*(0), 1–21.

Kordel, S. (2016). The production of spaces of the 'good life'—The case of lifestyle migrants in Spain. *Leisure Studies, 35*(2), 129–140.

Kou, L., Xu, H., & Kwan, M. P. (2018). Seasonal mobility and well-being of older people: The case of 'Snowbirds' to Sanya, China. *Health and Place, 54*(August), 155–163.

Leaver, R., & Wiseman, T. (2016). Garden visiting as a meaningful occupation for people in later life. *British Journal of Occupational Therapy, 79*(12), 768–775.

Liechty, T., West, S., Naar, J., & Son, J. (2016). Perceptions of ageing among older women softball players. *Annals of Leisure Research, 20*(3), 1–19.

Lister, J. J., & Nower, L. (2014). Gambling and older adults. In D. Richard, A. Laszczynski, & L. Nower (Eds.), *The Wiley-Blackwell handbook of disordered gambling* (First).

Loo, J. M. Y., Raylu, N., & Oei, T. P. S. (2008). Gambling among the Chinese: A comprehensive review. *Clinical Psychology Review, 28*(7), 1152–1166.

Loroz, P. S. (2004). Golden-age gambling: Psychological benefits and self-concept dynamics in aging consumers' consumption experiences. *Psychology and Marketing, 21*(5), 323–349.

Mair, H. (2009). Club life: Third place and shared leisure in rural Canada. *Leisure Sciences, 31*(5), 450–465.

Massie, A. S., & Meisner, B. A. (2019). Perceptions of aging and experiences of ageism as constraining factors of moderate to vigorous leisure-time physical activity in later life. *Loisir et Société/Society and Leisure, 42*(1), 1–19.

McGuire, F. (1984). A factor analytic study of leisure constraints in advanced adulthood. *Leisure Sciences, 6*(3), 313–326.

Mcguire, F. (2000). What do we know? Not much: The state of leisure and aging research. *Journal of Leisure Research, 32*(1), 97–100.

Mcguire, F., & Norman, W. (2005). The role of constraints in successful aging: Inhibiting or enabling? *Constraints to leisure*. Venture Publishing, Inc.

Meisner, B. A., Hutchinson, S. L., Gallant, K. A., Lauckner, H., & Stilwell, C. L. (2019). Taking 'steps to connect' to later life: Exploring leisure program participation among older adults in rural communities. *Loisir et Société/Society and Leisure, 42*(1), 1–22.

Millington, B. (2012). Use it or lose it: Ageing and the politics of brain training use it or lose it: Ageing and the politics of brain training. *Leisure Studies, 31*(4), 429–446.

Minello, K., & Nixon, D. (2017). 'Hope I never stop': Older men and their two-wheeled love affairs. *Annals of Leisure Research, 20*(1), 75–95.

Mortimer, J. (2011). Case study never too late: Older people and alcohol misuse. *Working with Older People, 15*(2), 71–79.

Nimrod, G. (2014). The benefits of and constraints to participation in seniors' online communities. *Leisure Studies, 33*(3), 247–266.

Nimrod, G. (2016). Innovation theory revisited: Self-preservation innovation versus self-reinvention innovation in later life. *Leisure Sciences, 38*(5), 389–401.

Nimrod, G. (2017). Older audiences in the digital media environment. *Information, Communication & Society, 20*(2), 233–249.

Nimrod, G., Janke, M. C., & Kleiber, D. A. (2015). Leisure and aging qualitative research 15 years into the third millennium. *Journal of Leisure Research, 8*(1), 12–14.

Nimrod, G., & Shrira, A. (2016). The paradox of leisure in later life. *The Journals of Gerontology Series B: Psychological Sciences and Social Sciences, 71*(1), 106–111.

Office for National Statistics. (2013, March). Chapter 1—Smoking (General lifestyle survey overview—A report on the 2011 general lifestyle survey), 14. Retrieved from http://www.ons.gov.uk/ons/rel/ghs/general-lifestyle-survey/2011/rpt-chapter-2.html#tab-Trends-in-alcohol-consumption-over-time.

Okvat, H. A., & Zautra, A. J. (2011). Community gardening: A parsimonious path to individual, community, and environmental resilience. *American Journal of Community Psychology, 47*(3–4), 374–387.

Paganini-Hill, A., Kawas, C. H., & Corrada, M. M. (2007). Type of alcohol consumed, changes in intake over time and mortality: The Leisure World Cohort Study. *Age and Ageing, 36*(2), 203–209.

Park, S. (2007). *Gardening as a physical activity for health in older adults* (Doctoral dissertation, Kansas State University). Retrieved October 28, 2020, from https://krex.k-state.edu/dspace/bitstream/handle/2097/459/Sin-AePark2007.pdf?sequence=1.

Park, S.-A., & Shoemaker, C. A. (2009). Observing body position of older adults while gardening for health benefits and risks. *Activities, Adaptation & Aging, 33*(1), 31–38.

Park, S., Shoemaker, C., & Haub, M. (2008). Can older gardeners meet the physical activity recommendation through gardening? *Hortechnology, 18*(4), 639–643.

Pettigrew, S., & Roberts, M. (2008). Addressing loneliness in later life. *Aging & Mental Health, 12*(3), 302–309.

Redhead, S. (2016). Afterword: A new digital leisure studies for theoretical times. *Leisure Studies, 35*(6), 827–834.

Roberts, K. (2011). Leisure: The importance of being inconsequential. *Leisure Studies, 30*(1), 5–20.

Ryu, J., & Heo, J. (2016). Relaxation and watching televised sports among older adults. *Educational Gerontology, 42*(2), 71–78.

Samdahl, D. M. (2005). Making room for "silly" debate: Critical reflections on leisure constraints research. In E. L. Jackson (Ed.), *Constraints to leisure* (pp. 337–349). Venture Publishing, Inc.

Samdahl, D. M., & Jekubovich, N. J. (1997). A critique of leisure constraints: Comparative analyses and understandings. *Journal of Leisure Research, 29*(4), 430–452.

Silk, M., Caudwell, J., & Gibson, H. (2017). Views on leisure studies: Pasts, presents & future possibilities? *Leisure Studies, 36*(2), 153–162.

Son, J., Kerstetter, D., & Mowen, A. (2008). Do age and gender matter in the constraint negotiation of physically active leisure? *Journal of Leisure Research, 40*(2), 267–289.

Stevenson, N. (2013). Television and cultural citizenship. In T. Blackshaw (Ed.), *Routledge handbook of leisure studies* (pp. 337–346). Routledge.

Subramaniam, M., Wang, P., Soh, P., Vaingankar, J. A., Chong, S. A., Browning, C. J., et al. (2015). Prevalence and determinants of gambling disorder among older adults: A systematic review. *Addictive Behaviors, 41,* 199–209.

Thurston, M., & Green, K. (2004). Adherence to exercise in later life: How can exercise on prescription programmes be made more effective? *Health Promotion International, 19*(3), 379–387.

Toepoel, V. (2013). Ageing, leisure, and social connectedness: How could leisure help reduce social isolation of older people? *Social Indicators Research, 113*(1), 355–372.

Van den Berg, A. E., Van Winsum-Westra, M., De Vries, S., & Van Dillen, S. M. (2010). Allotment gardening and health: A comparative survey among allotment gardeners and their neighbors without an allotment. *Environmental Health a Global Access Science Source, 9*(1), 74. Retrieved from http://www.pubmedcentral.nih.gov/articlerender.fcgi?artid=3001426&tool=pmcentrez&rendertype=abstract.

Van Der Goot, M., Beentjes, J. W. J., & Van Selm, M. (2012). Meanings of television in older adults' lives: An analysis of change and continuity in television viewing. *Ageing & Society, 32*(1), 147.

Walker, G. J., Courneya, K. S., & Deng, J. (2006). Ethnicity, gender, and the theory of planned behavior: The case of playing the lottery. *Journal of Leisure Research, 38*(2), 224–248.

Waller, S. N., & Martin, V. A. (2017). Research note: Religious doctrine and its influence on the choice to gamble as a leisure pastime among African American Methodists. *Leisure Studies, 36*(6), 866–876.

Wang, D., & MacMillan, T. (2013). The benefits of gardening for older adults: A systematic review of the literature. *Activities, Adaptation & Aging, 37*(2), 153–181.

Ward, L., Barnes, M., & Gahagan, B. (2011). Alcohol use in later life—Older people's perspectives. *Quality in Ageing & Older Adults, 12*(4), 239–247.

Wheaton, B. (2017). Surfing through the life-course: Silver surfers' negotiation of ageing. *Annals of Leisure Research, 20*(1), 96–116.

Wood, L., & Kulczycki, C. (2018). A different leisure life: Leisure experiences of snowbirds. *Leisure/Loisir, 42*(4), 481–504.

Yeomans, H., & Critcher, C. (2013). The demon drink. In T. Blackshaw (Ed.), *Routledge handbook of leisure studies* (pp. 305–315). London: Routledge.

York, M., & Wiseman, T. (2012). Gardening as an occupation: A critical review. *British Journal of Occupational Therapy, 75*(2), 76–84.

3

Investigating Private Leisure Lives

The questions of how people negotiate leisure in the context of everyday later life, and how they interact with metanarratives about ageing will inform this methodology. It explores what constitutes evidence and explains the need to find out not just what people do in their leisure lives, but how they negotiate a more leisurely life in a culture that presses for hyperactivity. My engagement with both quantitative and qualitative research in the background and literature review chapters comes from an understanding that research of all kinds works together, and the right methodology is the one that best answers the research question. There are many ways that the questions of how people negotiate leisure in the context of everyday later life, and how they interact with metanarratives about ageing could be addressed. Quantitative research is effective when making systematic comparisons to account for variance in a phenomenon of interest (Silverman, 2004). Large-scale surveys and demographic research referred to in the literature review have shown that the current understandings of constraints to leisure in later life are insufficient. There are cross-sectional and longitudinal studies that illustrate the problems with our current understandings of leisure in later life. But they cannot explain how we can create a different conceptualisation, a new

T. Wiseman, *Leisure in Later Life*, Leisure Studies in a Global Era,
https://doi.org/10.1007/978-3-030-71672-1_3

theoretical perspective on leisure in later life that reflects longer healthier later lives, only that we probably should. They highlight the problem and direct the development of further research. How and what questions are more often answered with qualitative methodologies (Silverman, 2004).

How people negotiate leisure in the context of everyday later life; and how they interact with metanarratives about ageing could be answered by a variety of methodologies, but if quantitative methods are to be used, the components would have to be delimited, named and framed and prioritised, grouped together by related concepts and organised into a questionnaire. The creation of the questionnaire would have to presuppose a great deal in order to create a comprehensive tool for this purpose, and as explained in the literature review this has been a focus of constraints research for many years. Another way to explore this would be to ask open questions, and perform content analysis of the answers, but in the recruitment of 'active agers' to answer a particular question, an identity would be elicited that may lead to predictable answers. Qualitative research is appropriate as it explores meanings that individuals attribute to complex concepts (Creswell, 2013). How people negotiate leisure in the context of everyday later life and how they interact with metanarratives about ageing, for me appears to be very much about social construction and therefore lends itself mostly to a qualitative approach in which people's own stories are fundamental to understanding how they construct their ageing. Observation and discussion constitute evidence when looking at lifestyles (Silverman, 2004). There is a long tradition of ethnography that considers lifestyles and culture, and to an extent this study is about culture, but it is also about how individuals negotiate the culture, more a critique of the culture of ageing, than a description of it.

In order to enter the subjective world of leisure in later life, observation would be insufficient, and hearing directly from informants would be desirable. This cultural interpretation of active aging suggests an ethnographic understanding would be a reasonable place to start the enquiry. There is a long tradition of narrative, or storytelling to explain the particular over the general. People often give accounts of their lives, in verbal and written form, meaning that some form of discourse or narrative enquiry is likely to generate the types of evidence required to address these research questions.

3.1   Narrative Inquiry

If we wish to understand how lives are lived, then one way of investigating this is through narrative inquiry. Narrative inquiry is a suitable approach within the qualitative tradition that explores what can be learned from studying stories (Creswell, 2013). This research will be based in the qualitative tradition, within a narrative frame of reference. This problem should be explored at a narrative level, because it is complicated by narrative conventions that ask for a story about life that is coherent. In life the story can be complex and messy, we can pull up trees and laugh out loud while still needing some help to get washed and dressed each morning. We know this, yet we search for a unitary coherent identity of an active and engaged older person, or one in need of help.

It will use an interpretivist epistemology, embracing my perspectives and reflections, recognising that preconceived ideas are impossible to eliminate. Reflexivity will be employed to ensure that my emerging ideas and biases are transparent (Finlay & Gough, 2003).

Narrative Inquiry is understood as both methodology and method, where the researcher is not a gateway to an authentic account but is part of the process through which a narrative is collectively assembled (Silverman, 2004). Multiple meanings, and the possibility that "*narratives directly challenge stereotypical cultural stories…collective stories that resist the cultural narratives about groups of people and tell alternative stories*" (Silverman, 2004, p. 157) mean this is a suitable way to address the research problem. Narrative inquiry explores the complexities of human life, thought, emotion and action (Webster & Mertova, 2007) and it is a form of inquiry commonly used for research in later life leisure studies (Nimrod et al., 2015). Narrative approaches are illuminating the complexity of later lives, allowing for a more subjective experience of ageing to be explored and reported (Humberstone, 2011, 2019; Phoenix & Bell, 2019; Phoenix & Sparkes, 2009; Phoenix et al., 2010; Pike, 2013; Randall & Khurshid, 2016). Narratives require context, stories are designed, told and interpreted for many functions and are historically situated (Riessman, 2008). Goodson argues that we are entering a period he refers to as 'the age of small narratives' (2017, p. 8), and cautions against decontextualized ahistorical writing of people's lives. So narrative approaches must be embedded in time and place in order to make sense and have meaning. Stepping outside of familiar academic boundaries to tell small stories creates the possibility of representing wider communities beyond the academy (Lorimer, 2003). Attention to small stories has its roots in postmodern approaches to narrative within the humanities, and pays attention to fluidity and contradictions, multiple layered meanings and how dispersed power influences and creates space for narratives (Lyotard, 1984; Tamboukou, 2013). If we listen deeply to the stories that people tell, of heroes and tragedy and comedy, rather than focus on the instruments of bodies, time, money, people and space, then we may come to better understand leisure in later life. The characters and scene are important, but the story is subject to apparently pre-determined narrative slopes of decline in later life (Morganroth Gullette, 2018) and conditioned by life course determinants of health. This is the case, but the story has still to be written, lives still have to be lived, whatever the backdrop. Stories are how culture gets into a person and moves between people, in this way the story is not told by the person, so much as it tells us about the person (Squire et al., 2008). This poststructuralist position is not from the same place as the humanist tradition in narrative (Bruner, 1999) which aims for holistic approaches, placing the person at the centre in the form of individual case studies, life histories and biographies, but the two are often used together, and this familiar form of narrative is influential to an extent in this book (Squire et al., 2008). Culture circulates in stories, if we want to change lives with our research then we must know the stories, and the stories behind those stories that people are telling about their lives. Bearing in mind what I have already said about the co-dependence of active ageing and decline, this will need to be approached subtly in order to find people who speak freely.

Narrative inquiry is the act of conducting case-centred research that retains context, keeping the story whole. The 'case' can be an individual, organisation, or subculture, but exploring the situatedness of the case is essential to the form of narrative inquiry. Here the case in question is the subculture of a leisurely later life at a particular time and place, the UK after 2008. Events are connected in sequence relating past, present and future consequences (Riessman, 2008). I am interested in how people interact with metanarratives, such as disengagement and active ageing. Narrative inquiry asks what stories people are drawing on to create their own. Narrative inquiry considers the story to be the 'truth', rather than looking to a story to uncover a 'real' truth. Narrative inquiry engages with the messiness of human reasoning, the contradictions, the lack of hard facts, and argues that we are all stories in the end. Bruner reminds us that narrative inquiry embraces Kierkegaard's idea that lives are lived forwards, but understood backwards, but Bruner, writing in his 81st year takes it further, 'No story, no self' (1999, p. 8).

The constructs of structure and agency, control and freedom are core to being human, and stories are a way of making sense of ourselves over time (Grant et al., 2012). Songs and theatre, religious texts, history, are all stories, their purpose is to make sense of life (Andrews et al., 2013). Social constructionism supports narrative inquiry because it focuses on uncovering the way that people maintain or change their social reality. This dynamic process of constructing reality requires continual re-affirmation for cultural ideas to persist. In narrative research this re-affirmation consists of the stories people tell, how they tell them, and why they might tell a particular kind of story, this is often referred to as the story behind the story (Riessman, 2008). The stories that we tell about ourselves create emotional states, a life lived well is a life with a culturally relevant story to tell. The animal is in the day to day doings, humanity is in the story, the story is what brings us into being, and we *are* human beings (Booth, 1983).

Bruner discusses Burke's pentad of agents, acts, goals means and settings, and the creation of a story depending upon disturbance. A typical story starts with a steady state, disruption ensues, agents act to restore order, if this fails a new order, or turning point must be found, then it needs to tidied up, so that we may get on with the ordinary act of living forwards, having 'fixed' the story by looking back (Bruner, 1999). There is a risk of fixing an account of ourselves too well, reducing subsequent opportunities, and Bruner warns,

"if the story is trouble free, it is likely to run out, to b[r]ing on death" and he suggests that "Which genre any particular individual in any particular culture adopts as a template for his own life story is partly a function of social position, and partly a function of luck. (Bruner, 1999, p. 9)

The importance of social position and luck feature in the earlier chapters, in relation to demographics and leisure research, and they will continue to run through this work as leisure lives are explored. A view on the idea of disruption requiring narrative remaking is offered by Abrams (2014), who discusses moments of epiphany which offer a different tone when compared to disruption, but amount to a change in perspective/reflection based upon an encounter or realisation of change. She writes that the epiphanic moment is part of a narrative strategy mobilised by a narrator "*attempting to align past and present selves, to make smooth or coherent story from a disjointed or incoherent life*". So, we find a narrative composure in terms of how a self is produced, and then again when this story is recontextualised and reproduced by the narrator (Abrams, 2014, p. 20).

Riessman outlines categories of analysis in narrative enquiry (2008). These techniques appear to be compatible with either analysis of narrative, or as part of a narrative analysis. Some of the forms Riessman explains are thematic analysis, structural analysis, dialogic/performance analysis and visual analysis (2008). Thematic analysis considers what is said, rather than how, to whom or why. Initially this appears to be a superficial form of narrative research, but it is clear from the examples given, that it has much to commend it. Riessman discusses four main forms of thematic analysis of narrative. One explores stories of illness; there is direction in the story relating to Aristotles memisis. The analysis considers time, with reflection on origin (past), and purpose (future). There is some element of locating the researcher in the work and interpreting the biographical disruption caused by illness (Riessman, 2008). Other thematic analysis of narratives explore acts of resistance where analysis focuses on the moral of the story. Riessman also discusses using archival documents to interrogate the data for stories and references to a particular concept (2008). The final category is working ethnographically exploring how a group identity is constructed, considering a range of data sources including documents, field notes and interviews. Analysis of narratives casts the 'participants' as 'narrators' whose stories are analysed (Riessman, 2008). Polkinghorne states "*In the storied outcome of narrative inquiry, the researcher is the narrator of the story, and often the story is told in his or her voice*" (1995, p. 18). The role of narrator is passed from participant to researcher during the production of the work. This understanding works well for analysis of spoken or written narrative. It is more complex when there are a variety of data types. Thematic analysis of narrative, involves drawing out generalisations, linking them to themes and it allows a large quantity of data to be synthesised and summarised (Alleyne, 2015; Riessman, 2008). It is usual for thematic analysis to occur across the full range of participants, looking for commonalities, with the overarching themes linking clearly to contextualised case studies.

How I represent my work, my representational practices impact on my research. Qualitative research has a difficult history; charges of developing colonial knowledge in order to control the 'native other' are discussed by Denzin and Lincoln (2008). More recent work in auto ethnography carries this argument into the 'self' and 'other' positions that health professionals assign to themselves and their patients. The reader becomes uncomfortably aware of their own 'othering' position (Grant et al., 2012). Debates around researcher identity and reflexivity have helped to develop my understanding of relational ethical practices. Many questions arise from this for my research. I aim to expose the 'unfamiliar' and accept it as such in order to develop self-awareness and increase positional validity (Krumer-Nevo & Sidi, 2012; Pillow, 2003). I aim to make visible this process of constructing the questions, collecting and selecting data, and carrying out analysis and representation. I anticipate that this will help to make a more accurate analysis of my research work. As I aspire to become consciously aware of my role in constructing the research, the problem, the setting and the findings, I challenge the assumptions that would lead me to write my participants, issues or setting as familiar (Pillow, 2003). This is my biggest challenge, having completed two prior research projects which asked about later life, published two peer-reviewed journal articles (Leaver & Wiseman, 2016; York & Wiseman, 2012), and two book chapters (Finnie et al., 2017; Wiseman & Sadlo, 2015) and I have supervised many master's projects that supported the development of key ideas. This specifically relates to the importance of reflection to the rejection of the familiar, the idea that I would continue to pursue prior ideas or carry on believing I understood the people when the research and the experience in the garden were telling me different stories. I aim to treat the new stories as exotic, and be open to unfamiliar messages, to expect the unexpected.

Aiming for an answer, a truth about my area of enquiry would work against the critical opportunity that reflexivity offers (Pillow, 2003). In effect it would be a simple uniperspective version of validity. I am not seeking the 'truth'. I should qualify this statement with intention. I do not mean to be seeking the truth. I mean to develop new understandings, there will be many truths. It will be messy and complex. This complexity is a concern across a spectrum of qualitative methodologies, for example Smith in discussing interpretive phenomenological analysis raises the notion of when an interpretation is good enough, not correct or rigorous, but '*good enough*' (2004, p. 46). There are at least two big concerns, one is of cherry-picking participants the second is what is done with their stories.

3.2   Reflexivity

Reflexivity is a way of understanding the politics of power in a researcher/participant/ context/wider community relationship (Andrews et al., 2013). Politics of power is a particularly important concept in this research, as discussed in the background chapter, in relation to power and influence over leisure lives. In order to practice reflexivity, it is important to have skills in reflection, and bring that skill to the researcher/researched relationship. Pillow (2003) discusses the importance of defining how reflexivity is used. How we practice reflexivity, and how these practices impact, open up or limit the possibilities for critical representations (Pillow, 2003) in order to address power relations in research. To be reflexive, then, not only contributes to producing knowledge that aids in understanding and gaining insight into the workings of our social world but also provides insight on how this knowledge is produced (Pillow, 2003). This can be interpreted as patronising, as the researchers aim to share their power with the research participants. Researchers aim to accept their own position of privilege, and thus move closer to their participants. The concept of cultural intuition is useful here, and applicable to my research. Cultural intuition involves bringing cultural and historical insight to the research process to ageism, agendas and social changes. This will impact on the development, process and analysis of the research. Reflexivity is linked with rigour, reflexive researchers explain how experience informs their research, they are encouraged to become aware of "thoughts, feelings, culture, environment, and history and their impact on interactions with participants, data analysis and research findings" (Genoe & Liechty, 2016, p. 470). Post positivist accounts of qualitative research consider rigour (Nicholls, 2009), the idea that reflexivity makes the positions of both researcher and researched transparent, is used to lend credibility to the research. However, the practices of reflexivity are based in finding the truth, and transcending our subjective cultural context, this is problematic to a postmodern viewpoint, but can work with a post-postmodern position, where the best of both is incorporated. Pillow concludes that reflexivity should not seek a happy transcendent ending, but acknowledge the messy realities of doing qualitative research (2003).

Lyotard (1984) explains that modernity is concerned with progress towards one of two possibilities; total knowledge or freedom. Active ageing engages with both modernist metanarratives; it invokes an evidence based, instrumental approach to generate total knowledge in order to control ageing, this is used in tandem with the promise of freedom, from illness, poverty and loneliness. Leisure studies also engages with both, with leisure as learning (Rojek & Blackshaw, 2013) and leisure as freedom (Blackshaw, 2010, 2014; Blackshaw et al., 2013). I argue in the literature review that the 'success' of successful agers is in large part a function of the conditions in which they find themselves, and the impact that can be made on health and longevity is limited. I also argue that much of the research on active ageing reflects the demographics of survivors, demonstrating that people with advantages compounded throughout life with 'middle class' active ageing lifestyles live longer, rather than people that take on 'middle class' active ageing lifestyles can change their odds and live significantly longer healthier, happier lives.

Lyotard offers a sharp view of the loss of traditional heroic metanarratives, his dismay about them being replaced by the dehumanising metanarrative of efficiency and profit that capitalism offers is clear in the following quote;

> *The decision makers attempt to manage these clouds of sociality according to input/output matrices, following a logic which implies that their elements are commensurable and that the whole is determinable. They allocate our lives for the growth of power. In matters of social justice and of scientific truth alike, the legitimation of that power is based on its optimising the system's performance – efficiency. The application of this criterion to all of our games necessarily entails a certain level of terror, whether soft or hard: be operational (that is, commensurable) or disappear.* (Lyotard, 1984, p. xxiv)

That familiar message in workplace and public life is the message that metanarratives about ageing are underpinned by: be operational or disappear.

Lyotard communicates a philosophy that rejects the idea of traditional, followed by modernist followed by postmodernist times, a serial time-bounded explanation does not work. Lyotard argues that these perspectives co-inhabit our experience, they are foregrounded or backgrounded, but one does not replace the other. He argues that postmodernist ideas are those at the vanguard of progress, disturbing existing systems of knowledge, he claims that postmodernist disturbances have occurred throughout enlightenment. The traditional hero narratives, and the modernist all-knowing and emancipatory narratives, and those same narratives repurposed in capitalism live side by side, or as Jameson suggests in the foreword to The Postmodern Condition, they have "gone underground, into our unconscious" (Lyotard, 1984, p. xii).

The role of books and literacy in bringing forward many ways of viewing the world is related to time; books retain the narratives of their time. They are trans historical, as Ricoeur says; "*All the books of the past lie open on my table. None is any older than any other*" (Dowling, 2011, p. 113). Therefore their narratives all inhabit our lives today simultaneously. Ricoeur and Lyotard consider narrative to be a "central instance of the human mind and a mode of thinking fully as legitimate as that of abstract logic" (Lyotard, 1984, p. xi). It is argued by Jameson that their work, with its focus on narrative ways of knowing is itself postmodern, through its unsettling of modernist ways of knowing.

Postmodernist thinking provides an unsettling perpetual challenge to the status quo, for Lyotard an "*avant-guard force within the upheavals of ...modernity that challenges and disrupts its ideas and categories, and makes possible new ways of thinking and acting that resist those modern dominant themes of progress and innovation*" (Malpas, 2003, p. 43). In my book postmodernist thinking will not be ascribed a time period, or conceived as a recent invention that has now retreated; but leading on from Lyotard it will reflect an attitude of scepticism towards metanarratives, particularly the enlightenment narrative (Lyotard, 1984). For Lyotard there is no end, history is open ended, and made by writers. There is also no postmodernist era, postmodernism is a nascent modernism, created and recreated as continual modernist transformation (Malpas, 2003).

Eclecticism, irony and anything goes, is not the mark of postmodernism, it is the realism of contemporary capitalism (Malpas, 2003, p. 45), it is neither radical nor subversive, it is economic consumption functioning effectively. Realism makes the world appear real, it appears true and natural. Modernism disrupts common sense realism, questioning the rules and postmodernism is at the forefront of this disruption. Nothing is safe from, or too sacred to be subject to, the instrumental logic of capitalism (Lyotard, 1984, p. xv). Through Lyotard we can begin to conceptualise the problems of the ageing metanarratives. Active ageing is grounded in capitalism and bookended by the modern speculative grand narrative of learning; if we can learn enough, we can slow or stop the ageing process; and the other grand narrative is of emancipation; whereby when we know enough we will be free from the chains of time. Lyotard feels that both of these ideas have lost credibility (1984). Disengagement is the alternative to being operational, and we have noted in the background and literature review that many people in later life do disappear, into the privacy of their homes.

Negotiation is a concept that is most often used in leisure studies in relation to how people manage particular constraints to leisure participation, in order to do particular activities (Jun & Kyle, 2011). Here it is more widely understood in a constructivist paradigm. A person lives a life, and that life involves understanding and applying the rules and regulations and norms of the culture within which a person finds themselves (Goffman, 1959; Lyotard, 1984). A person's preferences are not always in line with these rules and regulations. In order to live life there are choices to be made, small and big. When a person tells a story about what they have done, they explain their choices, and these explanations form one side of a conversation. The teller cannot know how these choices will be perceived by the listener and will guide the listener to understand their choices as reasonable. They construct one part of an argument for their choices. They imagine the responses from the knowledge they have of the cultural context, the messages that they accept as important. In this sense they negotiate legitimacy for their actions. They 'talk to', and 'do deals with' the cultural narratives (Bruner, 1999). Disengagement and active ageing are cultural narratives that are particularly pertinent to later life; personal responsibility to keep healthy and contribute to society in later life is a matter of public concern (Lassen, 2014).

To address this research question; to generate an open conversation about less active leisure lives; I need to access stories about how people negotiate leisure in the context of everyday later life without eliciting an aged identity and creating favourable response bias that illustrates active ageing. This is a problem inherent in asking people about their later lives. Narrative work already done about later life movement, advocates for people to exercise their capacity to move freely, with structural constraints relaxed, but recognises they can express not moving only in the sense of restoration or recovery (Phoenix & Bell, 2019). This research on later life movement was focused on two studies of physical activity in mid-later life, and one of disease that impacted on balance in early later life, all in southern England between 2012 and 2015, and calls for further research into people's aspirations to be active or otherwise. Conducting research about people's lives usually requires informed consent, to ask people directly about how they negotiate leisure in the context of everyday later life; and how they interact with metanarratives about ageing would potentially lead them to focus on an ageing identity and ageist ideas. To ask people to participate by virtue of their age, even without telling them about the purpose of the study would be to elicit volunteers with an age-focused identity for the duration of the interactions with the researcher (Randall & Phoenix, 2009). So to ethically investigate this problem without pre-conditioning the responses is difficult. Silverman challenges researchers to look beyond the predictable by examining how questions are framed, what lies behind them, and through this, to develop alternative paths for analysis (Silverman, 2004). A social constructionism ontology, along with an interpretivist epistemology and narrative inquiry and my researcher's role as intuitive and amplifier or curator of existing narratives and assembler of perspectives is offered for new critical understanding. These narratives will need to be framed in the context of everyday life, but not complicated by age or leisure and all the implications of virtuous activity that the term carries with it.

My overarching qualitative texts are Silverman (2004) and Denzin and Lincoln (2008). They give slightly different perspectives, allowing me to compare and contrast, and access a range of ideas. Narrative influences are Polkinghorne (1995), Pillow (2003), Riessman (2008), Andrews et al. (2013) and Alleyne (2015), all underpinned by Lyotard and Tamboukou (Lyotard, 1984; Tamboukou, 2013, 2017).

The 'natural history' of this research follows interspersed with the explanation of how I conducted this study in order to examine the framing of the questions and analysis.

3.3   Sustainable Research Methods

In recognition of the diversity of later life, a focus will be needed in order to answer the research questions. Good informants for this study would reflect some of the original context of the shush in the garden, so people in the UK, in the second decade of the twenty-first century will be needed. Additionally, a focus on people living in private homes would remove some of the complexity of social housing from the enquiry. Traditional methods of generating research data about leisure in later life are problematic for this research. Asking people directly about ageing and leisure elicits and highlights an identity of an older person with a level of activity. Leisure, particularly everyday passive leisure is vilified for this age group, and therefore open candid accounts of this kind of leisure are hard to co-create in a researcher/participant relationship, within a culture of 'active ageing'. This book focuses on how the everyday is negotiated, and this cannot be discussed without empirical 'everyday' data for context. Narrative offers different possibilities for generating data, and a range of possibilities for analysing the stories that are generated.

Life history research is a possible approach that involves in-depth interviews and other informal meetings, field notes and transcripts of interactions (Phoenix et al., 2010). It is proposed that direct interviews may be problematic for my research, because the discussion is with me, the researcher, I am identified as a health professional and could be cast as an 'agent of active ageing' by the participants (Katz, 2013; Moulaert & Biggs, 2012). In qualitative research, of any kind, data and stories are elicited according to the interaction of the people involved. Questions are designed, participant information is shared, and the researcher give clues to acceptable answers. A life history interview creates a different form of story, one that interprets life events, reevaluates relationships, and presents them in relation to the research context, a retrospective rewriting. Also people immersed in a particular subculture may feel obliged to focus on some forms of telling above others, drawing on narrative templates (Randall & Phoenix, 2009). So alternative forms were explored.

Another possibility is one of the forms of creative analytic practice, these include ethnodrama, poetic representations, and autoethnography (Phoenix et al., 2010; Smith, 2013). Creative non-fiction is an important narrative form (Gutkind, 2006), it is used in leisure studies research (Humberstone, 2011; Smith, 2013), and aims to present qualitative findings in an engaging and emotive way (Caulley, 2008). Stories about leisure in late life could be created by selecting stories, then weaving direct quotes together and adjusting tenses. The story could be written highlighting as much context as possible that emerges in the analysis. For the initial stages of my research this approach was adopted, creating emotive and engaging stories about later life leisure. This was the method of analysis and representation that was used for the transfer viva of this thesis, restorying accounts of leisure in later life. These stories went some way towards troubling "*conventional notions of ageing ....of an older person and the ways in which their sentient bodies become part of the world around"* (Humberstone, 2019, p. 106). They drew on narrative forms according to Ricoeur (1984), and enabled the creation of accounts of later life that were engaging and illustrative of a phase of life to look forward to. But there were two problems. One was the lack of space for intersubjectivity in the ideas of Ricoeur (Malpas, 2003), which meant that the communal nature of the stories was overlooked in the analysis and representation. The second was that it was not clear enough whose voice was being prioritised, and although I believed it was the participant's voice, the level of synthesis obscured this. A class of my Master's students read one of the stories from my early research, partially reproduced here:

I fall in step behind an ample rounded bottom, a joy to behold, distracted by a Staffie, I bend down to let him give me a lick, Staffies are my favourites, such doggy dogs, those big heads and small ears, the brown brindly ones are the best. We take up an advantageous position and wait, then the staggeringly loud roar of the Eurofighter splits the air, the rumbling makes feel ecstatic, shooting vertically up into the sky with its engine afterburners glowing red. The best things in life are free, and one of those is Eastbourne Air show! ....
More roaring jets, more laughs with my son and grandson, and the staffie goes past again. I like looking at pretty women. The ultimate star of screen is Elizabeth Taylor, a gorgeous lady. Attractive ladies on trains, in cafes, in galleries or anywhere who, when I'm really lucky, are happy to engage with me in conversation, a light flirtation, a dalliance; I think I must look harmless and not too insane when I smile at them. I have on a few occasions been tempted but have not yet cheated on my wife of 52 years. Of course I don't flirt now, with my wife here, having a conscience makes for good behaviour. Time to go home, setting off before the hoards, I can't abide hold ups on roads, so boring and such a waste of time, you never know how long it will be or what has caused it. You open your window and because engines are still on their exhausts stink and pollute the air. The state of the world is so awful, so many people being killed and maimed, often because of religious differences; opposition to totalitarian governments, the worst using torture on their foes. I don't think there has ever been so much dissatisfaction which results in misery for so many. Huge refugee camps, malnutrition, violence serving no purpose. So many distraught mothers... But not for me today, a day with the people I love, in the sun, good food, and great entertainment. We are home in no time, it's a lovely country drive. (Anthony, Wiseman 2015 transfer document)

Two of the students assumed that the voice narrating was mine because the contradictions in Anthony's story did not make sense to them. The main source of confusion was that his articulation, and the content of his stories were mismatched. This was the case in his data and this was conveyed in the story. However, the readers in search of a coherent version of Anthony sought to attribute the articulate creative side to my researcher narrating, and the love of staffies[1] and big rounded ladies' bottoms to a person of dubious character who they both described as having *'tattoos and a sweaty balding sunburnt head'*. The vivid picture that two readers independently shared of the person in the story was surprisingly detailed and stereotypical. They were quite clear, and quite different to the impressions of a third reader, who sat beside them. She was shocked at their description, she imagined a *'Sargent major type, gentile elderly man'*. The first two readers argued that those naughty thoughts could not possibly belong to a gentile elderly man. The other reader did not register the love of brown brindley staffies and appreciation of rounded ladies' bottoms as marks of distinction, she had engaged with his elegant use of language. My three readers were selectively attending to the story and finding two contrasting coherent unitary identities that they could recognise, and they ignored whatever did not fit. After discussing each other's impressions, they were astonished to re-read, and see the 'other' side of the character, saying *'I didn't see that at all, OMG!'* They turned the paper over and checked around the table indicating that they hoped that I had replaced the story with sleight of hand, that I was playing a trick on them. This level of interpretation by the readers was far beyond what I had imagined. I believed I had produced readerly text, the meaning quite clear and fairly fixed, but it transpired that the text was more writerly, with different cultural indicators being uncovered by the readers (Barthes, 1974). Their focus turned in on themselves and their rampant class stereotyping, and they felt quite embarrassed about their assumptions. What they did not see was the clever negotiations that Anthony was making with them. They told me that a bit of cheeky flirting never hurt anyone if it makes him happy. So, Anthony, with my

---

[1] Staffordshire Terriers are often confused with pit bull terriers, which are fighting dogs, banned in the UK due to association with a series of serious attacks leading to death and injury. https://www.bbc.co.uk/newsbeat/article/36367983/the-dog-breeds-that-are-banned-in-the-uk-and-why.

help, persuaded them that not only was his behaviour harmless, but it was also useful to his well-being. But I needed to question that out of them, the point of my Anthony story was subliminal for them, and that did not feel like a safe way to make a point for the purposes of this research. Also, it is not how I want to make my points. I want to tell readers what I have found more clearly and directly in my voice, and have them argue with me, rather than themselves or the participants.

It may be that this is the limit or power of creative non-fiction, or more likely, my newness to writing in this way that made it problematic. Smith (2013) published creative non-fiction about rehabilitation following spinal cord injury, and included four responses to it from different people, capturing the impact, and ensuring that the intended meanings were shared. Other authors say that it is an example of how narratives are co-constructed within the researcher-audience-response relationship (Gready, 2013) in unexpected ways, and this is a good thing. I want to provoke and surprise, but I also want to make my points more directly and fully in writing. Fortunately, there was time to do this. I was in a position to continue to develop my research skills, and drill further down into this 'problem' of how leisure in later life is understood. I want to share what I have come to understand, by being privy to these stories of later life leisure, through a reflexive and analytical iterative process of analysis and representation.

Thus far I have identified a need to use more oblique sources of empirical data. Not about ageing, not about leisure, but from people who are in later life, reporting on everyday lives. If it is not co-constructed in life history style, and not recorded in documentary style, then an archive approach could be profitable, generating data that foregrounds everyday leisure practices and reflections on them, while not directly eliciting ageing, active or otherwise, as an important factor. Using diary or other written narrative forms could enable a rich exploration of the research questions. In addition to the reduction of some of the bias inherent in qualitative research, storied memories, of the kind found in diaries and other written forms, often retain the complexity of the situation, and convey the emotional and motivational meaning behind the tale (Polkinghorne, 1995) this kind of data would enrich the enquiry.

In developing this thesis I have chosen to work with sustainable archive sources, written accounts of everyday leisure and will discuss this in more detail later. The words are the writers own, the choice and context and presentation in this book are mine. I am not aiming to be correct, because there is no 'correct' interpretation. I am creating stories about stories, then putting them together in a way that I hope will create different stories about leisure in later life from the ones we are used to. In this way this research is based on the structuralist narrative tradition (Andrews et al., 2013).

The writer has control until the eyes of someone else roam across their words, someone from a different world, an analytical world would use these words, as proof, as weapons, and vindication, as a source of power—to know the writer better and control them (Kushner, 1995). But when the researcher writes their own version of those words—plays with the context, chooses to focus on a particular point or idea, they are writing as much about themselves as they are writing about the originator of the text, perhaps more so. The use of the words data and originator are not accidental, it is an unusual mix, but no more so than a religious scientist, and this is in keeping with a post-postmodern stance. I consider this complexity of positions a strength in this work. There is a wide variety of choice in ordering and reinterpreting of the words, and careful consideration to making that process visible is important.

3.4   The Mass Observation Archive

Constructing candid accounts of later life leisure is problematic because it requires generation of data about people's leisure lives, and this area of life is private. People are constrained in their disclosures about leisure, but a research resource, The Mass Observation Archive allows a level of openness that enables a richer story to be told (Sheridan, 2000). With no connection between respondent and researcher the anonymity is stronger, and storied accounts are more candid (Sheridan, 2002).

The Mass Observations Archive (MOA) asks ordinary people to observe and write about their culturally embedded lives in Britain (Casey et al., 2014). The Mass Observation Archive holds materials from people that practice leisure and in all its diverse forms and record their understanding of it in day diaries and prose. The Mass Observation Archive is an anonymous transparent public data set in two parts. This research focuses on the second part of the collection, the post 1981 Mass Observation Project. Participants are recruited by The Mass Observation Project (MOP) which asks ordinary people to write about their culturally embedded lives in Britain (Sheridan, 2002).

MOP directives are sent out 3–4 times a year, and each has 2–3 'parts'. A directive is a set of open-ended questions, sent by post or email, asking about personal issues and wider social and political issues and events. Topics are initiated by researchers or prompted by culturally significant events. A researcher contacts the archive curators with an idea for a directive 'part', a member of the archive team then works closely with the research team to design a set of questions that will be acceptable to the correspondents in style and tone, and add continuity to their interaction with the Archive (Courage, 2015).

Sometimes an idea for a directive comes from the Archive team, for example the 2008 'Lifeline' directive was initiated by Dorothy Sheridan the longest standing curator of the Archive, she asked:

Part 2: Your Life Line

Mass Observation is all about people's lives looking back and forwards. in Part 2, could you draw us your "life line" marked up with the key events in your life. If you have never done one before, you start in the year of your birth and come up to the present. Then you mark off as many key events as you think are really important to you. I don't want to prompt you too much as part of the reason of asking you to do this is to see what you think ARE the key events. Just to give you an idea, you might want to mark up the year you started school, or began working for a living, moving house, major travelling experiences, meeting new friends and partners. If you got married or had children those dates might be included. But there are lots of other events which you may feel should be included (like, say, the day you joined Mass Observation!).

This can be as detailed as you wish, and can run on to as many pages as you need. Try to make it as legible as possible - PLEASE! Avoid using real names but if you are mentioning other people use initials and make sure you add their relationship to you (eg "my brother was born"). (Autumn 2008, part 2: Lifeline)

This directive may offer contextual information about people's lives. There is a current panel of over 500 correspondents, they have been recruited in various ways over many years, from a range of sources and usually people volunteer in response to reading or hearing about publications from the Mass Observation Archive materials. The same directive will be sent to all correspondents regardless of demographic or other identifying features. The archive keeps a private record of contact details and correspondents are asked to not name or identify themselves or others and use only the code which has been assigned to them. Responses are written anonymously, lay narratives, thoughts, stories and views on the given topic, sometimes the panellists give their own or another person's life history in response to a question. People that write for the archive are called correspondents and will be referred to as this throughout this work. Mass Observation correspondents write on a range of topics. For example, in the autumn 2015 directive there were three parts, one asked for people's opinions about fraud and scams, the second about bonfire night, and the third about the refugee crisis. In many of the directives there is a 'day diary' question, like this one from the autumn 2015 directive, which may offer insight into everyday leisure lives.

Bonfire Night day diary
Please keep a diary for the 5th November 2015 (or any other date that you attend a bonfire or firework party). Even if you don't do anything to mark this event, we are still interested to hear how you spend the day.
Remember to make a note of everything you do from the moment you rise to going to bed and record any references to bonfires or fireworks that you notice. We would also like you to document any preparations you do for the day; this might include arrangements to help you join in the celebrations or ignore them! We welcome photographs along with your diary, but, as always, please remember not to reveal your identity in these images. (Mass Observation Archive Directive, Autumn 2015, p. 3)

Their contribution is noted in a database, stored in the archive, and can be accessed by appointment by any researcher. The vast majority of the post 1981 archive is stored on paper, with a few directives digitised.

Many Mass Observation Project correspondents are representative of the demographics of people in later life (Parsons, 2013), and their participation in the activity of responding to Mass Observation directives is similar to other voluntary or educational 'active ageing' activities. Previous research on the Mass Observation Archive suggests this is the core group of later life correspondents (Bhatti et al., 2009). Mass Observation Archive has individuals that have answered a range of directives that include a day diary, which allows me to analyse a wide range of contributions, embedded in everyday life. The responses span several years, so can be considered in relation to a correspondents wider life, culture and life course. In effect it is longitudinal data with a direct focus on self-development and cultural context. The directives themselves arise from cultural events/structural changes and are embedded in a 'research culture'.

Some examples of the kinds of questions that have been asked of the correspondents have been given already, the purpose of this section is to explain what kind of data Mass Observation is, how it evolved, and why what I plan to do with it is close to the original purpose, and original methods. Presenting first-person narrative raises questions of what I have chosen, and why, and how I have contextualised it. Blackshaw questions if, "*in giving voice, the only voices that are really heard are those of the sociologists*" (2014, p. 6). He urges a move away from subjugated participants towards a more plural understanding of lives. He further suggests that, "*what we understand about the pluralized worlds in which we find ourselves is only knowable through some kind of story*" (Blackshaw, 2014, p. 10). He proposes new kinds of narrative that deconstruct binaries.

Contextualised stories of everyday leisure as part of life in the round will need to be generated. Stories that are messy and candid. We are all part of the culture of active ageing, but the people who are most clearly managing it are those in later life, so stories from people in later life from 2008 would be informative. Enough of a spread for 'life' to happen, but also post 2008 austerity measures and therefore with an increased focus on self-responsibility, this time period also covers the time of the shush in the garden, and my researcher lifetime.

I make a case that it would be reasonable to consider the Mass Observation writings as somewhat ambiguous, somewhere between front and backstage (Goffman, 1959). Between performance and reflection. They are at least as telling as a conversation, and often messier than interview data in terms of the presentation of self. Counter to expectation they do not present a tidy 'front', there are many lapses and contradictions. This ambiguity may in part be explained by people's motives in writing for the archive, some do so as social research, but others write for fun, or to reflect on their own situation, happy that they will not be judged for poor grammar or handwriting. Many report that they do not even think about who may read their writing and what they may do with it, they just want to make a mark (Holland & Wiseman, 2018, unpublished master's thesis). They have made a mark on me, taking me from an observer ethnographer to an archival researcher during the first sitting on 14 January 2015. While background reading for research about gardening in sheltered housing at the Mass Observation Archive I discovered, as this excerpt from my reflective diary shows:

> this data is so different, so blunt, my participants could never tell me this – I am the problem in my research – I am the agent of active ageing – I ask them to tell me how brilliant gardening is, and how much they need me, and how they love to age actively – but here these people laugh at that perspective, name the game, then tell the archive how it really is – I could never even dream to create data like this… It is me, I am the problem in this research. 14/01/2015

And again on 22/1/15

> how can I go on now with a broken project, when it is so clear now that if I really want to understand what it is to be managing the active ageing discourse in the UK in the 21st century that this is where I need to be looking. And these are the negative ones – losing the garden, and ageing and care and **euthanasia**, and yet still they paint a more hopeful picture of later life than anything else I have read or heard. These people are amazing – just like my ladies [gardening research participants], except they are saying so.

People go off subject, and are given permission to do so, they talk about what matters to them. They take their time, craft and consider. This method of data generation is not trying to catch a person off guard. This was when I first recognised the 'extraordinary older person' narrative where people report that they are old, but they are special, because they are not like 'other' old people. Triumphing despite the adversity of being 'old'. This is also when I asked myself how is it that *all of these people* are special, and different from 'other old people', who are these '**other old people**'?

Reading on active ageing confirmed for me that they are the people that we are warned about in the active aging adverts, they are poor and frail and visibly vulnerable (Martin, 2011). They did not save enough money, and they gave up on staying active. They should have tried harder. I know this is unfair, because the majority of influence on ageing well and wealthy is not within individual control. Further reading of demographic and sociological research led me to cast active aging as a 'myth of control' which is confounded by the long arm theory. Meaning that demographic studies show us that the likelihood of growing very old is predicted by structural inequalities. On average the older a group is, the better off they are. Cultural consonance is present for relatively well-off older people because the active ageing metanarrative reflects their lives. They do not identify with vulnerability and frailty, and more than that, they do not want to be reminded of the possibility of these things. A combination of 'love at first sight' of the archive data, or what Steedman would call archive fever (2001), and a rational elimination of other possibilities through experience and drawing on the experience of other researchers created a new opportunity.

I understand that archive research has an ambiguous status in social science research; I am fully aware that the social scientist in me is out of place at history conferences. But it is time to consider the interdisciplinary opportunity that this presents, rather than a novel method, this offers a credible enrichment of the way leisure is studied (Snape & Spracklen, 2019). One view point at one point in time could never be enough to appreciate the most complex of human experiences; leisure, at the most complex time of life; when we are old.

Archive research is not an easy option, it is not convenient, or something to do when you run out of time. It is awkward and intense and emotional. I go into more detail in the analysis sections about this. The decision to engage with the Mass Observation Archive came from a frustration with traditional qualitative healthy ageing studies. It is an active choice after many years of generating predictable data in other ways through interviews, focus groups, and action research. Mass Observation directives and diaries construct 'unimpeded' situated data that do not ask about ageing or leisure but elicit stories about everyday life. Mass Observation data is characterised as messy, big and awkward, but with that comes a sensuousness and intimacy, the contributors have an unusual role in that they are observing and observed giving detailed accounts of the every day, and the potential for longitudinal research, and research into later life is excellent (Casey et al., 2014).

I embrace the search for 'truth' in the 'archive fever' tradition (Steedman, 2001). The stories of later life have their own life world, they are true in their own terms. The archive I engage with aims to give voice to 'ordinary people' (Hinton, 2013). I have taken on the responsibility of bringing those stories out of the buff folders, and onto these pages in an ambitious attempt to illustrate plural understandings of what it means to be an 'active' ager for these correspondents, at this time.

3.5   Respecting the Genesis of the Data

Hinton's (2013) history of the early phase of the Mass Observation Archive highlights additional important points for my use of this data in this way. Madge and Harrison, founders of the archive in 1936, were privileged young men who were interested in what the masses thought at a time of social upheaval. The respondents in their initial Bolton project were working class, but literacy was always essential to engagement. With the academic inflation over the twentieth century, and increase in middle-class jobs, literate, engaged people write for the second phase of the Mass Observation Archive, the Mass Observation Project, except now they are middle class, and many of them are retired. Harrison started out as an ornithologist turned ethnographer in 1936, but within two years of managing a team of people observing and interviewing people in the ethnographic tradition of an immersive anthropologist he moved to respondent accounts, he was, according to Hinton, rather embarrassed and defensive about his U-turn, but convinced that the diaries and directives were a better way to know what people thought than watching what they did (Hinton, 2013). Everyday leisure was a focus of Mass Observation from the earliest stages and continues to be. The Mass Observation publication 'The Pub and the People' (Harrison, 1943) expresses concerns about the "*shift in emphasis of people's leisure from active and communal forms to those that are passive and individual…*" (Hinton, 2013). These concerns could have been written last week about people in the third age where concerns about social isolation pervade troublingly in contemporary leisure research (Glover, 2018).

The Mass Observation Project was conceived in turbulent times. It was recognised by Harrison, an ornithologist, and Madge, a Marxist, that the master narratives of the day around 'crisis' were not reflecting everyday life. The newspaper reports told readers what 'the man in the street' was concerned about without ever engaging with 'him'. There was intense speculation about a changing world around the abdication of Edward VIII, the rise of Fascism, and threat of war. This era parallels today with 'post-truth' politics, the rise of authoritarian leaders, the threat of terror, and crisis-led news. The 'crisis' that my book focuses on is the 'demographic boom' an ageing population is written as a threat to civil society, one that must be managed (Bazalgette et al., 2011), a matter of concern (Lassen, 2014). The plight of the 'poor' in the 1930s echoes the divide between political discourse and popular culture around ageing, with the 'plight of the poor frail elderly' disconnected from the everyday experience of later life (Humberstone, 2019). But there is a major difference in that people in later life are predominantly politically engaged voters and consumers, unlike the original Mass Observers. It is imperative to once again question what we now call the metanarratives of crisis, and ask what the people really think about living longer lives. The Mass Observation Archive was created for this purpose—to interrogate the popular and political narratives around what it is like to live a certain kind of life. The Mass Observation Archive can tell us if people respond to these narratives, and if so, how.

It took Harrison 2 years to turn his back on observation of people in the ornithological sense, and to realise that the best way to find out what people thought was to read their stories. It has taken 80 years for it to come back into fashion. All through modernity, to postmodern ideas, finally narrative has returned. The oldest form of meaning making, has become the newest form of presenting research findings.

The original survey materials from the 1930s to the mid-1950s cover wartime and beyond. The interest in the format tailed off in the 1960s, but as the materials grew older they took on historical significance, and more recently they have been made available online. The early Mass Observation Archive is mostly digitised, and historians, sociologists, and human geographers from all over the world use it to explore everyday life (Cairns, 2007; Casey, 2014; Harper & Porter, 1995; Knight et al., 2015; Moss et al., 2016; Robinson, 2012; Savage, 2007; Snape, 2013, 2015; Wood, 2015).

Since 1981 a second phase has been collecting writings about everyday life from a panel of around 500 members at any given time. Since 1981 there have been around 4500 writers that have joined the Mass Observation Project and left the panel, but there is a stable core, and some writers have been contributing throughout this time. Despite its longevity, and history Mass Observation research is still being introduced as method (Casey et al., 2014). Some researchers use to opportunity to work between both projects to explore cultural shifts over time (Cairns, 2008; Casey, 2014; Clarke et al., 2017). Other research works within the post-1981 archive which is moving away from methodologically niche publication into mainstream sociology (Baker & Geiringer, 2019; Dawson et al., 2017; Kramer, 2014; Lindsey & Bulloch, 2014; May, 2016, 2018; Smart, 2011; Stenner et al., 2012; Cook, 2017).

3.6   Strengths and Limitations of the Mass Observation Archive as the Resource for This Research

MOP correspondents are not representative of the general population (Sheridan, 2009). There are 500 active correspondents. It was heavily biased towards older women in the South East, but recruitment criteria targeting younger people from northern UK has been effective in rebalancing the sample. Currently, 59% of correspondents are female, 38% are over 50. In 2012 17% were aged 70+ The median number of responses from a correspondent is 5, although 10% have responded to 50+ directives (Parsons, 2013). The demographics of the people that create the data available in the archives should not be seen as weakness in the context of this study because people with cultural and economic capital, like these correspondents are suitable informants for this study.

The Mass Observation Archive correspondents are increasingly becoming representative of the general population, but many are from a more socioculturally privileged background, and writing in later life. It is perhaps more interesting to ask who the Mass Observers are, rather than whether they are representative (Lindsey & Bulloch, 2014), and this is explored in the introduction to the correspondents section in the findings chapter. Sheridan (2002) explains that the nature of the MOA means that authors are inseparably connected to the social situation which informs their writing; satisfying a need for their experiences to be contextualised within culture.

In summary the Mass Observation offers a breadth of leisure, not an activity focus, but as part of life in the round. Narrative inquiry considers the individual, and their cultural context. The data is narrative, talks about self-development, and is longitudinal. The longer term correspondents are active ageing people, for some studies this would be problematic because they are not representative of the general population. However, as noted a large proportion of people that survive into healthy later life are active agers, therefore it is important to generate new knowledge about this group's leisure.

Many Mass Observation Archive correspondents are representative of the core group of demographics of people in later life (Parsons, 2013), and their participation in the activity of responding to Mass Observation directives is similar to other voluntary or educational 'active ageing' activities, such as those carried out with the U3A (Hubble & Tew, 2013). Previous research on the Mass Observation Archive shows this is the core group of later life correspondents (Bhatti et al., 2009).

One limitation that should be embraced, is that correspondents will write what they want to write, they will not be corralled into writing about how wonderful gardening is, for example. They will say how much they dread it, what a chore it is, and how they have no interest in it, and they will write that for more than six double-sided pages, expressing how relieved they will be when it is no longer their responsibility, and they can visit parks that someone else looks after (Perris & Wiseman, 2019, unpublished masters thesis). This limitation, in this work, is the best thing that could happen, this is a missing voice in the gardening and well-being literature, it was the one that drew me in. It heralds a multiplicity of bold views.

In order to consider leisure as part of lifestyle a wide range of leisure pursuits needs to be explored. The Mass Observation Archive has many individuals in later life that have answered multiple directives about a wide range of leisure pursuits, and recorded several day diaries, which allows me to analyse a wide range of leisure pursuits embedded in everyday life. The responses span several years, so can be considered in relation to a correspondent's wider life, culture and life course. In effect it is longitudinal data with a direct focus on self-development and cultural context. The directives themselves arise from cultural events and structural changes and are embedded in a 'research culture'.

Mass Observation Archive directives provoke candid open accounts that enable leisure lifestyles to be analysed (Pollen, 2013). Mass Observation Archive data is excellent for applying Blackshaw's and Rojek's arguments to understand how leisure lives are negotiated and analysing relationships between self-development and culture (Rojek & Blackshaw, 2013). Mass Observation directives ask people about their beliefs and experience in a very wide range of matters, but do not presuppose that they will focus on being old, ill or lonely, and they do not aim to solve these 'problems'.

From a narrative perspective it is reasonable to say that we do not know what we think, and what we want others to know that we think until we write it down, the act of writing allows for reflection and consideration of what is important, what should go in, what should be left out, and whether it is worth it (Rolfe, 1997, 2016). With time for reflection it is potentially an ethically safer form of self-disclosure than perhaps focus groups or interviews. There are concerns about self-censorship in written accounts, if these were founded it would seem likely that these Mass Observation accounts of everyday life would contain more approval seeking cultural bias, be more idealistic, and present coherent, competent heroic writers. But they don't. The writers are candid, messy, contradictory, not just from season to season and year to year, but within a single directive. People say things they would never say out loud, tell secrets (Smart, 2011), and thus there is a need for some pragmatic protective censorship of the correspondents by the archive on particular issues, perhaps of extreme views that may be culturally unacceptable (Mass Observation Project, 2009). The material is still available to view but may not be reproduced without prior discussion and clearance. There is a system of adding a red paper sheet to any entries considered too sensitive or private to share in the lifetime of the correspondent, and correspondents can add time release embargoes to their own writing. It appears that the relationship with the archive is one of unconditional positive regard, and the writers can imagine their own accepting reader. This material is narrative. People write stories about what happened to them. These stories are influenced by larger narratives. What people write, and how they write it is influenced by metanarratives. It is the impact of these that I seek to understand, with a focus on active ageing.

In order to generate suitable evidence first-person candid accounts of a variety of leisure pursuits and day diaries were used. When correspondents explain their participation in a leisure experience, they negotiate its meaning with the reader. They construct a story that conveys their beliefs and values and these interact with the reader's beliefs and values (Polkinghorne, 1995). Explanations and persuasive language that tells the reader what is important help to illustrate negotiation skills (Alleyne,

2015). One of the strengths of the MOA data is an emphasis on subjectivity and self-representation (Parsons, 2013).

The risk in narrative research is when faced with a context, in this case, leisure in later life, researchers are inviting participants to produce a retrospective rewriting of history, an understanding of why they have come to this point (Silverman, 2004). A further problem with narrative is the idea of narrative slopes, the description of events over time, and how they are connected, and the relationship of that connection, whether they get better or worse, slope up or down (Josephsson et al., 2006). When this idea of narrative slopes is associated with ageing the assumption is of a single direction of travel, and in active ageing terms that direction of travel is down, but fighting all the way. One way of overcoming this is to ask people about events of the day and resisting the urge to impose a slope. In order to explore this topic a more open conversation is needed about lifestyles in later life, valuing a wide variety of leisure experiences, in order to create a new conceptualisation of later lifestyles.

Blackshaw (2010) suggests that we are all in constant transition in our leisure lives, in a constant contingent state, the directives chosen for my study were recorded over a ten-year period, long enough for life to happen. Drawing on everyday leisure stories with a belief that "*the locus of leisure forms and practices is subjective intentionality*" (Rojek, 2010, p. 7) this data is subjectively focused and presented. These two taken together mean that everyday leisure needs to be written at the time, not retrospectively and coherently, but candid and messy. An elicited identity as a Mass Observer encourages a candid, often messy writing of 'how it is', someone who aims to speak truth to power, rather than a 'person in later life'. This current writing also means that a person is responding to what is in the 'ether', interacting with day to day events and agendas.

The Archive materials are wonderfully awkward, responses are elicited by Mass Observation Project directives, brief examples of the kind of questions have already been given in this chapter, and further examples can be seen by searching the mass observation archive web pages. Initially the correspondent may have had thoughts and opinions about the topics, or possibly the ideas were new to them, but either way they have been asked to write about them for the archive. This has caused the correspondents to ponder the questions and then write about them; there is encouragement to write whatever is in mind so people do not always stick directly to the brief, or at all in many instances.

The responses arrive at the archive electronically or in paper form, hand written, or word processed. They are stored in paper form, with responses to each directive placed in up to three different boxes. They are kept in buff card folders in shallow A4 cardboard boxes. A directive box contains all responses to a single part of a directive, and this section may be further divided alphabetically by correspondents' codes, into multiple folders if there are large numbers of responses. Individual correspondent's contributions are therefore filed separately across different directive boxes. The majority of the post-1981 correspondence can only be accessed at the Keep, Sussex, UK. A reader's seat needs to be booked in advance for the day. Researchers can book up to three boxes in advance, each will contain multiple folders organised in alphabetical order. If many people have responded then the correspondence will be subdivided into folders, for example, a–b, c–d, etc. A researcher can view only one folder at a time, returning it before viewing the next one. A single folder can easily take a day to read if there are no selection criteria. In addition to this, reading and selecting, then transcribing handwritten materials is labour intensive. Developments in technology are reducing the labour involved for the word processed responses, including scanning on mobile phones, and character recognition software, so there is a great opportunity to use the MOA's rich archival data to build an understanding of people's lives. There is a £10 administration charge for each day of scanning, a record of scanned documents must be made and logged with the Archivists.

There is no personally identifying data such as names available to the researcher, which adds a layer of anonymity. The MOA organisation holds the correspondence and ensures consent and anonymity; copyright of archive materials is protected by the trustees, and publication of quotes must be agreed with the archivists. So working with the archive materials is a little awkward, but the archivists are as besotted with the correspondents as I am, and delighted when the stories are brought into the light, as one said to me:

I am so glad you are writing about xxxx he always uses such nice envelopes and interesting stamps.

It is a world of its own, with its own climate of chilled air conditioning all the year around I packed a large woolly blanket for each trip. The rules and regulations, a purposeful quietness, dull buff folders just waiting to burst into life, one surprising story after another just a page turn away, a shared passion and purpose of the archivists and the researchers. Each box I was interested in was booked, the relevant correspondents were identified, and their correspondence scanned to pdf. Each pdf was named by directive code (my own) correspondents' number (archives) and T or H for typed or handwritten. The typed responses were later put through character recognition software edited for accuracy and saved with the same name as a word document. Handwritten work was scanned to PDF at the Keep, then transcribed and saved as a word document with the same file name. This means that each file name is searchable by person and directive code and content. This was saved in a raw data file on a password-protected computer to ensure privacy and copyright protection of the archival data. The sense of community and adventure is gently shared, it is such a pleasure and privilege to be part of it. It is difficult to engage with concepts around the power of the archivists (Steedman, 2001) when we are all so besotted with the correspondents. Entering the 'special collections' room through the sliding glass door with my researchers ID created a sense of belonging to something very serious. Learning the competencies required to navigate the collection and becoming a Mass Observation Archive researcher is a precious gift from my doctoral studies.

Interviews and observations are commonly employed in narrative research, this means that the stories are co-authored from the beginning, and the person of the research interviewer introduces a 'wildcard' element (Randall & Phoenix, 2009). In a longitudinal study the element of interviewer variability increases, as interviewers change over time, or additional interviewers are employed in the generation of data, this can be further complicated by additional researchers analysing the data.

For longitudinal narrative studies, it can be argued that the consistency offered by the Mass Observation directives gathered over time is beneficial in terms of coherence. It can be further argued that a single situated, reflexive researcher can read and analyse and present those responses in a persuasive, coherent, and pragmatic way. Some sociologists are critical of Mass Observation data. Hubble explains that critics of the Mass Observation Archive naively describe it as unscientific, a middle-class adventure at the expense of the working class and a deeply flawed social survey (2010). If the paradigm is one of truth seeking, theory grounded in the data, seeing into the minds of others, understanding their experience then transferring that understanding to the minds of readers, then some of the criticisms of Mass Observation 'data' hold true. Because it is unrepresentative of the general population, and there is little or no connection between the researcher and the correspondents to facilitate this truth seeking (Bloom et al., 1993; Sheridan, 1996). However, in narrative terms persuasiveness, coherence, and pragmatism are the essential concepts to consider in evaluating the quality of a study (Riessman, 2008). The initial correspondence is constructed, and presented, entirely at the discretion of the correspondent, and available to view for any future reader of the research, this is valuable for their persuasiveness in narrative research. The analysis and interpretation of the single situated researcher aids coherence.

The Mass Observation Archive holds first-person storied data, writers provide biographical contextualised stories, carefully crafted to tell their story their way. I intend to retain context of quotes, situate them in the everyday from which they arose. I will add context and background and aim to retain the person and their every-day-ness, and arrange the story to make points that arise from their stories. I do not aim to catch them unawares, and get to a 'real truth', because I do not believe that a 'real truth' exists. There are multiple truths within and between people, and when people write to the archive they are writing themselves, securing an autobiographical footprint (Sheridan, 1993). Some Mass Observation researchers use thematic analysis of a single directive (Adams & Raisborough, 2010; Busby, 2000; Harper & Porter, 1995; Knight et al., 2015; Lindsey & Bulloch, 2013; Noakes, 1996; Thomas, 2002; Wilson-Kovacs, 2014; Wood, 2015). Others compare themes across two different time points (Casey, 2014; Knight et al., 2015; Kushner, 1995) Or explore two connected directives (Bhatti, 2006; Bhatti et al., 2009) or use and additional data source such as a survey to complement the Mass Observation data (Bhatti & Church, 2000, 2001). Others take a longitudinal biographical perspective and follow individuals across several directives (Garfield, 2004; Hinton, 2010, 2016; Hubble & Tew, 2013; Lindsey et al., 2015), rather than seek to produce typical cases, researchers engage with 'telling cases' (Bloom et al., 1993; Sheridan, 1993) or they treat the responses as rhetorical, assuming the writing is social commentary (Bloom et al., 1993). All of them employ abstracts from the Mass Observation responses and allow people to speak for themselves. The more engaging ones give fuller quotes, ensure that the social and political context and the sense of a complex multi-layered narrative is retained (see for example Hubble, 2010). I want to analyse the stories in order to understand how they are interacting with grand narratives around leisure and later life. Then I will curate and write my critical interpretation of this. Any reading of the correspondence is a situated re-reading, and any writing about it is situated rewriting. I am to make that process as transparent as possible to create a persuasive, coherent, and pragmatic thematic analysis of narrative of leisure in later life.

The Mass Observation Archive material has been cast as 'secondary data', and therefore in some way inferior. There are shifting attitudes about the use of secondary qualitative data, and this turn has created opportunities to make better use of the Mass Observation Archive. There is policy and practice to encourage the use of qualitative data by researchers that have not generated it (Lindsey & Bulloch, 2014; Lindsey et al., 2015; Moore, 2007; Neale, 2013). Data collected by a person other than the researcher is framed as 'secondary data', for some research paradigms this is discussed as problematic, and.

> *the concerns centre on conducting secondary analysis whilst also retaining a sense of the way in which the data were produced.* (Lindsey & Bulloch, 2014, p. 2)

In the UK there has been debate over the secondary use of qualitative data, and the concerns settle around the original construction of the data, but these concerns underestimate the contemporary context, and the reflexivity of re-users of data (Holland, 2011). Despite this concern qualitative databases are being encouraged as a sustainable research resource (ESRC, 2015). In addition to this, there is a call from research funding bodies to re-use data from publicly funded qualitative research, including the Economic and Social Research Council Open Access Policy (ESRC, 2015) and the Research Councils UK (2013). The boundary of what is primary and what is secondary is more fluid than it would appear; it is common practice for a research assistant to conduct interviews for analysis by a lead researcher, but this is not considered to be a secondary analysis. The primary or secondary generation of data is not always clear cut, but with my use of the Mass Observation Archive it is clear that I had nothing whatever to do with the generation of the data, it was created by other researchers. So to me it is indeed secondary in this sense. However, the charge that secondary data is in some way inferior belongs to a different paradigm to the one I am working with, and this will be discussed next.

Historians and biographers, and literary and theology researchers have no choice but to use pre-produced data and artefacts, in these disciplines archives are considered a primary source, and the writings produced about them are considered to be secondary sources. So this is not as simple as it first appears. These Mass Observation Archive directives are first-person stories, primary sources, requested by a research organisation, rather than by me which makes them secondary data in some social science terms. I think the treatment of these primary archival sources as secondary data is misleading. I think that this is primary narrative data.

I think that the disconnection between researcher and correspondent brings some advantages. This data is not free from interference; but importantly it is free from *my interference* on the critical active ageing perspective, I have not created artefacts in my construction of research questions and participant information sheets. I have not asked people what they think about the dominance of active ageing discourses, I have not encouraged them to tell dismissive and subversive stories about active ageing. I have not nodded vigorously when they object to being told what to do or wrinkled my nose when they tell of others that are 'conforming'. I have simply found writers that write at length and in multiple directives, people who write for the archive voluntarily. I have looked to see what their everyday lives are like, and if there are signs of how people negotiate leisure in the context of everyday later life; and how they interact with metanarratives about ageing.

Kozinets et al. claims that historically, 'archival data' has rarely been used to develop concepts and theories in research (2008). More commonly, researchers who are collecting interview or observational data use the archival data for context, as I did in the beginning. A possible reason for this is the complexity of navigating the directives may be off-putting, as already touched upon. But clearly Kozinets is writing about a narrow range of concepts and theories, because, as already discussed, archival research is core to many subject areas.

I did not co-create the written responses that the research draws on, in the way that literary or historical researchers do not generate their sources. I asked a question of these fixed accounts on paper and in time, and created a 'story' from them that illustrates later life, and how that later, mostly leisurely, life interacts with metanarratives about ageing. The co-creation is in how I have sought, selected, read and presented their stories (Alleyne, 2015), this will be discussed in detail in the analysis chapter.

There is opportunity for authentic persuasive accounts as there are lots of temporal stops because the directives are focused on particular dates, and there are reports on external events in the correspondence. Some of these are stories that I recall in my life, some I am not part of, but know of, and others are new to me. The correspondents and myself share similar aspects of being in the world in temporal terms, we are exposed to many of the same stories outside of the world of the correspondents' text (Ricoeur, 1984), and share an interest in growing older in the UK in the twenty-first century, mine is more academic and personal, theirs more personal and autobiographical.

I read the stories, the big narratives and the little ones, I was not guiding their telling with my approving nods, or my disapproving raised eyebrows. I was reading them with my approving nods and raised eyebrows. I could respond openly and with no control by the correspondent over how I should feel about some information, and this partly told me where my own views were situated. I know that the correspondents are writing about their lives, but it is not very relevant whether it is 'true', whatever that might mean, because what I am interested in is which narratives they are interacting with, and how they are using them when they write to the archive. Readers of my transfer document stories asked what happens on a bad day, implying that the stories paint too rosy a picture, and it must surely be worse than this to be old. Research nearly always focuses on the crisis days in ageing, what it is like to live with injuries, illness, and bereavement, there is plenty of research like that. It appears that Mass Observation correspondents are too busy to write in very bad times, for example one person has a gap which covers bereavement, another one that covers injury. It is important to remember what this enquiry is, it is an enquiry into the everyday, the norm, and crisis, by definition, is exceptional and not the focus of this research.

Although I did not co-create the stories that the correspondents contribute, I acknowledge that the 'institution' did co-create this data, it has an historical, ethnographic background. People are not writing themselves from their own starting point, but in response to direction, it is like a very long, open interview which allows time to ponder and create a good answer. Because I did not co-create this data there are no field notes from my perspective, but I argue that my 'view', much like an ornithologist's view, would tell me little about how a person sees themselves in their culture, only how I see them, which is not relevant to this particular enquiry. I am interpreting how they report they are interacting with active ageing.

Field notes suggest a literal truth, they report what was seen—'the person was unkempt and smelled but explained that they were returning from a very important business meeting'. This suggests some delusion. I want to know people's delusions, illusions, self-aggrandisements, aspirations, disappointments in others who have no say in the work, including but not limited to friends, family and neighbours. If they matter to the correspondent, they matter to me. However, the very nature of the data, the candid and subversive expression in the archives suggests a level of openness is achieved that I, as a situated researcher with a leading participant information sheet, and a self-fulfilling set of questions could never hope to achieve alone.

The perspective I am re-telling the Mass Observers stories from is that of a person critical of the active ageing agenda, critical of the appropriation of leisure in the name of promoting individual health and well-being. I am interested in whether people interact with the metanarratives about ageing, and if so, how so? I am taking a micro-analytic approach, considering the stories of individuals to be personal sense-making strategies, drawing on Lyotard's 'petit récits', or little narratives (1984), and analyzing how these relate to and confirm dominant metanarratives, but also subvert and resist them (Bamberg & Andrews, 2004). It would appear to be a risky strategy to look for contradiction in carefully constructed stories, written for the Mass Observation Archive, but many writers comment on the complex messy and contradictory nature of the Mass Observation data (see for example Casey et al., 2014; Hinton, 2010, 2016; Pollen, 2013; Uprichard et al., 2013; Wilson-Kovacs, 2014). For my project, as theirs, this messiness is ideal. My selections, omissions and curation of the stories will be discussed throughout the analysis section.

I am arguing that as a reader of archival materials, particularly a researcher reader, that I am writerly; that is, I construct my own meanings, understandings and insights based on what I read (Barthes, 1974). These may be close to the writer's ideas, or very far from them. If I re-tell my version, my interpretations, my construction and presentation of this data is then open to other readers who are free to interpret it from their own unique perspectives.

3.7   Ethical Considerations

Consent, anonymity and confidentiality need to be addressed within qualitative research studies (Silverman, 2004). The voluntary respondents are self-motivated in their correspondence (Pollen, 2013). Anonymity and confidentially are upheld with a unique participant Mass Observation code number, of the form A833, R1418, etc. reducing exposure to personally identifiable information within the research process. The code is allocated when the correspondent joins the project and remains the same throughout their time. Further potentially identifiable information used by respondents within the written data was anonymised during the analysis process. Password protected computer guaranteed protection of stored data. I upheld the Mass Observation Archive terms of access (Mass Observation Archive, 2009). Procedural ethical approval was obtained through the School of Environment and Technology, University of Brighton. There is a risk that bringing peoples' diverse directives together can create such a rounded picture that the correspondents could be identifiable, however, care was taken to mask their identity through changing potentially identifying items, such as niche activities, or combinations of places, people and activities that could be identifying. Small snips of handwriting are included to give a closer representation of the material form of the correspondence, but only for people that have not given away secrets. This section, and all quotes and pseudonyms were shared with and cleared by the Mass Observation Archivists.

In traditional anthropology there is a long arm of European colonialism, danger of exposing 'others', knowing them in order to lambast them, manage them or raise them up as exemplars (Behar, 1986). In traditional ethnography with the researcher participating in day to day life, the knowing is with 'others' that both see and hear the researcher. The researcher may participate, be aloof, be vulnerable or engaged, but they will be seen, and to an extent they will be known. With the Mass Observation Archive it is different, and potentially more exposing. The material is intimate and candid, told to the archive, with an understanding that there is a researcher somewhere that may read, but that researcher is imbued with familiarity, spoken to in personal terms by the correspondents, as an old friend might be. Their writing addresses a reading public/future public, this could be compared with other forms of personal correspondence, and personal correspondence is often used in archive research (Tamboukou, 2013) and the construction of biographical work. But it is different to the intimate writing of personal letters in some ways, yet in a sense still personal:

> And so ended my working day, and if you're still awake, dear reader, good night to you and pleasant dreams! (D1602, a working day 2010)

Please excuse my writing, I broke my wrist in February and my cast is now off but my wrist is a problem. (S496, What makes you happy 2013)

I am not their friend, but they draw me in to feel like I am like I know them, but they do not yet know me. I respect them. I understand that they have thought carefully about what they have shared, and that they want these stories to be out there in the world. The ethics of representation is a heavy responsibility when it is not possible to review and request permission from the correspondents to use their material in the way that I have. This means that careful attention has been paid to changing details to ensure anonymity. I have not changed the context of events in order to sensationalise them; I have aimed to tell the stories that illuminate later lifestyles. I have worked closely with the archivist on everything from pseudonyms to the quoted content of the findings chapters, seeking permission to share what I have written. Correspondents sometimes describe, in their correspondence, reading Mass Observation Archive research reports and looking for themselves. I hope they will find themselves in my work.

Ethics of representation is a challenge in this work. It has already been discussed in relation to using creative non-fiction, that the restorying of data has unpredictable outcomes. An engaging and emotive account of people's lives could be achieved through use of the first person, staying close to the data, and developing the skills for this style of writing, is part of my post-doctoral plan. For this stage of the project a more direct approach was taken. The restorying of the correspondence is constructed by the researcher, the narrative weave of the stories is clearly from this perspective, using third person 'about' people. This is supported with first-person explanations from the correspondents. In order to ensure that people have been represented well the data was read and re-read, immersion into the language use and focus of the correspondent was aspired to, before using NVivo software to assist analysis, which is discussed in the analysis section in detail. I have aimed to explain my part in choosing who and what is represented from this large and complex data set in the Methods: analysis chapter that follows.

When quoting from or referring to several sets of directive replies, researchers are asked by the Mass Observation Archive Trustees to specify which directive each quotation came from (Mass Observation Archive, 2009). The use of pseudonyms is frequently adopted by Mass Observation writers, with permission from the trustees (Mass Observation Archive, 2009). Due to the large number of directives for each correspondent a table was used to collate this information.

Traditional notions of trustworthiness and rigour in qualitative research do not fully support evaluation of the quality of narrative studies; Reissman (2008) suggests that the concepts of persuasiveness, coherence, and pragmatism are essential concepts to consider. In this research the reader will be the judge of whether the stories are persuasive, coherent, and pragmatic. In order to enhance these qualities a change was made during analysis from a rather remote third-person narrative, to first-person narrative, with explicit researcher commentary and analysis, to ensure that I am clearly located in the research (Riessman, 2008). A reflexive diary facilitated reflection on the researcher's responses to data, before, during and after analysis. This involved acknowledging feelings and opinions raised by the correspondence, to enable a self-critiquing platform and explore assumptions (Finlay, 2014). It identified and embraced emotional responses to the stories, and the people telling them.

The materials were consulted at the Keep, in Sussex, and through recording conventions of the participant's code and the directive, the materials used in any given research project can be verified or reviewed by other researchers at any time. This transparency has been a feature of the Mass Observation Archive for over 80 years.

References

Abrams, L. (2014). Liberating the female self: Epiphanies, conflict and coherence in the life stories of post-war British women. *Social History*. Taylor & Francis.

Adams, M., & Raisborough, J. (2010). Making a difference: Ethical consumption and the everyday. *British Journal of Sociology, 61*(2), 256–274.

Alleyne, B. (2015). *Narrative networks, storied approaches in a digital age* (C. Rojek, Ed.). Sage.

Andrews, M., Squire, C., & Tamboukou, M. (2013). *Doing narrative research.* Sage.

Baker, J., & Geiringer, D. (2019). Space, text and selfhood: Encounters with the personal computer in the mass observation project archive, 1991–2004. *Contemporary British History, 33*(3), 293–312.

Bamberg, M., & Andrews, M. (2004). *Considering counternarratives: Narrating, resisting, making sense.* John Benjamins.

Barthes, R. (1974). *S/Z* (R. Miller, Ed.). Blackwell.

Bazalgette, L., Holden, J., Tew, P., Hubble, N., & Morrison, J. (2011). *Coming of age.* London. Retrieved from https://dspace.brunel.ac.uk/bitstream/2438/6237/2/Fulltext.pdf.

Behar, R. (1986). *The vulnerable observer: Anthropology that breaks your heart.* Beacon Press.

Bhatti, M. (2006). "When I'm in the garden I can create my own paradise": Homes and gardens in later life. *Sociological Review, 54*(2), 318–341.

Bhatti, M., & Church, A. (2000). 'I never promised you a rose garden': Gender, leisure and home-making. *Leisure Studies, 19*(3), 183–197.

Bhatti, M., & Church, A. (2001). Cultivating natures: Homes and gardens in late modernity. *Sociology, 35*(2), 365–383.

Bhatti, M., Church, A., Claremont, A., & Stenner, P. (2009). 'I love being in the garden': Enchanting encounters in everyday life. *Social and Cultural Geography, 10*(1), 61–76.

Blackshaw, T. (2010). *Leisure.* Routledge.

Blackshaw, T. (2014). The crisis in sociological leisure studies and what to do about it. *Annals of Leisure Research, 17*(2), 127–144.

Blackshaw, T., Long, J., Nicholson, M., Stewart, B., Taylor, P., Gratton, C., & Hughes, J. (2013). Routledge handbook of leisure studies Tony Blackshaw. In T. Blackshaw (Ed.), *Handbook of leisure studies* (pp. 37–41). Routledge.

Bloom, D., Sheridan, D., & Street, B. (1993). *Theoretical and methodological issues in researching the Mass Observation Archive* (The Mass Observation Archive Occasional Papers Series, pp. 1–22). Retrieved from https://www.massobs.org.uk/occasional-papers.

Booth, W. C. (1983). *Rhetoric of fiction* (2nd ed.). The University of Chicago Press.

Bruner, J. (1999). Narratives of aging. *Journal of Aging Studies, 13*(1), 7–9.

Busby, H. (2000). *Health, sickness and the work ethic* (The Mass Observation Archive Occasional Papers Series, No. 11, pp. 1–16). Retrieved from https://www.massobs.org.uk/occasional-papers.

Cairns, T. M. (2007). *Class gender and education in the 20th century: An exploration of educational life histories of correspondents to the Mass Observation Archive.* University of Sussex.

Casey, E. (2014). "Mass gambling" from 1947 to 2011: Controversies and pathologies. *Sociological Research Online, 19*(3), 1–10.

Casey, E., Courage, F., & Hubble, N. (2014). Special section introduction: Mass Observation as method. *Sociological Research Online, 19*(3), 1–7.

Caulley, D. N. (2008). Making qualitative research reports less boring: The techniques of writing creative nonfiction. *Qualitative Inquiry, 14*(3), 424–449.

Clarke, N., Jennings, W., Moss, J., & Stoker, G. (2017). Changing spaces of political encounter and the rise of anti-politics: Evidence from Mass Observation's General Election diaries. *Political Geography, 56,* 13–23.

Cook, M. (2017). AIDS, Mass Observation, and the fate of the permissive turn. *Journal of the History of Sexuality, 26*(2), 239–272.

Courage, F. (2015). *Collaborating on a Mass Observation Project Directive.* Retrieved from https://www.massobs.org.uk/the-archive/collaborating-on-research.

Creswell, J. W. (2013). *Qualitative inquiry and research design: Choosing among five approaches* (3rd ed.). Sage.

Dawson, M., McDonnell, L., & Scott, S. (2017). Note on recruitment as an ethical question: Lessons from a project on asexuality. *International Journal of Social Research Methodology, 20*(3), 255–261.

Denzin, N., & Lincoln, Y. (2008). *The landscape of qualitative research.* Sage.

Dowling, W. C. (2011). *Ricoeur in time and narrative: An introduction to temps et recit.* University of Notre Dame.

ESRC. (2015, January). ESRC framework for research ethics. *Economics and Social Research Council* (pp. 1–51). Retrieved from https://www.esrcsocietytoday.ac.uk/about-esrc/information/framework-for-research-ethics/index.aspx.

Finlay, L. (2014). Engaging phenomenological analysis. *Qualitative Research in Psychology, 11*(2), 121–141.

Finlay, L., & Gough, B. (2003). *Reflexivity: A practical guide for researchers in health and social sciences.* Blackwell Science.

Finnie, K., Wiseman, T., & Ravenscroft, N. (2017). Rambling on: Exploring the complexity of walking as a meaningful activity. In M. C. Hall, R. Yael, &

N. Shoval (Eds.), *The Routledge international handbook of walking* (pp. 253–263). Routledge.

Garfield, S. (2004). *Our hidden lives: The everyday diaries of a Forgotten Britain, 1945–1948*. London: Ebury.

Genoe, M. R., & Liechty, T. (2016). Using our whole selves: Our experiences with reflexivity while researching a community arts-based leisure program. *Leisure/Loisir, 40*(4), 469–492.

Glover, T. D. (2018). All the lonely people: Social isolation and the promise and pitfalls of leisure. *Leisure Sciences, 40*(1–2), 25–35.

Goffman, E. (1959). *The presentaion of self in everyday life*. Penguin Books Ltd.

Goodson, I. (2017). *The Routledge international handbook on narrative and life history* (A. Antikainen, P. Sikes, & M. Andrews, Eds.). Routledge.

Grant, A., Biley, F. C., Leigh-Phippard, H., & Walker, H. (2012). The book, the stories, the people: An ongoing dialogic narrative inquiry study combining a practice development project. Part 2: The practice development context. *Journal of Psychiatric and Mental Health Nursing, 19*(10), 950–957. https://doi.org/10.1111/j.1365-2850.2012.01921.x.

Gready, P. (2013). The public life of narratives: Ethics, politics, methods. In C. Squire, M. Andrews, & M. Tamboukou (Eds.), *Doing narrative research*. Sage.

Gullette, M. M. (2018). Against 'Aging'—How to talk about growing older. *Theory, Culture and Society, 35*(7–8), 251–270.

Gutkind, L. (2006). The 5 Rs of creative nonfiction. *Creative NonFiction, 6*, 1–4.

Harper, S., & Porter, V. (1995). *Weeping in the cinema in 1950: A reassessment of Mass-Observation material* (The Mass Observation Archive Occasional Papers Series, No. 3, pp. 1–34). Retrieved from https://www.massobs.org.uk/occasional-papers.

Harrison, T. (1943). *Mass observation: The pub and the people, a worktown study*. London: Victor Gollancz, Ltd.

Hinton, J. (2010). *Nine wartime lives: Mass-Observation and the making of the modern self*.

Hinton, J. (2013). *The Mass Observers, a history, 1937–1949*. Oxford University Press.

Hinton, J. (2016). *Seven lives from Mass Observation*. Oxford University Press.

Holland, J. (2011). Timescapes: Living a qualitative longitudinal study. *Forum Qualitative Sozialforschung, 12*(3), Article 9.

Hubble, N. (2010). *Mass Observation and everyday life, culture, history, theory*. Palgrave Macmillan.

Hubble, N., & Tew, P. (2013). *Ageing, narrative and identity: New qualitative social research*. Springer.

Humberstone, B. (2011). Engagements with nature: Ageing and windsurfing. In B. Watson & J. Harpin (Eds.), *Identities, cultures and voices in leisure and sport LSA Publication No. 116* (pp. 159–169). Leisure Studies Association.

Humberstone, B. (2019). Embodied life-long learning in nature, narratives and older bodies—'quit or crash.' *Journal of Adventure Education and Outdoor Learning, 19*(2), 101–110.

Josephsson, S., Asaba, E., Jonsson, H., & Alsaker, S. (2006). Creativity and order in communication: Implications from philosophy to narrative research concerning human occupation. *Scandinavian Journal of Occupational Therapy, 13*(2), 86–93.

Jun, J., & Kyle, G. (2011). The effect of identity conffiict/facilitation on the experience of constraints to leisure and constraint negotiation. *Journal of Leisure Research, 43*(2), 176–204.

Katz, S. (2013). Active and successful aging: Lifestyle as a gerontological idea. *Recherches Sociologiques et Anthropologiques [En Ligne], 44*(1). Retrieved online 7/2/14. https://rsa.revues.or.

Knight, A., Brannen, J., & O'Connell, R. (2015). Using narrative sources from the Mass Observation Archive to study everyday food and families in hard times: Food practices in England during 1950. *Sociological Research Online, 20*(1), 1–14.

Kozinets, R. V., Hemetsberger, A., & Jensen Schau, H. (2008). The wisdom of consumer crowds. *Journal of Macromarketing, 28*(4), 339–354.

Kramer, A. M. (2014). The observers and the observed: The "dual vision" of the Mass Observation Project. *Sociological Research Online, 19*(3), 1–11.

Krumer-Nevo, M., & Sidi, M. (2012). Writing against othering. *Qualitative Inquiry, 18*(4), 299–309.

Kushner, T. (1995). *Observing the 'Other': Mass—Observation and 'Race'* (The Mass Observation Archive Occasional Papers Series, No. 2, pp. 1–15). Retrieved from https://www.massobs.org.uk/occasional-papers.

Lassen, A. J. (2014). *Active ageing and the unmaking of old age*. University of Copenhagen.

Leaver, R., & Wiseman, T. (2016). Garden visiting as a meaningful occupation for people in later life. *British Journal of Occupational Therapy, 79*(12), 768–775.

Lindsey, R., & Bulloch, S. L. (2013). *What the public think of the 'Big Society': Mass Observers' views on individual and community capacity for civic engagement*. Third Sector Research Centre (Vol. 95).

Retrieved from https://socialwelfare.bl.uk/subject-areas/government-issues/ social-policy/thirdsectorresearchcentre/145228LinkClickwp95.pdf.

Lindsey, R., & Bulloch, S. (2014). A sociologist's field notes to the Mass Observation Archive: A consideration of the challenges of "re-using" Mass Observation data in a longitudinal mixed-methods study. *Sociological Research Online, 19*(3), 1–14.

Lindsey, R., Metcalfe, E., & Edwards, R. (2015). Time in mixed methods longitudinal research: Working across written narratives and large scale panel survey data to investigate attitudes to volunteering. In N. Worth & I. Hardill (Eds.), *Researching the lifecourse: Critical reflections from the social sciences* (Vol. 1, pp. 43–61). Policy Press.

Lorimer, H. (2003). Telling small stories: Spaces of knowledge and the practice of geography. *Transactions of the Institute of British Geographers, 28*(2), 197–217.

Lyotard, J.-F. (1984). *The postmodern condition: A report on knowledge.* Manchester University Press.

Malpas, S. (2003). *Jean-Francois Lyotard.* Routledge.

Martin, W. (2011). Visualizing risk: Health, gender and the ageing body. *Critical Social Policy, 32*(1), 51–68.

Mass Observation Archive (University of Sussex). (2015). *Autumn 2015 directive, part 2: Bonfire night.* Accessed at http://www.massobs.org.uk/images/ aut_2015_final.pdf.

Mass Observation Project. (2009). *The Mass Observation Project Notes for research students Referencing guidelines for working with the directive.* https:// www.massobs.org.uk/images/Referencing_Mass_Observation_material.pdf. Accessed 29 Nov 2020.

May, V. (2016). When recognition fails: Mass Observation Project accounts of not belonging. *Sociology, 50*(4), 748–763.

May, V. (2018). Belonging across the lifetime: Time and self in Mass Observation accounts. *British Journal of Sociology, 69*(2), 306–322.

Moore, N. (2007). (Re)Using qualitative data? *Sociological Research Online, 12*(3), 1–14.

Moss, J., Clarke, N., Jennings, W., & Stoker, G. (2016). Golden age, apathy or stealth? Democratic engagement in Britain, 1945–1950. *Contemporary British History, 30*(4), 441–462.

Moulaert, T., & Biggs, S. (2012). International and European policy on work and retirement: Reinventing critical perspectives on active ageing and mature subjectivity. *Human Relations, 66*(1), 23–43.

Neale, B. (2013). Adding time into the mix: Stakeholder ethics in qualitative longitudinal. *Methodological Innovations Online, 8*(2), 6–20.

Nicholls, D. (2009). Qualitative research: Part three—Methods. *International Journal of Therapy and Rehabilitation, 16*(12), 638–648.

Nimrod, G., Janke, M. C., & Kleiber, D. A. (2015). Leisure and aging qualitative research 15 years into the third millennium. *Journal of Leisure Research, 8*(1), 12–14.

Noakes, L. (1996). *Gender and nationhood: Britain in the Falklands War* (The Mass Observation Archive Occasional Papers Series, No. 5, pp. 1–15).

Parsons, S. (2013, May). *Mass Observation Archive British birth cohort studies.* Retrieved from https://www.closer.ac.uk/wp-content/uploads/CLOSER-resource-report-1-Mass-Observation-Archive-S-Parsons-May-2013-FINAL.pdf.

Phoenix, C., & Bell, S. L. (2019). Beyond "move more": Feeling the rhythms of physical activity in mid and later-life. *Social Science & Medicine, 231*, 47–54.

Phoenix, C., Smith, B., & Sparkes, A. C. (2010). Narrative analysis in aging studies: A typology for consideration. *Journal of Aging Studies, 24*(1), 1–11.

Phoenix, C., & Sparkes, A. C. (2009). Being Fred: Big stories, small stories and the accomplishment of a positive ageing identity. *Qualitative Research, 9*(2), 219–236.

Pike, E. C. J. (2013). The role of fiction in (mis)representing later life leisure activities. *Leisure Studies, 32*(1), 67–87.

Pillow, W. (2003). Confession, catharsis, or cure? Rethinking the uses of reflexivity as methodological power in qualitative research. *International Journal of Qualitative Studies in Education, 16*(2), 175–196.

Polkinghorne, D. E. (1995). Narrative configuration in qualitative analysis. *International Journal of Qualitative Studies in Education, 8*(1), 5–23.

Pollen, A. (2013). Research methodology in Mass Observation past and present: "Scientifically, about as valuable as a chimpanzee's tea party at the zoo"? *History Workshop Journal, 75*(1), 213–235.

Randall, W. L., & Khurshid, K. N. (2016). Narrative development in later life: A novel perspective. *Age, Culture, Humanities*, (3). Accessed at https://ageculturehumanities.org/WP/narrative-development-in-later-life-a-novel-perspective/.

Randall, W. L., & Phoenix, C. (2009). The problem with truth in qualitative interviews: Reflections from a narrative perspective. *Qualitative Research in Sport and Exercise, 1*(2), 125–140.

Research Council UK. (2013). *RCUK policy on open access and supporting guidance*. Retrieved from https://www.rcuk.ac.uk/RCUK-prod/assets/docume nts/documents/RCUKOpenAccessPolicy.pdf.

Ricoeur, P. (1984). *Time and narrative* (Vol. 1). Chicago University Press.

Riessman, C. K. (2008). *Narrative methods for the human sciences* (2nd ed.). Sage.

Robinson, E. M. (2012). *Women and needlework in Britain, 1920–1970*.

Rojek, C. (2010). *The labour of leisure: The culture of free time*. Sage.

Rojek, C., & Blackshaw, T. (2013). The labour of leisure reconsidered. In T. Blackshaw (Ed.), *Routledge handbook of leisure studies* (pp. 544–559). Routledge.

Rolfe, G. (1997). Writing ourselves: Creating knowledge in a postmodern world. *Nurse Education Today, 17*(6), 442–448.

Rolfe, G. (2016). *Exercising the nursing imagination: Putting values and scholarship back into research Chaos in the Brickyard*.

Savage, M. (2007). Changing social class identities in post-war Britain: Perspectives from Mass-Observation. *Sociological Research Online, 12*(3). Accessed at https://www.socresonline.org.uk/12/3/6.html.

Sheridan, D. (1993). Writing to the archive: Mass-Observation as autobiography. *Sociology, 27*(1), 27–40.

Sheridan, D. (1996). *"Damned anecdotes and dangerous confabulations" Mass-Observation as life history* (The Mass Observation Archive Occasional Papers Series, No. 7, pp. 1–17). Retrieved from https://www.massobs.org.uk/occasi onal-papers.

Sheridan, D. (2000, December). Reviewing mass-observation: The archive and its researchers thirty years on. *Forum Qualitative Social Research, 1*(3), Article 26.

Sheridan, D. (2002). Using the mass-observation archive. In A. Jamieson & C. R. Victor (Eds.), *Researching aging and later life* (pp. 66–79). Buckingham: Open University Press.

Sheridan, D. (2009). *The mass observation project: Background to material collected since 1981*. Brighton: University of Sussex.

Silverman, D. (2004). *Doing qualitative research* (2nd ed.). Sage.

Smart, C. (2011). Families, secrets and memories. *Sociology, 45*(4), 539–553.

Smith, B. (2013). Sporting spinal cord injuries, social relations, and rehabilitation narratives: An ethnographic creative non-fiction of becoming disabled through sport. *Sociology of Sport Journal, 30*(2), 132–152.

Smith, J. A. (2004). Reflecting on the development of interpretative phenomenological analysis and its contribution to qualitative research in psychology. *Qualitative Research in Psychology, 1*(1), 39–54.

Snape, R. (2013). All-in wrestling in inter-war Britain: Science and spectacle in Mass Observation's Worktown. *International Journal of the History of Sport.* Taylor & Francis.

Snape, R. (2015). The new leisure, voluntarism and social reconstruction in inter-war Britain. *Contemporary British History.* Taylor & Francis.

Snape, R., & Spracklen, K. (2019). Introduction: Robert Snape and Karl Spracklen. *Leisure/Loisir, 43*(2), 155–158.

Squire, C., Andrews, M., & Tamboukou, M. (2008). Doing narrative research introduction: What is narrative research? *Doing Narrative Research* (September 2014), 1–22.

Steedman, C. (2001). *Dust: The archive and cultural history.* Manchester University Press.

Stenner, P., Church, A., & Bhatti, M. (2012). Human-landscape relations and the occupation of space: Experiencing and expressing domestic gardens. *Environment and Planning A, 44*(7), 1712–1727.

Tamboukou, M. (2013). A Foucauldian approach to narratives. In M. Andrews, C. Squire, & M. Tamboukou (Eds.), *Doing narrative research* (2nd ed., pp. 103–121). Sage.

Tamboukou, M. (2017). Reassembling documents of life in the archive. *European Journal of Life Writing, 6*, 1–19.

Thomas, J. (2002). *Beneath the mourning veil Mass-Observation and the death of Diana* (The Mass Observation Archive Occasional Papers Series, No. 12, pp. 1–32). Retrieved from https://www.massobs.org.uk/occasional-papers.

Uprichard, E., Nettleton, S., & Chappell, P. (2013). "Food hates" over the life course: An analysis of food narratives from the UK Mass Observation Archive. *Appetite, 71*, 137–143.

Webster, L., & Mertova, P. (2007). *Using narrative inquiry as a research method: An introduction to using critical event narrative analysis in research on learning and teaching.* Routledge.

Wilson-Kovacs, D. (2014). "Clearly Necessary", "Wonderful" and "Engrossing"? Mass Observation correspondents discuss forensic technologies. *Sociological Research Online, 19*(3), 1–16.

Wiseman, T., & Sadlo, G. (2015). *Gardening: An occupation for recovery and wellness.* In *International handbook of occupational therapy interventions* (2nd ed.).

Wood, H. (2015). Television—The housewife's choice? The 1949 Mass Observation television directive, reluctance and revision. *Media History, 21*(3), 342–359.

York, M., & Wiseman, T. (2012). Gardening as an occupation: A critical review. *British Journal of Occupational Therapy, 75*(2), 76–84.

4

Navigating Archives, Going Native and Falling in Love with 26 New People

Altogether there are 26 correspondents in later life represented in this research, each contributing material from between three and ten directive responses, with a total contribution varying from eight to 33 pages, with the majority at the higher end, around 15,000 words being the median per correspondent, the range 3500–18,000. All explain what it is currently like to be in later life in the UK. The mechanics of how they were chosen from the 500 correspondents is explained next, and they are formally introduced in the 'introducing the correspondents' section.

> *Different people understand the same story differently precisely because the stories they already know are different. Understanders attempt to construe new stories they hear as old stories they have heard before. They do this because it is actually quite difficult to absorb new information. New ideas ramify through our memories, causing us to have to revise beliefs, make new generalizations, and perform other effortful cognitive operations. We prefer to avoid all this work. One way to do this is to simply assume that what we are seeing or hearing about is just the same old stuff. The real problem in understanding then, is identifying which of all the stories you already know is the one that is being told to you yet again.* (Schank & Ableson, 1995)

© The Author(s), under exclusive license to Springer Nature Switzerland AG 2021
T. Wiseman, *Leisure in Later Life*, Leisure Studies in a Global Era, https://doi.org/10.1007/978-3-030-71672-1_4

The old story about the Mass Observation correspondents that I already knew was that middle-class 'active ageing' older ladies were hiding in those archive boxes. At two recent conference presentations I was told, not asked, that the people in my study must be a certain kind of person, to be involved in the Mass Observation Project, a kind of academic posh person, not like proper, normal old people. One of the questioners had himself conducted research with University of the Third Age participants, and felt they were closer to the common experience than his stereotype of Mass Observers. The correspondents are characterised as middle-class older ladies from the south east of England, retired librarians or academics. An echo, or perhaps a lazy reproduction of the competitors critique of the original project, that it was a middle-class experiment at the expense of the working classes (Hubble, 2010). So a strategy to ensure that I was neither avoiding nor selecting the expected people was required. This next section is concerned with that selection process, and the organisation and management of the chosen material. When I have explained that I will engage with the same problem around the telling of 'new' stories from the data. But I will start with the selection of correspondents.

Selection of participants is not usually discussed in great detail. I am explaining the process of selection here because it is problematic for researchers working with the Mass Observation Archive on a theoretical level (Baker & Geiringer, 2019; Pollen, 2013), and on a practical level (Moor & Uprichard, 2014). There is also the underlying concern reported about the representativeness of the Mass Observation Panel (Baker & Geiringer, 2019). There is further critique of how each research project selects which writers to include. Some sample the first folder, which includes all those with the surnames beginning with A and B (Savage, 2007), others aim to find a representative sample within the sample, thus reducing both of these major concerns (Clarke et al., 2017). However, there is a risk in my study of leisure in later life that the use of pre-existing indicators to find a sample from the panel of 500, may miss some people that are not 'indicated'. I decided to choose through inclusion criteria led by the background and literature review chapters, which led me to choose by age, work status and answering useful directives.

The selection of participants in Mass Observation research is often obscured. The sheer volume of data creates problems for a researcher, and the only way of engaging until recently has been to read through, and therefore be influenced by whatever juicy quote catches the eye. Recently a new database was introduced, that enabled me to choose correspondents in a less subjective way. This process of participant selection was very effective in creating a much more socially diverse group than expected. People that answered the lifeline question were selected, to ensure a big story to add narrative context (Phoenix, 2013). People who had retired by 2008 were chosen, it was hoped that this would be indicated in the lifeline. Then a transition period of six years was chosen in order that they were not in the early stages of adjusting to role change. From those people, correspondents that had completed day diaries in both 2014 and 2015 were selected. Additional directive responses relating to particular interests expressed in the lifeline or diaries were also retrieved from the archive. This selection process is expanded upon, and justified in the participant selection section that follows. How I used these resources to choose and then introduce a story, and how it was contextualised with information from other writings of the correspondents will also be explained in the analysis section. Recognising my truth seeking behaviours, the archive fever that Steedman mocks so effectively (2001) and maintaining a plurality of truths, the correspondents 'telling it as it is' and my multiple filters, the ambition was to work it all together in hope of producing new knowledge about how people negotiate leisure in the context of everyday later life; and how they interact with metanarratives about ageing.

4.1   Choosing Suitable Materials to Analyse

I had a choice of many directives that would give rich detailed information about leisure in later life. A Mass Observation Archive researcher needs to be aware that if they are interested in a particular question within a directive, the only way to know whether it has been answered is to view the correspondence at The Keep. Although it may be a directive that has been responded to, there are three parts within each directive, and several questions in each part. There are many reasons that a person may not answer a particular question within a directive, they may get bored of a particular subject, miss the questions at the end, they may not notice a question, they may not like a question, they may feel that question is irrelevant to them, or find it offensive. The question may be time bounded, and they may not notice it until later, this is often the case with day diary questions. Indeed it is worth considering the implications of someone not answering a question, the missing voice is very loud in the archive, and people will sometimes explain why they have not answered a question, and those responses are some of the most telling.

> *I used to complain gently (well maybe not gently!) to Dorothy [Archivist] about the way some directives lumped inappropriate things together and would add throwaway questions needing many pages of reply. I see whoever has drawn up Part 2 has learned this well! This is about care of the elderly in our society. And then – quite off the cuff it seems – you throw in questions about what is a good death which is a bit tangential, and a question about euthanasia, which is really something very different to the rest of what you ask. So I will not deal with that here. [And I insert this point having got to the end: asking about people's own experiences is valuable, asking them about things they can have little knowledge of [euthanasia] is largely pointless.]*
> (B2710, Ageing and Care)

I remembered this quote that I transcribed in January 2015, largely because of the sinister connection of the ideas of ageing and euthanasia in the minds of the researchers that must have designed the directive. The two topics were entirely unconnected for this 81-year old-correspondent and myself, and his refusal to play along with this conflation of ideas is powerful.

I also noted how unreliable topic areas are, while background reading about gardening in supported housing, I noted:

> *I am looking at how people imagine being without their garden, and how their experience of care in later life informs their stories about it. I am interested in how some respondents tell better stories about gardening in the Ageing and Care directive, and more telling stories about old age care in the gardening directive.* (My notes, 22.1.2015)

With these points and illustrations in mind my sampling had to accommodate that people may not answer directly, on topic, or at all, so I needed to over-sample, and chose which directives I used to create a sample carefully.

In looking at the available directives I read correspondence from two directives that included a day diary. I noted that Working day 2010, and the Jubilee 2012 diaries had everyday contemporaneous stories about leisure lives. Many of the other questions in the directives prompted retrospective writing, much like life history approaches, already considered and not pursued for my research. The day diaries had everyday contextualised information, as suggested by the example of the bonfire night diary question earlier in the methods chapter. The other directives helped me to understand the broader context of peoples lives. For example 'Families and holidays' gave me a lot of social history, holidays all through people's lives, but I was concerned that families and holidays are not a routine part of all lives, mindful that it might exclude particular groups of people. While presenting at the Mass Observation at 80 conference I met a research team from the University of Southampton. Rose Lindsey discussed a 'Life line' directive, which they were using as part of volunteering research (Lindsey et al., 2016). It was a particularly interesting directive, which asked people to write a time line, listing significant events in their lives. It is mentioned in the methods chapter, as an example of the style of Mass Observation directives. Having already viewed the Families and Holidays responses, I was able to anticipate that this would add some rich background material.

There are many potential directives relating to leisure, but the every day is the focus of the day diaries, and my research project. The most recent directives that contained day diary requests had different topics, which I reasoned between them would attract a varied response. The days were Eurovision 10th May 2014, Remembrance Sunday 9th November 2014, Election Day 7th May 2015 and Bonfire Night 5th November 2015. These directives were chosen because they share rich and contextualised stories about everyday leisure. They are culturally defined events, but they are not as formalised as, for example Christmas or a park run or a music festival. They are also not planned events in the sense that commercial participation is essential, although it is an option (Getz &

Page, 2016). In this way a person will be aware of the name of the day but may not participate in any organised element of it, they may not vote, or watch the Eurovision song contest, but it is something that they are likely to be aware of. Having prior experience of a 2010 working day diary, and the 2012 Jubilee diary it was anticipated that the day diaries would focus on the whole day, not just the event.

Choosing the most recent day diaries led to 'no choice' about subject. For example, I had absolutely no interest in bonfire night as a leisure event, it was just one of the four available day diaries. Now that I have analysed the days, I would like to claim how clever I was in choosing this diverse set of days, the almost ambiguous nature of them in relation to the studies of organised leisure events. But it was not clever, just pragmatic, in the general sense of the word.

I decided to focus on these five directives, the Lifeline, and the four most recent diaries, and supplement them with additional material from the other directives that were indicated by the content of the day diaries. The day diaries give a structure, explaining leisure as part of life in the round, and the supplementary directives add subjective meanings, and deeper insights into people's leisure lives.

4.2   Participant Selection

I designed a sampling strategy around the Lifeline 2008 directive and the most recent day diaries from 2014 to 2015. In order to satisfy concerns about cherry picking correspondents, systematic selection criteria were established. Purposive sampling was used to choose people in later life. A cohort approach was taken, choosing people that were born before 1965, and therefore part of the UK 'baby boomer' generation and older that makes up the new large population of people in later life in the UK. In order that some lifelong context was available to me, only people that had contributed to the Lifeline directive question were included. This was the directive question quoted earlier that asked them to contribute a 'lifeline', in which they give a brief history of their lives. This adds context to their stories about leisure in later life. I believed the lifeline response would indicate time in retirement, and it was six years before the day diaries.

People that identified in the lifeline directive as in paid employment were excluded, as working people of this age group report time as an overwhelming constraint to leisure and it is well documented that the 'early' stages of retirement are complex, non-linear and a new lifestyle takes some time to develop (Moffatt & Heaven, 2017). This avoided the overwhelming concept of worker role loss and financial readjustment in transition to retirement being a primary focus of the day diaries, which while very important, is already the subject of other research (See for example, Genoe et al., 2016; Liechty et al., 2017), and not the focus of this book.

This became possible because a new database was developed.[1] It was launched in June 2016, following the work of Lindsey and Bulloch (2014). I accessed it in January 2017 many times and learned how to 'work it'.

I know that many researchers do not discuss the detail of how they sample at the Mass Observation Archive, and this is perfectly acceptable in qualitative research. Some do, notably Lindsey and Bulloch (2014) and Savage (2007). However, it was a challenge that I decided to take up, this means that I can challenge some criticisms that I would otherwise have had to live with, about who the Mass Observers are, and about my choice of correspondents. I would recommend it to any budding MOA researcher, I believe it has helped me to meet more varied correspondents.

The data base lists every response to the Mass Observation Project directives. It lists the code number, year of birth and other demographic details for each entry. Each line of the 65,768 represents a response to a single directive by an individual person.

There are some limitations to this database:

- Some of the biographical data, such as employment status and marital status, and living arrangements is from the 1990s, or when writer joined the MOP if that was later. Therefore the data does not reflect recent developments.
- Occupations have been categorised by the creators of the database using the Standard Occupational Class (SOC) classifications provided by the Office of National Statistics measure of class.

---

[1] Accessed at https://database.massobs.org.uk/.

- There is data missing; for example when date of birth is used to organise entries, from line 64,011 to 65,768 date of birth is incorrectly formatted or missing. I investigated and one correspondent, A833 had one directive misfiled that was not in the inclusion criteria, so this had no impact, he was still excluded. 15 additional people who had answered any of the chosen directives were cross checked to find out if they met the inclusion criteria and they did not.
- Keyword searches of the responses are not possible.
- It is not built for complex searches.
- It does not indicate if someone has answered all parts of a directive.

Database strengths

- Keywords searches from the directives are effective.
- Searches by age are effective.
- Searches by which directive has been answered are effective.
- It is possible to download and save the database into an excel format and explore the data.
- It is possible to create multiple sheets, and therefore record an audit trail of decisions.

This enables people to find things like: Y2498 born 1912, started writing in 1990, stopped in 2012, I could spend all day finding examples like this, I love a good database. It is important to recognise that some people will be excluded by errors in the database, the database is not perfect, so critical reading of searches and checking of decisions should be done. It is easy to make a mistake, at one point I put people in alphabetical order during a trail sampling, then noticed that on the third level of exclusion I had inadvertently left several columns out of the re-ordering, so each line entry was a hybrid of two people and I needed to start again.

However, it is an excellent resource for *informing* a sampling strategy, the researcher should consider that many participants who look as if they will meet the criteria on the data base, will be ruled out when the correspondence is viewed at the Keep. Biographical and occupational data are the least useful organising factors, and age and answering a particular directive are more reliable. Mass Observers are known for their wilful interpretations of questions, it is possible, for example, to search for 'divorced' people but if the 'divorced' observer believes that to be none of your business, it will not be a productive search. Correspondents who pride themselves on their subjectivity, cannot be expected to provide reliable objective data for sampling purposes. That is asking to have your cake and eat it. If you want your candid individuals neatly packaged up into demographic bundles, then you will have to do that work by reading what they have written.

Inclusion criteria:

Age: Generation baby boomers and older (born before 1966), retired by 2008.

Particular directives:

- Lifeline 2008
- Day diaries: 2–4 days over a two-year period, 2014/15, at least one Thursday (election and Bonfire) and at least one weekend day, from Saturday (Eurovison) or Sunday (remembrance), giving at least one weekend day and a weekday.

The database enabled the choice of participants to be narrowed down to baby boomers or older that had answered lifeline, and 2 different day diary directives in 2014/15. This identified 58 potential participants, I sought and gained permission from the MOA to share transcribed lifeline directives from Rose Lindsey's research team at the University of Southampton. In order to screen for retired individuals I reviewed the lifeline directive, 17 clearly identified as working in paid employment in 2008, leaving 41 potential participants. My prior experience about how people answer directives meant I anticipated that around half of them would not have completed the day diary question that I was looking for. I would find this when I visited to screen for completed day diaries, this is recorded in Table 4.1.

This tells us little about the sample or those that were rejected; it was simply a method of choosing a number of informants; their participation in these particular directives means they are likely to give information to the study, but those that are not included are no less representative and

Table 4.1 Participant selection

Criteria	Excluded	Remaining
From the data base: Number of people who answered Life line directive		160
From the data base: People born before 1965	37	123
From the data base: Those that answered at least 2 of 4 day diary directives 2014/15	65	58
On screening the Lifeline correspondence: Those that identified as not working by 2008	17	41
On screening the correspondence at the Keep: No diaries, minimal/partial diaries completed	9	
One diary or only weekend or Thursday diaries completed	6	
Two full diaries weekend/weekday		9
three		7
four		10
Those that completed at least 1 weekend and 1 weekday diary		26

may have been just as interesting, but happened to be busy at the time of these particular directives.

I visited the Mass Observation Archive at the Keep in Sussex to screen the day diaries. I did this one directive at a time, scanning each directive looking for any correspondence from my selected sample of 41 people. I did this for each of the four day diary directives. I saved each scanned page to a password-protected laptop. I collated all the typed ones into a single word document, editing and correcting the imperfect character recognition. I collated the transcribed data from the hand-written responses and filed the handwritten PDFs for easy reference. Then transcribed the day diaries, and inserted screen clippings of the supplementary material. I organised and read the multiple directives for each correspondent in chronological order. Contributions to individual directive questions varied in length from a few lines to eight densely handwritten or typed pages. Each person's contributions were incorporated into a single word document, the average contribution was 15,000 words. They were listed in alphabetical order ready for analysis. I developed a simple system of organising the reading from A–Z, one at a time.

This section introduces the correspondents, giving an overview of their demographic details in their own words. It then shares their political leanings, and information about housing, money, relationships and their day to day routines. The next chapter explores what all this means for them in their day to day leisure lives. It is initially overwhelming to meet 26 people all at once, but the aim of this chapter is to enable the reader to engage with the people and thus the complexity of leisure in later life.

Whatever I write cannot do justice to this data, every person surprised me, each unique life written about. Adventures relayed, quiet lives, busy lives, cosy lives, conflicted lives, trials overcome, troubles managed and moved on from. Where there are troubles they are related to illness or bad luck by correspondents, rather than ageing, and it is fair to say that many of the illnesses and luck mentioned are not directly relatable to ageing. A brain tumour, a pulmonary embolism, the death of a child. What follows is some information that helps to relate these people to demographic markers, aiding the reader to identify with them. In the UK, after establishing where someone has come from, we ask what they do. When they are retired, we will enquire further, to ask what they did. This information is volunteered in the tiny biographies of the participants written at the top of each directive: Each person was given a Pseudonym, and their mini biography as presented by them is included, with examples of the actual presentation of the handwritten ones in Fig. 4.1. Where people have identified a small village or town that may lead to their identification it has been replaced with a descriptor that aims to keep the essence of their disclosure, such as 'Market town' or 'small village'. Throughout the work details such as birthdates, bus routes, etc., have been changed to reduce the identifiability of the correspondents.

4.3   Introducing the Correspondents

To do justice to the materiality of the correspondence, this picture of the mini-biographies is offered. The remainder of the selected correspondents use a computer to write their contribution.

Having got to 'know' these 26 people, I felt it important to the persuasiveness of the research that the reader should also have that opportunity.

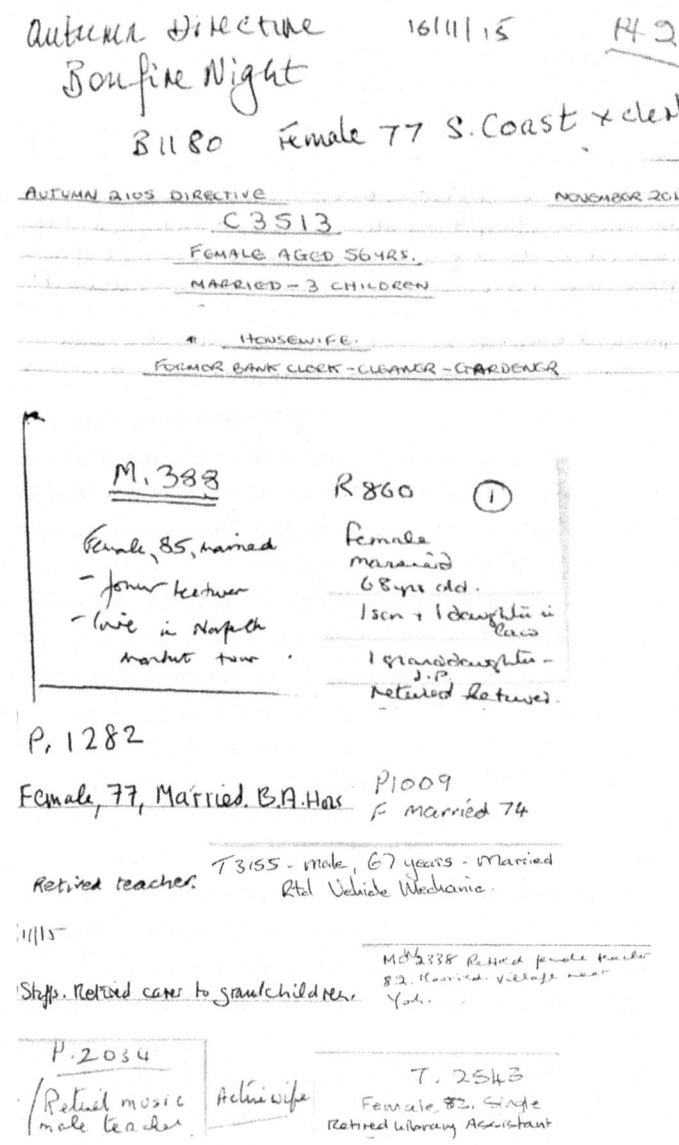

Fig. 4.1 Samples of handwritten mini biography

Further readings were made in order to review initial impressions, and demographic data was collated from the directive responses, in order that the reader might know more about the correspondents. To aid transferability, basic demographic information and other contextualising detail is presented next. The following is each person's favoured description of themselves, with the assigned pseudonym. Do take time to read this list as it is their first statement in any interaction with the archive and therefore is important. What they include or omit matters, as if words were precious, but space more so.

Brenda: B1180 Female 77 S Coast x clerk.

Barbara: B 1771 Female age 79 Widow, village, Surrey, Retired Secretary.

Cathy: C3513 Female aged 56 yrs. Married—3 children. Village Essex, Housewife, former bank clerk—cleaner—gardener.

Charles: C3603. Male—born 1944, Married—Living in a village, Sheffield, Retired Youth & Community Officer.

Freda: F218, I am a 69-year-old Mum of two sons 42yrs. and 44 years, respectively. We live in a small market town in Suffolk.

Marjorie: M388 female, 85, married—former lecturer—live in Norfolk market town.

Matthew: M3231; Male, 66 Years Old, Single Residence—village, Wigan. Occupation: Physicist (Retired).

Mary: M3408; Female 69, Married, Coventry, Retired Nursery Teacher.

Peggy: P1009 F Married 74, Market town, Worcestershire, retired teacher.

Pauline: P1282 Female, 77, Married. B.A. Hons. Small village, staffs. Retired carer to grandchildren.

Patricia: P1796; Female; Age: 69. Married; market town; Dorset; Administrator.

Peter: P2034 retired music male teacher, 88, market town in Nottinghamshire. Active wife.

Paul: P3204 male 76, married, village, East Yorkshire artist.

Rachel: R860, female married, 68 yrs old. 1 some and 1 daughter-in-law. 1 grandaughter. JP, retired lecturer. Large town near Manchester.

Rosalind: R.1025. 72-yr-old housewife, formerly book-keeper, living in Milton Keynes with husband, retired engineer.

Richard: R1418. Male aged 93: widower ret. decorator. Derby.

Rodney: R3032. Male, 73, widower, retired civil servant, Cardiff.

Sophie: S1399 female 65, Married, large affluent southeast town.

Teresa: T2543 Female, 82, single, retired library assistant, Large town, West Midlands.

Terry: T3155. Male, 67 years—Married. Rtd. Vehicle Mechanic, Village in Derbyshire.

Timothy: T 3686. Male. Aged 78. Married. Living in London. A retired trade mark attorney.

Winifred: W632. F/74/widow/Small town W.Sx retired Business Analyst.

Wendy: W633. Female, 72, retired journalist, Market town, County Durham, Married, one daughter, 39, not living at home.

Vivien: W1813. Female, 65 years Retired teacher Married, Market town, Staffs.

Violet: W2338. Retired female teacher. 82. Married. Village near York.

William: W3176 Male 74 Married village near Blackburn (Lancs) Retired Teacher.

4.4 Getting to Know Them a Little Better

These 26 micro-biographies, start the categorisation process in the reader, 'frail hand writing', 'confused information', 'computer literate', 'different backgrounds', 'different ages', 'Active wife?', 'widow'. These things are culturally relevant, and as has been discussed in the introduction and the literature review are relevant to later life leisure participation. The following section summarises the correspondents' other priorities.

The correspondents are from all over England and Wales (Fig. 4.2). The sampling strategy has produced a diversity in the areas of geographical region, previous work, education and political opinions.

4.4.1 Overview

Age has little influence on length of retirement in this group (Fig. 4.3). All 26 identified as not working in the 2008 lifeline. 17 people give a year of retirement in the 2008 lifeline directive but nine gave no specific date of retirement.

Of the nine that did not give a year of retirement, Cathy, Sophie and Rosalind identify as housewives, William and Peggy identify as retired teachers; Paul as an artist; Pauline moved from caring for her children, to doing a degree, to caring for her grandchildren; Marjorie is a 'former

Fig. 4.2 The correspondents' region of residence

lecturer' and Richard a 'retired decorator'. Marjorie says in her lifeline response.

> *As I think about the key events of my life, I wonder if age has a marked effect on perceptions. I think there are fewer 'key events' I'd list now than perhaps 20 years ago. Things/events that mattered great deal at the time have merged with other things since to take a less important role in my life line.* (Lifeline, 2008)

One of those things appears to be retirement. Other people do focus on retirement as a milestone and their time in retirement is indicated in Fig. 4.3 above. Retirement is prompted by a range of things including early deaths or life-threatening illnesses of parents, siblings and friends. A correspondent's own ill health can result in retirement, Mary retired three times on health grounds, but recovered each time, so went back to work, echoing her three career starts earlier in life. Rachel retired in 1990, and had ill health until she entered 'retirement', where she is hyperactive and community engaged. Wendy retired hating the job she once loved, and quite unwell as a result, Rodney states

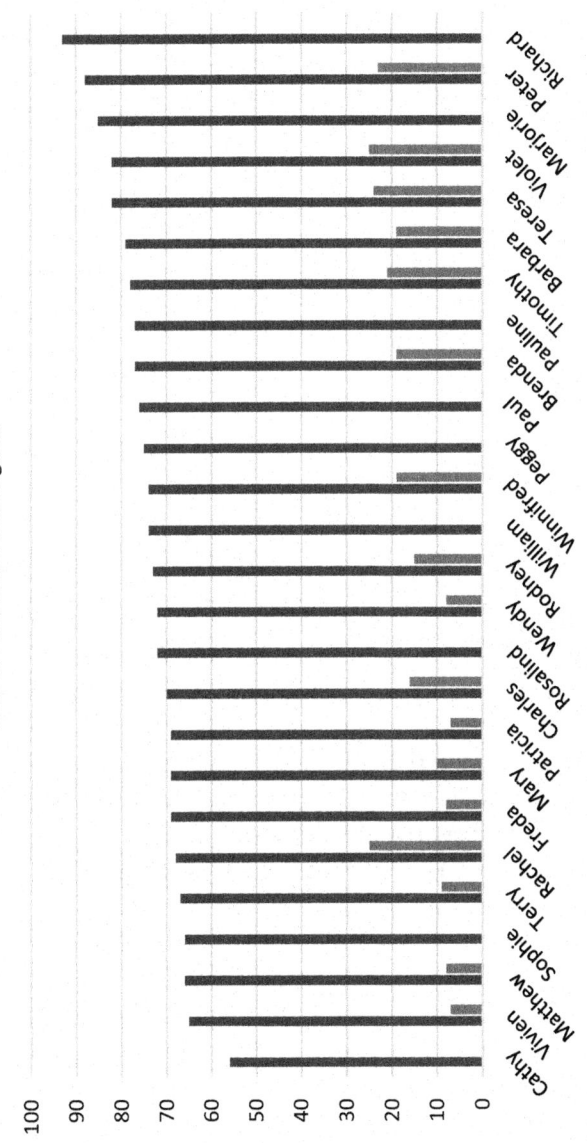

Fig. 4.3 Pseudonym, age and years in retirement where indicated

I decided to retire early, and did so on my 58th birthday, did an OU degree.

For Winifred it is simply stated

Aug1996 - voluntary redundancy, early retirement - great pay off, big party, May 1997 - husband died.

Vivien was unsure of what was to follow when she wrote in 2008.

both just taken retirement from teaching.

Teresa retired in 1991, and tells us that.

partner younger and still worked until 2006.

In Terry's case

2007 Endured the contortions of not regularly working, and justifying our existence to ourselves. (Lifeline, 2008)

Overall the correspondents are varied in age and length of retirement, they identified as not working in 2008 lifeline, and still identify this in the 2014 and 2015 diaries.

The Mass Observation writers are a self-selected group, and these participants were chosen according to their age and self-declared work status, and the fact that they responded to at least three of the five chosen directives. They were not chosen for the quality or quantity of their correspondence and were not sampled to give a demographic spread. They may or may not be representative of the archive correspondents, the selection was intended to remove my choice and it did. For example, given the choice I would have chosen typed responses, as they are easier to manage and transcribe, but there were risks of choosing only computer literate people and skewing the sample. I have, at times, been accused of having too optimistic a view on later life, choosing 'unusually' good days to present, and in avoiding my own positive selection bias, I have found a rich, diverse and inspiring set of stories about leisure in later life.

These correspondents have had more opportunities in education than others in their age group. Sixteen people mentioned the 11 + in their lifeline. Five failed it, and eleven passed in an era where approximately a third to a quarter of children passed the 11 + exam and went to grammar school. Five people missed the introduction of the 11 + exam as they were too old, the remaining five did not mention it, including three who attended fee-paying schools which did not require it. Nine correspondents went to university. Five from Grammar schools, one from a secondary technical, one from a convent high school, one from a fee-paying school, one was not clear. Of those nine, seven had careers supported by their degree. The proportion of graduates is high, but there is variation in the sample, with nine people leaving school at 14 or 15, and the remainder attaining GCE qualifications.

In the 2015 general election, ten voted labour, seven voted conservative, three voted UKIP, one Green, four kept their vote secret, one did not vote, and has not voted since the Thatcher years. Many people discussed the fight to get the vote, and responsibility to vote. Patricia speaks for many of the correspondents when she says.

if you don't vote then really and truly you cannot complain... (Election, 2015)

Only Freda expresses housing insecurity, stating that she may have to downsize due to the 'bedroom tax'.

I still live in a 3-bedroomed house and manage to keep it decorated and would quite happily spend all day in the garden. Some doubt this year that I will have to contribute £30 p.w. for 2 bedrooms vacant so I may have to downsize or ship out. (Remembrance, 2014)

The remainder are in secure housing. There is a route to home ownership explained in their lifelines for those that did not have wealthy parents, their families lived with grandparents or in low-rent housing, moving onto privately owned housing later.

Money is discussed by all of the correspondents, and their own financial security is a matter that they share in their correspondence. Overall they are financially stable. Only Brenda expresses worries about money in both years,

> Draw out money to pay council tax £118. Dwindling savings". (Remembrance 2014), and with characteristic black humor reports the contents of her post in 2015 "A letter from the funeral directors inviting me to an 'open day'. How Thrilling. I recently buried our remaining brother, and they were v. gd. One from the Halifax, informing us that interest rates have halved. O Goodee. (Bonfire, 2015)

Sophie experiences a different kind of poverty:

> I started Sunday upset as I had worked out on Sat. that I had £1/4 million in cash in 3 accounts (unable to access as don't know PINS etc.) & I found when I undressed for my weekly bath, that none of the clothing I was wearing had been bought/made for me – all 2nd hand, charity shops, Jumble sale, given to me – nothing was mine. All that money & I have no working account and no clothes. (Remembrance, 2014)

Paul speaks for many of the remaining correspondents when he says.

> I have some fears as to what an unfettered Tory government will now do. I am a pensioner with a good standard of living and no money problems, so maybe I should be quite content. From another aspect I am not complacent because I wonder how poorer and the less fortunate people will be affected. (Election, 2015)

Twenty of the correspondents live with a spouse or partner, with many celebrating their 40th and 45th wedding anniversaries, but some of those anniversaries pass by unmarked. Only William remarried in 2002, following the death of his wife in 2001. Winifred is a widow, and lives with her son and his family. The remaining five live alone; Freda divorced in the 70s, Barbara, Richard and Rodney are widows. Matthew has always been single.

It is important to explain that people write about themselves and their relationships and interactions purely from their own perspective and report the reactions of others from their own perspective too. Some people, like Sophie and Richard write themselves as characters who frequently disagree with others. There are some who write themselves as loving and caring, characters such as Mary and Vivien and Freda. It is not possible to say if people are in 'happy' situations, but it is possible to illustrate days together, and days apart. The next section shares a variety of these stories.

Each person's day to day life was analysed in relation to their lifeline, day diaries and supplementary directives. The day is similar in structure, whatever the person's socioeconomic, marital or educational situation. Everyone gets up, they all get ready, they all have media habits, they all interact, they all do active and passive things, they all go to bed. They all spend most of the day at home, unless on holiday, mini-break or day trip. Things that structure the day are sleep, self-care, media, food, other people and animals. The narratives about everyday life that I have assembled, of this 'group' that I have constructed were analysed, and the themes that emerged are illustrated in the section that follows.

4.5 Thematic Analysis of Narrative

This chapter explains the process of corralling complex, contradictory and incomplete stories into an account of how the correspondents negotiate leisure in the context of everyday later life; and how they interact with metanarratives about ageing. There is no best way to analyse Mass Observation correspondence (Pollen, 2013). The material is embedded in everyday life, which produces a complex set of temporal connections between each individuals diaries, and the diaries of the others in the sample. Thematic analysis is a usual approach to analysing archive material such as this (Riessman, 2008), and is a method of analysis used in leisure studies and sociological Mass Observation research (Adams & Raisborough, 2010; Wheaton, 2017; Wood, 2015). Thematic analysis of narrative embraces prior theory as a resource that supports the interpretation of data (Riessman, 2008). Literature and policy reviews were carried out for theories of ageing, active ageing, leisure theory, leisure studies and leisure constraints research to ensure that the emerging themes were theory informed throughout the process, and theoretical positions were understood. Additional literature was consulted when novel ideas were presented during the process, to reduce ignorance of other ideas.

The Lifeline and day diaries gave a structure, explaining leisure as part of life in the round, and the detailed supplementary directives added context and subjective meanings, and deeper insights into people's leisure lives. The collated data was then subject to thematic analysis of narrative (Polkinghorne, 1994, 1995).

Narrative research can engage with the story as expression of internal state or social circumstances, in this way it has the potential to be conflicted (Andrews et al., 2013) but if the enquiry is about the space, or lack of space, between the individual and their culture, then stories are well placed to aid exploration of this nexus. Narrative research supports the analysis of the effectiveness and conditions of public narratives (Gready, 2013), such as active ageing, and focuses on how people negotiate and perform social identities with shared meaning (Salmon & Riessman, 2013). The focus is on sense making (Riessman, 2013), how people explain their day to day lives, and how I make sense of it all through the interpretive process is explained next. Each person's day diaries were analysed for everyday leisure, and when a topic of special importance to the writer is highlighted then a directive related to it in their Archive writing was retrieved and added to the information for that person, to add subjective detail, to the rhythm and structure of the day. It is the case that people that have contributed to these directives are consistent contributors, and there is therefore a rich resource of many directives that write directly about leisure experience.

The process of analysis was iterative and immersive. It can broadly be described in three interrelated stages. Stage one was the initial immersion in the full data set, stage two was a line by line thematic analysis of just the day diaries using NVivo software to support the process. This took place intensively over a four month period of study leave, the third stage was analytical reframing of the stories using three additional analytical frameworks in the year that followed.

Initial immersion involved the construction of narratives raises the question of "which kinds of practices, linked to which kinds of external conditions determine the discursive production of narratives under investigation" (Tamboukou, 2013, p. 90) I have been as open as I can in explaining the influences. The responses of each correspondent were read and re-read, noting key ideas, repetition of themes and recognising key features of the stories that added context and depth. Important stories for each individual person were highlighted. Efforts were made to understand and represent the rhythm and routine of daily life and illustrate the negotiation of leisure lives. Key ideas such as active ageing policies and concurrent big news items were considered, to see if they had an impact, and if they did, what that might be. Narratives were treated as having multiple meanings and how different stories interconnected was considered, (Tamboukou, 2013), within the correspondence of each person, between correspondents and with stories and practices within and without the lifeworld of the correspondence.

The order of analysis was decided by archive code, from A–Z, rather than arranging people by age or any other organising factor. This meant that although I was not age blind when reading, I was at least not reading from youngest to oldest, or the reverse, with an assumption that age matters. Each person's correspondence was read and transcribed in date order, from earliest response to most recent. A second reading for each individual was made where my responses to the data were recorded on the document.

I had not fully considered the impact of reading about whole lives. In a life there will inevitably be tragedy, there will be serious illness, bereavement, and these significant events will be reported with the good times. To read 26 condensed life stories, with intimate knowledge of the writers opened up the frequency and intensity and impact of major life events. This made me sad, it made me panic. The correspondents were very real to me, and their losses, their challenges over 26 long lifetimes were many. Their management of them was inspirational, because people just got on with it, and if they were writing then they had survived. Their good times are also inspirational, and although the lifetime incidents alarmed me, the day diaries soothed that alarm.

Following Tambouko, another archival researcher (Andrews et al., 2013; Riessman, 2008), I educated myself about the historical context of their lives and times, with a focus on representations of ageing.

This included reading biographical work, theoretical work, and research, watching news, film and TV documentary and drama. In addition to this I also spent time sitting on one of the many benches on the seafront promenade in Eastbourne and watched as the walkers, many of whom were in later life, strolled back and forth, to get a sense of how the things I had been reading may play out in the world. I loved the 'real marigold' style documentaries,[2] and almost daily news articles about 'game old people' having adventures, one about a man who took off from nursing home in Brighton and travelled to France for D-day celebrations with no money or documents ran in local news headlines for days. I saw news items about the problems of getting work over the grand age of 50. I read the excellent non-autobiographies of Penelope Lively and Dianna Athil, both accomplished writers in their 80s bluntly refusing to write autobiographies, both actively refusing to 'finish' their stories.

An iterative approach to primary data meant it was compared to other scholarship and events. In the writings of the correspondents it was clear that much leisure in later life happens at home and is solitary and passive. For four months I immersed myself in 'at homeness' and read over and over the stories they had written. I referred to documentary information to add context, for example, the prominence of the 11+ in their life stories led me to research the history and ongoing debate in England around academic selection at age 11.[3]

It was important to reflect on my own habitus and consider resonance and dissimilarities with the correspondents in the study. I found this privileged peek into the private lives of 26 people enriching in ways I could not have imagined. I am a middle-aged mother of two

---

[2]Following the success of the film 'The best exotic Marigold Hotel' where older people retire to a holiday lifestyle in India, https://www.imdb.com/title/tt1412386/.

A series of documentaries with older celebrities took them first to India for a 'real life' version of the film, then on tour to explore being retired in other countries. https://www.bbc.co.uk/programmes/b09hztft. They have since been camper-vanning around the UK, which was fun to watch.

[3]A school based assessment was introduced in 1944 for all 11 year olds in the England and Wales. It was called the 11+. Until this time private education was expensive or available on a scholarship after age 14, two tiers of schools were supported, grammar school for those that passed the 11 + , and secondary moderns for those that failed. It became compulsory to stay at school until 15. The 11 + was phased out by 1976, but still exists in some counties in England, and continues to be divisive.

teenagers, a university lecturer working full time in a financially stressed environment, completing a part-time Ph.D., so my leisure life is somewhat limited. In order to better understand their stories I borrowed immersion techniques from ethnography. On the recommendation of one correspondent I visited the Peak District National Park for a walking weekend, where I had a dramatic and muddy fall and thought I had fractured my hip. I spent many Sunday mornings hiking in the Sussex Downs and having tea or coffee in cafés. The years of the two world wars do not feature in all of the lives in this book, but for many they are mentioned unprompted in the lifeline, and again in the Remembrance Day directive. Also Suffrage was a very firm presence in the election-day directive. Because of this, and frequent recommendations in the remembrance Sunday directive, I was moved to visit the Imperial War Museum, mainly inspired to get a better sense of context to some of the longer lives that informed this book, but also because the economic and social inequality of those times is said to mirror our own (Piketty, 2014). I watched all of the political party leaders' conference speeches in Autumn 2017, to more fully appreciate the correspondents' spread of political views. I watched television programmes and listened to radio programmes they mentioned. A wide variety of daily papers were read by the correspondents, so a review of headlines and front-page news for each online version was made in an effort to get myself out of my own media bubble. I took a novel morning stroll to the supermarket to buy a local paper. I had a drink in my local pub during an afternoon 'trip to the shops'. I whizzed around the block on my bike in the rain. I spent an afternoon in the bath, I cannot remember regularly bathing since I was pregnant. I even flea combed my cats, which was very satisfying. I stood and watched a sunset and caught sight of a murmuration of starlings as a bonus, and I discovered that there is a plump robin guarding the grapes in my garden. I cancelled a bonfire party that the children have got too old for and threw a PIMS sleepover for twenty 16-year-old girls 'come on mum—what's the worst that could happen?' Being woken at 5am to the sound of them roaring with laughter, teaching each other how to lap dance apparently. I planned an all-night computer gaming party for a gang of 14-year-old boys, a 'wakeover' rather than a sleepover. I cancelled the sale of our camper van, deciding we needed it in retirement. I booked a half board winter sun holiday without consulting my family. I popped out to meet a friend for a coffee and we shared three bottles of wine.

Overall it would be fair to say that these correspondents were a bold influence on me, by bold I mean I felt encouraged to be culturally rebellious, and I liked it. I liked it a lot. I resolved to retire every weekend and be more playful in the working week. Middle age for me and my husband was fraught because we allowed it to be so, rather than learning from our elders not to worry so much, because most of what we worry about we cannot control. Learning not to judge so fast, not to make our bubble too small, to appreciate the pleasure in the everyday, be open to experience and new people, have mini adventures, and make sure that we take care of ourselves and others in ways that are personally satisfying. These realisations of how to live a better life, came along with warnings not to wait to do that. I decided it was also a good idea to have various plans for the future, just in case things do not go the way we imagine. This was all elicited in me in the first round of reading. The process of analysis needed to manage and explore this response. The findings needed to be constructed interactively, paying attention to both audience and context. Back and forth, between data, theoretical sensibilities and reflections, themes linked to other material sources, it was narrative, the narratives from the correspondents, interacting in my mind with narratives from mixed media, and mimicry through my participation in external experiences. Focusing in on apparently unimportant topics, taken for granted ones, holding them up to the light in order to:

> *focus on the act the narrative reports and the moral of the story.* (Riessman, 2008, p. 62)

There are correspondents who have not had a partner, and do not miss that company, they have happy, rich days; there are some who have a difficult partnership, and some who have happy partnerships. I did not mean to look at love and grief, but it kept finding me, big losses, little ones, making me cry. I started to form themes around this mood. The sad stories in-particular drew my eye.

A bridge was needed from the overwhelming emotionality of 26 lifetimes to deeply considering the day to day, and from there to explore how people negotiate leisure in the context of everyday later life; and how they interact with metanarratives about ageing. This involved moving briefly away from the individuals, although immersed in their stories, to more critically consider what is said in the day diaries 'in general'.

Thematic analysis can be a process of merging the particular into the general, but here it is used to identify important stories about everyday leisure lives of correspondents in a more dispassionate way, and to explore perspectives available from looking at the stories in a different way. Thematic analysis of narrative is the usual approach to diaries, biographies, and letters, and correspondence provides fertile primary data (Riessman, 2008).

Riessman explains the importance of what is said rather than how it is said, in thematic analysis of narrative, suggesting that materials are read first at a surface level (2008). I carried out a line by line thematic analysis of just the day diaries. Asking the question what do the correspondents do? I believed this to be a reasonable starting place, to know what they do before asking how they negotiate it, and whether or not it is leisure for them. This was conducted using NVivo software in order to ensure attention to the variety reported in their day diaries. This line by line analysis of the narratives highlighted important features of people's leisure lives, their leisure activities and day to day life. At this nominal level of analysis words and phrases were highlighted with a focus on stories about leisure activities that they described. These initial themes were about what people do, but why is personal, so a list of 'simple pleasures' and chores, was not very enlightening. The first stage of consolidation involved using Nvivo tools to check for overlapping categorisations, and test for distinct themes. Following this each of the remaining themes was checked against direct quotes, and it became apparent that the themes did not stand alone. I had analysed the day diaries, but the context of the rest of the writing for each person stayed with me, and heavily influenced the way information was coded. Apparently simple statements carried meaning and context through my knowledge of the correspondents' complete writing. I had information about what their doings meant to them in the day to day, and how that related to their biography, why something may unexpectedly raise an eyebrow or a tear. Who people are and who they are not. These day diaries echo the stories that people tell about who they are in the world, and who they are not. They reported their loves, their losses, their beliefs about what it means to be themselves, and how their days play out.

In this way the themes that emerged from the day diaries retained the context of the people's lives because having been immersed in the life-lines, and diaries and supplementary directives for several weeks I already knew them well. It gave an additional perspective, but these initial themes lacked depth. They illustrated everyday leisure, what people do, and how they describe it, but in order to get the most understanding from this narrative inquiry I needed to return to the embedded stories, in the context of all of the correspondence from each person, the thematic analysis helped me to focus on the everyday-ness of leisure in later life. These initial themes from contextualised line by line analysis of day diaries explained what the correspondents talk about. Three key themes were generated.

- Windows on the world
- Sociable active ageing
- reminiscence.

They highlighted what is important in the day to day, which re-focused me from the lifetime drama, to the micro politics of cultural engagement in the day diaries. But there was still another level of understanding to be gained from this data.

I discussed earlier concerns around the co-construction of narratives, and the dilemma of representation. I take the opportunity here to comment more upon my approach in co-constructing the narratives. I have tried to remain close to what has been said, and have derived themes from common meanings found across the dataset. So, there is a realist approach to acknowledge, this links back to my discussions around the idea of being post-postmodern, appreciating the value of complex positioning that a critical realist would recognise. But I acknowledge too that there is a variety/plurality of possible readings, so there is a gap between narrative and interpretation. I would start to defend the process of reframing and contextualising the stories by acknowledging that my interpretive practice is also mindful of an audience of practitioners and researchers that are interested in active ageing. There is also a pragmatic, in the research sense of the word, thread that runs through this book, in asking how people negotiate leisure in the context of everyday later life; and how they interact with metanarratives about ageing. It can only be answered from a complex position.

I explored the idea of active ageing as culture (Moulaert & Biggs, 2012; Moulaert & Paris, 2013). I asked where it was, this culture, was it in the ether between them, within them, was it fluid and flexible. I explored terms like cultural consonance (Dressler, 2012), that explores cultural comfort, and concordance that engages with individual love of an activity, and conviviality, the idea of comfortable social engagement (Neal & Walters, 2008). I want to express engagement with a culture of active ageing in a way that does not isolate the internal processes from the thoughts of other people, and knowledge of society. These words, consonance, concordance and conviviality allow for that overlap, they provide the in-between concepts that are sometimes missing in exploring culture and individuals. If we believe that culture gets into a person then we must define it and the person as separate entities. So these ideas are needed so that we can understand how it may be possible to see leisure in later life differently. If a person and the people and ideas they interact with are part of the creation and reproduction of culture, we need a language that works across the constructed boundaries of self, other and society. I tested these words to see if they could work as interfaces. My analysis engaged with how a culture of active ageing is expressed in the correspondence.

I revisited the whole data set, considering the elements of cultural capital that appear to characterise active ageing. I looked at how the correspondents were expressing their cultural capital, the economic, physical, intellectual, caring and civic engagement elements of their stories. I considered the performative nature of this and the reproduction of these ideas in the telling of stories about everyday leisure in later life.

I considered whether engagement with an active ageing culture could be explained and defined, and if not, then could a plural perspective of active ageing be more useful here. I asked where the correspondents' place that culture, if they engage with it, what stories do they tell about active ageing and what those stories do in their world.

While reading I kept notes about the correspondence, and my own responses, to aid reflexivity

'Somehow, I have no idea how, the UKIP voters are in the later part of the sample – perhaps the archivists tuck them at the end of the alphabet – knowing how most people only manage a-b. Really though it gives me issues – I cannot impartially present them in alphabetical order if they are so skewed, and they start out liberal and end up at UKIP, it will look like a strange set up. I also am finding it strange to be transcribing things like "I'm glad I voted UKIP" and "I agreed with a great deal that Farage said". (T3155). It helps me recognise just how lefty I am, how I judge, I have to hold and understand them in the round, aware of political leanings, but not mocking, or portraying unfairly. It would be amazing if I could be so impartial that the reader could not tell where I stand – but obviously my topic is a lefty topic, I will not fool anyone. I must be respectful, each of these people brings something to the research, careful reading, and respectful representation is the only way to do justice to their contribution'. Reflexive diary 29.9.2017

It is important to note that careful attention was paid to the representations that follow, in order to respect the stories. The following section explains the outcome of the analytic process. I have aimed to clarify the relationship between the voice of the correspondents and my curation and control of their stories, and my contextualised representation of their words (Gready, 2013; Pillow, 2003). I aimed to frame the issues raised in complex ways, rather than frame them simply as good or bad, active or passive, third or fourth age. My ambition is that the gap between the original telling and my re-telling is not too wide, so that the precious detail in the correspondence is retained, and to re-phrase Crouch (2016), the nuanced happenings and gentle, and sometimes brash, politics of everyday life are visible.

References

Adams, M., & Raisborough, J. (2010). Making a difference: Ethical consumption and the everyday. *British Journal of Sociology, 61*(2), 256–274.

Andrews, M., Squire, C., & Tamboukou, M. (2013). *Doing narrative research.* Sage.

Baker, J., & Geiringer, D. (2019). Space, text and selfhood: Encounters with the personal computer in the mass observation project archive, 1991–2004. *Contemporary British History, 33*(3), 293–312.

Clarke, N., Jennings, W., Moss, J., & Stoker, G. (2017). Changing spaces of political encounter and the rise of anti-politics: Evidence from mass observation's general election diaries. *Political Geography, 56,* 13–23.

Crouch, D. (2016). *Flirting with space.* Taylor and Francis.

Dressler, W. W. (2012). Cultural consonance: Linking culture, the individual and health. *Preventive Medicine, 55*(5), 390–393.

Genoe, M. R., Liechty, T., Marston, H. R., & Sutherland, V. (2016). Blogging into retirement. *Journal of Leisure Research, 48*(1), 15–34.

Getz, D., & Page, S. (2016). *Event studies: Theory, research and policy for planned events.* Routledge.

Gready, P. (2013). The public life of narratives: Ethics, politics, methods. In C. Squire, M. Andrews, & M. Tamboukou (Eds.), *Doing narrative research.* London: Sage.

Hubble, N. (2010). *Mass observation and everyday life, culture, history, theory.* Palgrave Macmillan.

Liechty, T., Genoe, M. R., & Marston, H. R. (2017). Physically active leisure and the transition to retirement: The value of context. *Annals of Leisure Research, 20*(1), 23–38.

Lindsey, R., & Bulloch, S. (2014). A sociologist's field notes to the mass observation archive: A consideration of the challenges of "re-using" mass observation data in a longitudinal mixed-methods study. *Sociological Research Online, 19*(3), 1–14.

Lindsey, R., Bulloch, S., & Metcalfe, L. (2016). *Volunteering 1981–2012.* Retrieved from https://longitudinalvolunteering.wordpress.com/.

Moffatt, S., & Heaven, B. (2017). "Planning for uncertainty": Narratives on retirement transition experiences. *Ageing and Society, 37,* 879–898.

Moor, L., & Uprichard, E. (2014). The materiality of method: The case of the mass observation archive. *Sociological Research Online, 19*(3), 1–11.

Moulaert, T., & Biggs, S. (2012). International and European policy on work and retirement: Reinventing critical perspectives on active ageing and mature subjectivity. *Human Relations, 66*(1), 23–43.

Moulaert, T., & Paris, M. (2013). Social policy on ageing: The case of "active ageing" as a theatrical metaphor. *International Journal of Social Science Studies, 1*(2), 113–123.

Neal, S., & Walters, S. (2008). Rural be/longing and rural social organizations: Conviviality and community-making in the English countryside. *Sociology,* *42*(2), 279–297.

Phoenix, A. (2013). Analysing narrative contexts. In M. Andrews, C. Squire, & M. Tamboukou (Eds.), *Doing narrative research.* Sage.

Piketty, T. (2014). *Capital in the twenty-first century* (Translated). Harvard University Press.

Pillow, W. (2003). Confession, catharsis, or cure? Rethinking the uses of reflexivity as methodological power in qualitative research. *International Journal of Qualitative Studies in Education, 16*(2), 175–196.

Polkinghorne, D. E. (1994). Transformative narratives: From victimic to agentic life plots. *The American Journal of Occupational Therapy, 50*(4), 299–305.

Polkinghorne, D. E. (1995). Narrative configuration in qualitative analysis. *International Journal of Qualitative Studies in Education, 8*(1), 5–23.

Pollen, A. (2013). Research methodology in mass observation past and present: "Scientifically, about as valuable as a chimpanzee's tea party at the zoo"? *History Workshop Journal, 75*(1), 213–235.

Riessman, C. K. (2008). *Narrative methods for the human sciences* (2nd ed.). Sage.

Riessman, C. K. (2013). Concluding comments. In *Doing narrative research* (2nd ed., p. 273).

Salmon, P., & Riessman, C. K. (2013). Looking back on narrative research: an exchange. In M. Andrews, C. Squire, & M. Tamboukou (Eds.), *Doing narrative research* (2nd ed.). Sage.

Savage, M. (2007). Changing social class identities in post-war Britain: Perspectives from mass-observation. *Sociological Research Online, 12*(3).

Schank, R. C., & Ableson, R. P. (1995). Knowledge and memory: The real story. In R. S. J. Wyer (Ed.), *Knowledge and memory: The real story* (Vol. 33, pp. 33–3602–33–3602). Lawrence Erlbaum Associates.

Steedman, C. (2001). *Dust: The archive and cultural history.* Manchester University Press.

Tamboukou, M. (2013). A Foucauldian approach to narratives. In M. Andrews, C. Squire, & M. Tamboukou (Eds.), *Doing narrative research* (2nd ed., pp. 103–121). Sage.

Wheaton, B. (2017). Surfing through the life-course: Silver surfers' negotiation of ageing. *Annals of Leisure Research, 20*(1), 96–116.

Wood, H. (2015). Television—the Housewife's Choice? The 1949 mass observation television directive. *Reluctance and Revision. Media History, 21*(3), 342–359.

5

Negotiating Leisure Lives in a Culture of Active Ageing

A word cloud was generated from the diary entries, and this illustrates the main focus of the diaries, which was getting the day going. I include this, knowing that this is a form of quantifying content analysis, but it is also intriguing, allowing the reader to play with words and construct sentences, consider meanings. This is, after all, what I have done on a grander scale (Fig. 5.1).

The findings of the analysis were constructed to express the nature of leisure experiences explained by the correspondents. This chapter presents the themes from the thematic analysis of narrative with some contextualising references. Here in the findings section, texts, research and background material is added to explain ideas and comments raised by the quotes. A fuller discussion follows in the next chapter that returns to the leisure constraints literature to support an analysis of how people negotiate leisure in the context of everyday later life; and how they interact with metanarratives about ageing.

During the analysis the idea of 'windows on the world' became very important. The first part of this section will focus on illustrating that

© The Author(s), under exclusive license to Springer Nature Switzerland AG 2021
T. Wiseman, *Leisure in Later Life*, Leisure Studies in a Global Era,
https://doi.org/10.1007/978-3-030-71672-1_5

Fig. 5.1 Word cloud generated from correspondents day diaries

idea. The sociable nature of much of the leisure discussed by participants is the next idea explored in this section, including reminiscence.
Then the themes start to address how people interact with metanarratives about ageing. The correspondents report deeply connected busy
lives, with moments of freedom. They negotiate their leisure time mainly
in relation to work, civic duty, home and body maintenance and social
labour.

> Windows on the world
>> A pleasant couple of hours in good company
>> Other people's fun
>> Reminiscence was a joy
>> I was honoured
> No great virtue in all this active ageing
> His Lordship goes off to work,

A balance is struck
Discord as work trumps leisure
Other old people: 'Active wife' to 'Courageous intrepid lady'.

5.1   Windows on the World

They are paying attention, not so much the curtain twitching kind of paying attention, but there is a writing that demonstrates concern and connection, environmental and generational. Like societal parenting, nearly stewardship, but without that explicitly being the remit. The theme of 'Windows on the World' relates to the prospect and refuge home offers for the people writing, but also expresses multifaceted connection, and concern with and for others.

Much leisure in later life is home based. It is cheap, familiar, comfortable and hidden from prying eyes. There is choice in this because all but one of the correspondents are not 'house bound', they choose to be at home, enjoying passive educational and connecting leisurely pastimes. The day revolves around radio, newspaper, internet, tv, reading. There are 'trips out' which are mainly for shopping or other consumptive leisure activities, and there are some holidays too.

On first reading the everyday lives are explained as familiar and routine, expressing continuity. Anything 'out of the ordinary' is the focus of the micro narratives, contrasting to the expected run of events. News and entertainment media is very important, with most days starting with a favourite radio programme and a preferred newspaper. A trip out to fetch a newspaper allows for a walk that is not in itself leisurely but provides opportunities to be in the world, see other people and acknowledge the dark mornings that indicate the time of year. In this way these leisure routines, focused around media consumption, serve to embed people in the world around them, from the comfort of home, the comfort of 'as usual'.

Woke as usual at 7.40am. Also, as usual, I read the paper after breakfast but this morning it was different. I looked out of the window to see a fox gazing back at me; he was about to go into the garage. There's nothing edible in there

but I didn't let on. I like the idea of having Mr Fox around so left him to it.
(Paul, Bonfire, 2015)

I woke at around 5.30 (as usual) and drifted on as usual half listening to Radio 4; I did hear the Sunday Bells (half muffled) at 5.45. I then listened to the 7 o' clock News before making tea to drink while I dressed (after a shower). Then out for the paper, which I started over breakfast. (Rodney, Remembrance, 2014)

I battle to the newsagent in strong wind, but no rain. On return I see a chubby young chap in school uniform on his way to Breakfast Club. It's still dark. My husband has the pot on and I curl up with the crossword and plan my day. (Brenda, Remembrance, 2014)

We got up soon after 8 and had breakfast after listening to the news on radio 4. And had a quick look at the paper. We had to get a move on as normally our church service starts at 10.30 but this morning we were starting at 10.00. (Peggy, Remembrance, 2014)

TV takes a central role in many lives, offering far reaching views of the world, entertainment, education and pleasure. People record programmes from advertising channels, and fast-forward through the adverts to save time, missing out on the popular culture embedded in TV advertisements. Marjorie is the only person to describe herself as 'registered as disabled', note that she has a similar habits to others in the group, with media and world events an important part of her day.

Now I can't get out by myself, and I know I am a problem for my more aged husband, so I have stayed at home whilst he goes to the local service at the war memorial in the centre of our town. I do what I've done each year since a fall had me registered as disabled, and that is: the usual getting up, showering, breakfast… preparations for lunch, then a sit down for watching and listening to the BBC1 transmission from the cenotaph. I continue till it finishes at about 12.30pm. I think of my father. The rest of the day amounts to the usual household chores (which I am very slow at), lots of rests in between with news bulletins, and 'Downton Abbey' later. (Marjorie, Remembrance, 2014)

Tonight Bonfire Night, follows a normal day of domestic activity. After a normal supper I'll watch Autumn Watch for an hour or so then read and do the crossword from the paper… Bed will be at about 11.30pm. (Marjorie, Bonfire, 2015)

She reaches out into the world through TV news, live events, autumn watch and TV drama, and normal routines. We could consider if she is describing herself as disabled, what she actually says is '*a fall had me registered as disabled*'. We could consider her externalisation of this event, and its impact on how she is now 'registered', and what that means for her, as this registration reaches into her life. There is no official registration of disability in the UK.[1] But there are processes of assessment for eligibility for a disabled car parking permits, free or reduced-price public transport, and some disability-related benefits, and it may be these that Marjorie is referring to.

People have TV, computer, laptop, tablet and phone all on the go at the same time, with a focus on current affairs. They are learning skills and exploring new ideas through this engagement. TV in particular can be connecting, both to self and others, in the present and across time.

Over the years I always watched it [The Eurovision Song Contest] with my family, mostly with the younger members. The Daily Mirror had a few pages with entrants and places to mark your favourites. Children love doing that sort of thing and we used to discuss the various talents as if it mattered! Stand out winners have included Lulu with Boom Banger Bang, Sandie Shaw with Puppet on a String, Cliff Richard with Congratulations and Brother hood of Man with Save Your Kisses for Me and who could forget the supreme ABBA with "Waterloo". The music on offer nowadays is pretty mundane and I can't see anything selling globally.

I don't usually watch nowadays but my daughter (51) and her partner love watching and she wanted me to compare notes…I put "Eurovision" on and my daughter and I texted and phoned each other back and forth. She was being fair in her judgements and I was my usual scathing self. One entry,

---

[1] https://www.nhs.uk/common-health-questions/caring-carers-and-long-term-conditions/how-do-i-register-as-disabled/.

Poland I think, had placed a buxom woman on a milking stool, apparently a non singer but I suspect an escapee from a porn show who behaved lasciviously bending over and wriggling about - they didn't win! When I had had enough I went to bed but did put the small television on in my room. I noticed that we were nowhere near currying favour let alone winning. Quel Surprise! A bearded Austrian male singer dressed as a woman won with "Rise Like a Phoenix". She did have a beautiful voice. What next? Conjoined twins on stilts? (Barbara, Eurovision, 2014)

There are different levels of connection expressed here; with her daughter now and in the past; with her own sense of taste, related to a global music industry; and with popular culture. Barbara writes expressively about lascivious behaviour and her surprise about the winner's appearance. In this way television viewing can offer excitement and cultural challenge and connection.

My wife sat down in our lounge to watch Eurovision Song Contest 2014. At 8.00pm (BBC One). After a day in the garden I had a bath & appeared in the lounge at approx. 9.15. she told me about the initial entrants. I was much impressed by the Lighting & flashing. Such a huge effect. Wow, terrific!!

Of course Austria's Conchita Wurst won. A good song, "Rise like a Phoenix", sung alone with inspiring charisma... We did not vote... (Peter, Eurovision, 2014)

The majority of correspondents are completely surprised by '*a lady with a beard*' winning the Eurovision song contest. Peter quoted above, describes himself as a retired music master, and was the only person that commented but did not mention the beard or mock the performer. Others, like Barbara above, were challenged by the concept of a lady with a beard, some of their comments are difficult to repeat, many are oblivious to the cultural turn, and the millions of votes from 195 million viewers around the world,[2] some rejected it as 'ridiculous' or wrote it off as a novelty. Others took the opportunity to find out more, turning to the internet to clarify "the situation".

---

[2]https://eurovision.tv/story/eurovision-song-contest-2014-reaches-195-million-worldwide.

My husband was on his laptop and had a look at Facebook (that is how
we keep tabs on our 18 grandchildren.) One of my granddaughters seemed
to have grown a beard! Then another appeared to have a beard also! My
oldest grandson was saying 'Concita to win!' Then someone showed this very
glamourous woman with long hair, sparkly earrings and a dark beard. Very
strange! However it turns out that 'she' is really a drag act, and obviously
captured the populations imagination, to go on to win the Contest for Austria.
(Pauline, Eurovision, 2014)

Brenda reports that she heard on the radio that "*a chap with a beard*
won" (Eurovision, 2014). She did not watch the contest so did not know
that it was 'a lady with a beard' and was therefore unable to engage with
the political statement that informed the performance or learn anything
new about developments in cultural expression supported by the contest.

In the house, in the car, on the bus, in bed, radio, TV, newspapers,
books, magazines, internet articles, phones, letters, fiction and factual
reading, metaphorical and literal windows on the world influence the
way the correspondents write about their lives. Charles tells us about his
favourite news sources, and comments on the changing media of political expression, noticing the lack of posters during the election campaign
from his car as he drives out to the supermarket.

Up at 9-00am. Need to pace myself - long day and night ahead!

Breakfast - then read daily paper. I subscribe to the 'i' which has had very
comprehensive and unbiased coverage of the election. Yesterday's edition had
an excellent 3-page summary of the policies of all the major and minor
parties. Much easier to comprehend and digest than wading through the
actual manifestos.

9-30am - checked incoming emails (personal stuff) - and then looked at news
headlines on the net. I prefer the BBC website to any other news broadcaster.
Also viewed 'PoliticalBetting.com' - my favoured source of political news and
comment. I haven't placed any bets on the outcome of this election - but
'PoliticalBetting.com' features all the opinion poll data - and detailed analysis.
I have referred to this site every day for months.

10-15 - Drove with my wife the 4 miles… to do our weekly shop. **Didn't see a single poster for any political party.***That was a surprise. In past elections many houses have sported posters on boards - or in windows. Perhaps people are using social media instead to show which party they are supporting.* (Charles, Election 2015, emphasis added)

Winifred also notices the lack of political posters, through the windows of the bus.

1pm - Turn on BBC1 lunchtime news and eat whilst watching starlings (in the garden) squabble over the mealworms. Wash up pots and leave to drain, fold washing, get a coffee. Find my Labour rosette and pin it to my jacket to go to the supermarket, 10min bus ride away, for cash and a few bits- cat treats, peanuts for the birds, toiletries - the family get the main shopping and anything I ask for. I **didn't see one sign for any political party anywhere along the route.** *(Winifred, Election 2015, emphasis added)*

This change is interesting to both, Winifred actively participates in the democratic process, but the form of participation has evolved. Winifred became a local politician for six years after she lost her husband, just as they entered retirement. She now organises her day around feeding the birds and fussing the cat. She follows the political excitement on the TV with a Campari and soda, but still has fun provoking intergenerational political debate on the bus.

At the bus stop a little girl, about 5 or 6, asked why was I wearing the badge and I said "it is voting day" and she asked what was it for and I said "to show I support the red party" she was with her mother and granny who were totally involved with her older sister having a tantrum, A middle-aged couple got on the bus after asking if it went near where they were going and only had a £20 note and Euros, so obviously not normal bus users, the driver said to sit until later when he might have some change and drove off, I offered two £10s which they took, mock checking if they were genuine, I said "freshly laundered" and held their £20 up to the light, so they could pay their fare. He said I should have voted Tory as they would double the pension, I said "I'm alright it's the grandchildren who need the help". (Winifred, Election 2015)

Winifred reports the banter, exaggerates the intergenerational mistrust, and her expression of 'not normal bus users' with euros allows her to express the identity that so many of the correspondents hint at, that of the selfless boomer. She is aware of the talk around housing shortages and older people blocking the way for the younger generation (Kneale et al., 2013), as a politically engaged woman she knows that her generation are being offered up as a cause of intergenerational injustice (see for example of this rhetoric: Willetts, 2010). Her own experience of growing up in an era of cheap rent, then council housing from 1964 meant that Winifred could afford to buy her council flat. She lists the important events in her lifeline, there is repetition of families staying close and supporting each other through the three generations that are included, and she highlights the importance of housing in this. This is Winifred's story, but it is also the story of post war housing in the UK, and the changing role of women in property ownership and the workplace, and the emergence of a leisure lifestyle afforded by rent free housing and a pension in later life. She has helped her sons to buy their own homes but knows the grandchildren will need something more radical to help secure their housing for later life.[3] This echo down the generations of Winifred's family is one that will eventually become resounding, because the pathway to becoming a property owner, and therefore living rent free in later life when incomes fall, is currently disrupted. This route to property ownership of cheap council housing, or cheaper living with grandparents, was described in most of the lifelines of the homeowning correspondents. Home as a leisure space is clearly important in the directives, and tenancy is important in all the lifelines. Because home is a place of leisure that is less public, less subject to critique and social pressures, tenancy is very important to leisure studies in later life.

Mary was thrilled by the election coverage, enjoying the twists and turns in the coverage, and the excitement of 'winning'.

---

[3]Winnifred is definitely not a mail reader, but she is politically engaged, and would have followed these stories. Daily Mail (2011) Over-60 bedroom blockers 'should be taxed out of their homes' to encourage them to leave 'too large' family houses. October 20th 2011. https://www.dailymail.co.uk/news/article-2050800/Over-60-bedroom-blockers-taxed-homes.html (accessed 20.12.2017).

At quarter to three I was wide awake and got up and switched the TV on. The results that were coming through were already giving weight to the exit poll. Amazing. I stayed up until I was pretty sure that whatever station I turned to, the Labour Party was completely trashed. A couple of hours sleep and I was up again before seven to be glued yet again to the small screen that was telling such a big story. At this point I went in and woke my husband up to tell him we appeared to have wiped out Labour, Liberal Democrats and UKIP. As the morning rolled on we kept the television on and kept returning to stay abreast of developments. When the results that gave the Tories a clear victory came in I really did go into a state of euphoria. I'd had so little sleep and yet I was so fuelled up with excitement I wasn't in the least bit tired or concerned about the threat of the SNP but just celebrating the moment. (Mary, Election, 2015)

This initial theme highlighted important ideas about the multiplicity of connection and the refuge of home. The familiar routines and habits of media consumption discussed at the beginning of the windows on the world theme mean that people are potentially living in a bubble, bordering on tribal, and this idea continues in the sub themes that follow, moving away from mass media interactions, and looking on in the world, to participating in social life.

5.1.1   A Pleasant Couple of Hours in Good Company

There are many different expressions of sociability, from seeking out spaces away from the home to experience the company of other people such as visiting the pub or a social club, to forms of sharing and connection with family members, to travelling as a couple and experiencing moments together. There is a sniff of adventure, but from a comfortable and familiar base.

We Were Met by Our Guide and Driver and Transferred to Our Hotel in the City, then, as We Had Opted, the Rest of Our day Was Free to Rest, Walk, Sleep or Eat as We Wished…

Bangkok was full of people, cars, fumes and noise as we wandered up one side of the street and down the other. We stopped in a supermarket to buy some sort of spirit - we object to hotel prices for a nightcap - and chose rum in the end.

Later we went out to eat at a Thai restaurant (amid all the Chinese, Indian, Malaysian and western restaurants, there aren't as many as you'd think!). It was open on two sides and filled with locals (always a recommendation). It was a bit of a 'greasy spoon' place with sticky plastic tablecloths and staff buzzing about like flies trying to deal with dozens of people at once, but the food was wonderful - probably the best red curry we've ever had (with rice, spices, chicken and vegetables) and fried chicken with noodles and egg. The beer was very acceptable too. (Vivien, Bonfire night, 2015)

The importance of freedom on holiday is expressed, free from time constraints, and free to choose what to do, where to eat, what to pay for a drink. Being out and about with a partner in crime is a feature of many of the days in the diaries, but also adventures without a spouse are reported. These adventures are not about reaching across social difference, which is a key part of how sociologists have conceptualised conviviality as part of social comfort (Jones et al., 2015; Neal & Vincent, 2013), rather this grows from the comfort of existing familial relationships and friendships. This lack of diverse interactions in an otherwise very sociable life will be further considered in the discussion. Violet has a difficult relationship with her husband, and enjoys regular respite with acquaintances;

I was staying in [the lake district] with a group of 12 friends on a short walking holiday. I have a postal vote on a permanent basis so had voted 3 weeks before the election. There was a TV in the house but was not used during our stay. I had a radio by the side of the bed, permanently on and could hear it through and ear piece so as not to disturb my room mate.

7.00 am Up and made a drink & back to bed to listen to the radio.

8.00 am Up and breakfast – hardly any mention of the election – I imagine most of the group would have different views from me.

9.30 am. In the car and off to xxxxxxx reservoir then a 9 mile walk along the Pennine Way over very difficult terrain for the first 3 miles, then beautiful scenery – wild flowers (gentians) birds and views in glorious spring sunshine and no thoughts of the election at all. (Violet, Election, 2015)

She notes that she imagines most of the group are different to her politically, but no discussion is reported and no examples given, the silence on this topic that is so important to the majority of correspondents may be indicative of the place of political discussion as removed from the everyday, and consumed in private. The informal company of TV or acquaintances is important;

I recorded the song contest as there is so much waffle going on that it is easier that way and I only have to watch the bits that I want to. So after we'd had dinner and washed up, we wrapped up some birthday presents for my grandson's birthday which we will be celebrating on Sunday.

I started watching the programme at about 8.30 and my husband went upstairs and was on the computer all evening. He never watches the contest but will usually watch the results coming in, but this time he didn't even do that. (Rosalind, Eurovision, 2014)

I went to coffee morning (my only chance in the day to have a conversation with someone other than my husband) but the election wasn't mentioned a great deal because there had been three deaths in the village in the preceding couple of days and obviously this was of more pertinent news to most people. (Rosalind, Election 2015)

Organised socialising around newly developed interests creates opportunities, and there is some sense that 'who died recently' does form the basis of a new interest. Wendy's new interest is more about self-expression and mastery.

The group started about three years ago; I joined, encouraged by the friend who's in Scotland, about 18 months ago. There's no audition, anyone is welcome and xxxxx, who runs it, is a great encouragement to us all. Some are good singers, others like me got told to shut up at school yet, amazingly, after a few months of proper vocal and physical warm-ups and learning parts phrase by phrase, everyone gains confidence. I'll never be more than a back row alto, but the buzz of holding a part in anything from a Beach Boys' number to the seven-part introduction to Zadok the Priest is terrific. (Wendy, Working day, 2010)

Wendy was driven out of a hard won career, causing illness, and has begun to express her competency in learning difficult vocal parts for her choir, the 'buzz' she describes in this deeply social activity gradually takes over from the stories about the cruelty of her colleagues. The encouragement she receives as she becomes more involved in musical activities, some of which she has enjoyed throughout her life, supports her to express acceptance and competency. Matthew expresses his competency in more subtle ways;

I find quite easily most of the items I want, except for shampoo. I wander around the area for men's shower gels, deodorants, etc, thinking it was much easier when men did not use such stuff. I find the shampoo I want on a shelf some distance away. It is busy at the checkouts. I join a queue, and after a little while an assistant asks me if I want to go to another till which is just opening. As I am heading there I see a couple of women dash to get ahead of me. I walk a little quicker and get there before them. I act as if I have not seen them. As I put my purchases onto the conveyor belt one of the women starts to put her purchases on as well. The area l have to put them on gets smaller as the assistant is putting my items through the till. Eventually the woman realises that she will have to move her purchases back to allow me room. I put my purchases in my car, and drive home. (Matthew, Bonfire, 2015)

He describes asserting himself but does not directly engage with the women, he expresses subtle satisfaction as he holds his place as they try to get past him in the supermarket queue. Their company is not so good, but the interaction, and the outcome are both worth writing about. Shoppers age and stage of family life cycle do have an impact on how people behave and different generations do not tend to accommodate each other (Kohijoki & Marjanen, 2013). In other directive writing, and in his lifeline, Matthew expresses annoyance at being overlooked throughout his career, as younger more assertive people were promoted ahead of him, and he was repeatedly turned down for promotion. He retired early, sorry that he had not been properly appreciated, and more recently he expresses satisfaction in having a rewarding retirement, able to express many competencies.

I start to watch a DVD I have made of a holiday I took during June. The DVD contains photographs and video I took on the holiday, and includes maps, titles, information and background music…I will spend the evening writing DVDs, the tomorrow I will produce labels and put them on the DVDs. Some of these will be distributed to friends and relatives. (Matthew, Bonfire, 2015)

He is close to his sister and is in regular contact through their shared interest in family history.

I get onto the internet to spend a few minutes looking up family history information.1½ hours later I finish having found some information about the family of a possible ancestor. I email the results to my sister. (Matthew, Remembrance, 2014)

He is a lifelong cricket fan and has 'played the long game' in life, quietly assertive, winning in the end. He has always lived alone and connects with friends and family daily, sharing his adventures through his skilled use of computers.

Rachel's days combine entertaining family, organised pastimes and informal socialising, all before lunch.

10.00. Started to peel potatoes and apples in readiness for tonight. We have son and daughter in law and 10 mth old baby coming for fireworks and dinner. I made beef in red wine last night together with mince, onions and steak and onions as I do bulk cooking and decant into little containers and freeze – which I did this morning.

10.45am. left for my needlework class – no tutor today just 5 of us. Afterwards

12.40 – a friend and I went to local pub for lunch and did a little shopping – 4 toffee apples, treacle toffee. (Rachel, Bonfire, 2015)

With acquaintances or loved ones, whether they are there or not. Stories about socialising, researching, holidays and day trips bring out the prevalence and importance of the sociable in the correspondence.

10.55 pm: Home again after a pleasant couple of hours in the good company of my local pub. Quieter night in there than is normal and that might have been due to the non-arrival of the pianist. Again in the interests of this diary I did ask those sharing the same table if any had been watching Eurovision. The general response was "Not bloody likely!" and "What? That rubbish?" It has to be said though, they were long past their own dancing days.

Anyhow, I am back to the comfort of my chair and on the small table at its side awaits a large measure of whisky, a can of beer, and from the music centre comes my kind of music and that is not a bad note on which to end this report. (Richard, Eurovision, 2015)

It also highlights the freedoms that having comfortable relationships affords, the private space for relaxation, and the comfort of familiar routine. Some loneliness within married life is expressed. Some stories of intergenerational pith are told, with hints at perceived ageist behaviour, that is managed outside of these familiar relationships. How work life ended, particularly if it was difficult or disappointing, has an influence on the stories that are told. Mainly people seek comfortable and reliable social opportunities with people of their own age.

5.1.2 Other People's Fun

This sub theme introduces ideas about vicarious participation, inclusion, exclusion and how they are explained. It mainly focuses on bonfire night, which provided fertile ground for expression of these ideas. Peter enjoys views of local displays of fireworks from his windows, vicarious participation in an event that is usually reserved for families with children to hand. Participation is enjoyable, cosy and easy.

Tea at 5.00, after some gardening. Good seat in our lounge at 6.00 onwards for super display. Local Scout hut area?? Lasted to approx. 8.30. Various venues perhaps. 7 November same views but fewer fireworks that we could see. We certainly heard them. Bed at 10.45, on both days!! (Peter, Bonfire, 2015)

Peter enjoys the display as he enjoyed the Eurovision song contest, Teresa who comments below watches fireworks, but is not entirely sure that she approves,

Haven't really participated in any Bonfire Night activities, though I did go up to the window to watch a few fireworks which were being let off in gardens of the houses in the next street. Few youngsters living in our road, so little interest in the celebrations near to us.

Our main Bonfire festivities…organised by the council…is the nearest I shall come to any Bonfire Celebrations, from our house 2 miles away we can hear the loudspeaker & recorded music of the show, usually the fireworks display is out of sight, blocked by trees, but his year we watched it for ¾ of an hour from the back bedroom window. Must have been bigger or better fireworks – that's where our Council Tax goes! (Teresa, Bonfire, 2015)

This idea of vicarious participation in other people's fun is expressed by involvement in the activities of others, known or not, watching fireworks displays from the comfort of home engages with the activity in a different way.

6.15 pm Heard my first 'banger' of the night. Wonder then if the rain has stopped. I will take the trouble to find if this is so…and yes, so it has. This pleases me because of my concerns over disappointed children having this spectacular celebration spoilt for them…It would seem this lull in the wet weather is being made the most of; rockets are swishing skywards and creating their own bangs more colourful than any of my reminiscences. (Richard, Fireworks, 2015)

But the 'opportunity' to participate is not really a choice, unlike many public events the noise of this one is intrusive, and the sound of other people fun is not enjoyable for everyone.

Some fireworks had gone off late into the night and sounded more like bombing which made me quite cross. Went up to bed and watched" Question Time which had Victoria Coren-Mitchell on who criticised the Tories so much she made the audience laugh at Justine Greening because Tory soundbites are extremely irritating! Such as "Hardworking families" "Long term economic plan" "Northern powerhouse" absolute bollocks! Caught a bit of "This Week" then switched off to put LBC radio on which blocked out some of Bonfire Night but there were huge explosions around that went off into the early hours. (Barbara, Bonfire, 2015)

11pm. Off to bed. Stuck head out of back door earlier, intending to stretch legs. Blown back in by enormous explosion. This is fun? All in all what my mother used to call an "indawsy day". She and I both fresh air fiends. But there are limits....This is a "school" night so will have to endure Fri + Sat no doubt. (Brenda, Fireworks, 2015)

By mid-evening there are explosions outside as if we are in a war zone. All went quiet by 10pm. Our son says that there was plenty of activity in his village (2 miles away). The family's pet cats utterly terrified and one has gone missing. Some of us have to grit our teeth and accept that this is Guy Fawkes' Night and put up with it. (Paul, Fireworks, 2015)

The lifelong experiences of these writers have led them here, to writing/rewriting their relationship to this intrusive intergenerational event. Some find ways to vicariously participate, others turn up the TV, grit their teeth and hang onto their pets. This research is beginning to explore what lies beneath these responses to other people's fun. The diaries were elicited close to the 2015 general election in the UK, where all political parties courted 'hard working families'.[4] Bonfire night is also aimed at people who qualify for inclusion in this group. It is notable that only those with grandchildren who live close by can participate, and only then if they organise the event. The idea of not being in the group of 'hard working' or 'families', as it is conceived for the purpose of

---

[4]The idea of the hardworking family excluded most people, as humorously analysed in this newspaper article. https://www.theguardian.com/media/mind-your-language/2015/mar/20/welcome-to-the-election-but-only-if-youre-a-hardworking-family.

that election, and the bonfire celebrations is excluding. Whether watched from a window, or not, these events are other people having fun that is not inclusive.

5.1.3 Reminiscence Was a Joy

This sub theme explores leisure that is not observable, the reminiscence examples given here suggest that the meanings of everyday, potentially mundane activities cannot always be found in the everyday. They emerge in the lifelines and other directives, Brenda has a close connection to her role as a mother enhanced through memories of ironing that make it a pleasure on a wet and windy day, as she explains:

I think the satisfaction of seeing a crumpled rag transform into a pristine garment helps. But there is also the smell. Bringing the washing in fresh from the garden, and the process. Providing you don't rush it.

A very happy day was spent when our youngest returned from a summer in Corsica. A suitcase bigger than her was full of dirty washing, but hurriedly rinsed through and strung out up a line, criss-crossing our garden and pegged out all her pretty clothes. When it came to ironing them, I could imagine her wearing the flowery blouses in hot sunshine. At 21, she was quite capable of doing this chore. That's the difference. It wasn't a chore. It was a joy. (Brenda, Happy, 2013)

I Arrange the Washing on the Radiator, and Fish Out the Shirts to Iron. A Nice Warm Job, on a Wet and Windy day. (Brenda, Remembrance, 2014)

This quote complicates reminiscence, there is reminiscence on a holiday that Brenda's daughter enjoyed as a young woman, Brenda was not free to enjoy that holiday herself, but now, many years later, she reminisces on that feeling, and once again temporarily joins in with her daughter's holiday. Ironing is a joy to Brenda, appreciating the movement and smells and warmth, not rushing, taking her time. This quote may also reflect distancing of her daughter, from a time when she was becoming independent, and the moments of connection, and time for reflection that the routine of washing and ironing clothes offers.

Vivien has a double dose of sociability, at the end of her night out in Bangkok she describes her usual Guy Fawkes night, the thoughts of it connect her with her child, grandchild, her inner child and her ever-present husband.

> *Every year at home we mark Guy Fawkes Night (which is what it was always called when I was a child) with sparklers and baked potatoes. We don't have a child at home any more and my daughter, son-in-law and small grandson live too far away, so we don't bother with fireworks, though we do go out to watch other people's if we hear them. But it is a tradition that we light sparklers and I (still) run round the back garden waving them wildly and enjoying the strange orange/white circles and curves the light makes. I am still a child at heart!* (Vivien, Bonfire night, 2015)

Brenda expresses freedom from the mundane, drifting off to sunny Corsica. Vivien expresses freedom to play and express youthfulness. Ideas of freedom from and freedom to, present in many of the stories presented here, are important to expressing the relationship between leisure and freedom (Carr, 2017). These ideas work even in reminiscence on a daughter's holidays, thirty years earlier; and a 'tradition' of lighting sparklers that may or may not be an annual event, but is an expression of freedom to play and expression of acceptance of that freedom within the relationship.

5.1.3.1   I Was Honoured

Having formal social roles is important to some of the participants. Engagement with organisations that enable them to contribute to society and have that contribution acknowledged is often a repayment for kindness received earlier in life. Freda was the only child of Jewish refugees. Her mother died soon after she was born, and she was fostered throughout her childhood, she states.

I was always the outsider… Somewhere along the line, my foster parents and my father were showing dislike of each other's lifestyles. My foster people looked upon my father as a too rich person; and my father endlessly told me that they were working class and I was not to model my lifestyle on theirs'. (Freda, Lifeline, 2008)

Freda was married for 6 years, and had two sons,

When the lads were young, under the age of 10, we had caravan holidays in a friend's caravan at Felixstowe. It was heaven for us all as the owner took us to the site and picked us up at the end of the holiday. She was a shining light in the Red Cross but so kind. 1 was a single parent and wouldn't have got there without these kind people. (Freda, Holidays, 2010)

She has never felt the need to look for another partner. She is not senti-mental, when her old Jack Russel dies, it is not explained, he is just replaced in her stories with a lively 2-year-old dog. Freda is civically inclined, when she retired from her care work in an 'old peoples home' she continued to work as a volunteer in a charity shop, and within a year became the secretary to the Women's Section of the Royal British Legion, which she finds 'a bit stuffy', but she enjoys meals and outings with them, and explains that it has broadened her horizons to a certain extent.

Being part of the British Legion, I set off as an escort to our standard- bearer - got there before her. There was a new Parade Marshall who wouldn't let me march alongside her which upset my equilibrium. We were led by the Royal Engineers Band, resplendent in their red tunics and gold buttons, and their spurs on their boots. Our soldiers in khaki not long back from the war in Afghanistan (hopefully not to have to go back again) were cheered and applauded all the way.

Our new mayor and council leaders and church officious on a platform led a service. A schoolboy played a cornet and literally hundreds of primary, and playschool lined the route and sang word for word two war songs they had learnt at school were "Pack Up Your Troubles in your own kit bag and smile,

smile" and "It's a long way to Tipperary" very moving. A quartet from St. Marys Church.

I accompanied with pride but couldn't keep quite keep in step with the 6' 4" Paratrooper beside me. Evidently our town lost 74 men. An Apache helicopter flew overhead. Anybody who was somebody went for refreshments at the Legion Club. (Freda, Remembrance, 2014)

Freda is busy and civically engaged in all of her day diaries.

Day spent usual. Walking dog morning and evening. Afternoon accompanied my Age UK rep to a new lady needing help. Never turn anyone down but in this case I don't think I can proceed.

Prepared Buster [dog] for a relatively safe indoors without me. Our charity evening went well with the new Mayor and I enjoyed my chicken and chips. (Freda, Fireworks, 2015)

Timothy has many things in his life that he is proud of, he was president of his professional organisation and received an OBE (Officer of the Order of the British Empire) when he retired for services to industry.

Getting an OBE was probably the proudest moment of my entire life. My wife and I had been away on holiday and of course there was a mound of post awaiting us on our return one Sunday evening. I was gradually working through this when I came upon the letter from Buckingham Palace offering me an OBE. I leapt into the air with a great shout! I went to the Palace to receive the medal...from the Queen. (Timothy, Lifeline, 2008)

This was followed by the presentation of a Silver Plaque received on resignation from a government committee, another proud moment, shortly followed by an award of merit from his international professional body. On Remembrance Day he tells us;

This year (2014) I was honoured to be able to lay a wreath. I am currently Chairman of our local amenity group and as such I joined in a small service outside a local church on November 11. We assembled in the churchyard around a mulberry tree that had been planted in 1945. There was a 2 minute silence, signalled by a trumpeter, and a small service. Wreaths, in addition to mine, were laid by a representative of the British Legion, our local MP, a Chelsea pensioner, the church, and a host of schoolchildren all of whom had made their own poppies. (Timothy, Remembrance, 2014)

His civic engagement extends to being a patron of the arts;

I did pay for 2 of the poppies that were planted in the moat of the Tower of London. As I write, these poppies, representing one for each of the servicemen and women killed in WW1, are being removed, packed up and posted to those people - like me - who have paid for them. Of all the memories of the war this year this display, entitled "The Blood Swept Lands of Sea and Red", has attracted enormous popularity so much so that on occasions the nearest tube station to the Tower, Tower Hill, has had to be closed because of the crowds. My wife and I had the enormous pleasure of standing in the Tower moat on the evening that a poppy was planted in honour of Edith Cavell. (Timothy, Remembrance, 2014)

His civic duties are taken very seriously;

My wife has already voted by post but I rather like the discipline of walking down the road to the Polling Station which, as usual...is a caravan parked temporarily at the end of the street. There were 3 officials inside and a portable loo outside. There was no problem with my vote but my daughter is registered as an Overseas Elector and has named me as her proxy. At first the officials could not find her details but these were eventually identified and I cast my second vote. (Timothy, Election, 2015)

Peggy is amazing, keeps on going, keeps on caring, keeps on helping, and is royally rewarded in 2012 with a palace garden party and a Jubilee concert for 35 years of volunteering with the Citizens Advice Bureau (CAB). She is still enjoying the memory of the fireworks three years later in 2015. Her voluntary work with the CAB is modestly underplayed and her husband's twice a week hospital visiting mentioned in passing. However, her civic concern for the thousands of people she has met as a teacher and CAB volunteer is expressed after the 2015 general election;

I don't know what will become of the U.K – as a CAB worker I have seen the damage they have done in their first five years & don't think another five will do us any good at all. I am afraid there may be public unrest because of the tremendous difference between the 'haves' & the 'have nots' & goodness knows how they will raise another 12 billion from benefits when they have been cut to the bone already. They have consistently refused to say what these cuts will be but I am quite sure the well-off will not be too affected. (Peggy, Election, 2015)

Vivien was very sick as a baby and young child, and had ground breaking surgery in the 1950s, her mother fought for her then and again when she failed the 11+ through illness. She attended a grammar school and went on to teach RE, marry and have a daughter. Civically minded Vivien writes to MP's and fears for the vulnerable, and 'us all' on the election of a Conservative majority government in 2015. In her 60s Vivien regularly drives for over an hour to visit her mum and dad and help them with the house and garden. She drives several hours round trip to collect her toddler grandson for weekend visits. She tells us;

In London, on Remembrance Day itself a thirteen year old cadet (rather inappropriate, I think) will place the last ceramic poppy at the Tower of London. 888,246 ceramic poppies, one for every British and Commonwealth soldier who died in the First World War, form a work called 'Blood-swept lands and Seas of Red' and it has had a deep emotional effect on many who have seen it as it brings into sharp focus the sheer numbers of those who gave their lives. Five million people have been to see it, but after Remembrance Day it will be dismantled and the poppies sent out to those who paid £25 to own one. (They had all been sold before I even knew you could buy them and I wasn't pleased to find that there was no limit to 'one per household' or some such. Someone else will have my poppy!) (Vivien, Remembrance, 2014)

I could not resist the punchline to the Timothy story, his sense of being a patron of the arts being rumbled by Vivien, her exposure of the way that access to the poppies was affordable, but only for those with connections. These kinds of inequalities are not apparent within the stories people tell about their lives, because people do not really mix beyond their own friends and family. Timothy and Vivien have very different stories, different material wealth, but they both have chores and duties to navigate. Timothy may have Vivien's poppy, but she has a lot more fun, and both of them are valued members of society, dutiful, selfless boomers, as many of the participants are.

5.2   No Great Virtue in All This Active Ageing

This theme enfolds examples of pragmatic engagement with active ageing concepts. Active ageing as an idea is not so bad. The stories cover a range of activities, including exercise, healthy eating, moderate alcohol intake, and life-long learning. They provide context to begin to explore the idea that people engage with active ageing advice on their own terms, bold heroes of their own stories. This is how they tackle a cultural concept and take what they want from it.

> *I have the TV on and am forever checking the updates on the voting. I go to the gym and as all the equipment has TV on, I am enthralled with the programmes on the election. The numbers seem to be rising for the Conservatives and not for Labour. The Labour Party have been wiped out in Scotland and I still worry that the SNP will have too much hold over the UK government but relief is sweet when the final votes are in and despite the opinion polls the Conservatives got in with an overall majority of 12, slim I know.*
> (Patricia, Election, 2015)

Patricia mentions exercising at the gym, but it is the TV coverage of the election that makes the trip exciting. The gym is a chore, pragmatically engaged in, but much enlivened by televised election coverage, which she is on the winning side of. Engagement in physical exercise for these correspondents in later life rarely aspires to enthrallment, this is nested activity, with the leisure in the entertainment that televised politics, particularly when winning, offers. The gym and any exercise that may have happened are barely mentioned. Cathy discusses the following 'regular' exercise;

> *The teasmade woke us up at 6.30am as usual. Drank our tea in bed with our books. Then up and dressed and out by 7am for what we call our 'brisky'.*

This is a fast walk we do every morning along the bridle path and back - 2 ½ miles total. Mild morning. Lots of beautiful coloured leaves, carpeting the woods we pass through. (Cathy, Bonfire, 2015)

But it only appears once, this is one of many 'as usual' events reported by correspondents as done regularly, but in her other diaries habits and physical routines focus on an allotment, and the benefits of home grown vegetables she produces. Healthy eating is explained pragmatically by Wendy;

That done, I put a buffet tea on the dining room table (at weekends we have our main meal at 1pm). Home- made pumpkin-seeded bread, low fat spread, lower fat Ardennes pâté and tomatoes for sandwiches, home-made hot cross buns from the Easter surplus in the freezer and Jaffa cakes. No great virtue in all this, merely common sense as my husband comes from a family with heart problems and has had one heart attack. (Wendy, Eurovision, 2014)

Her husband's heart attack has prompted a shift to lower fat produce, but their tea still involves cake and plenty of saturated fats. Barbara tells us about bad luck and fate that meant her parents had three daughters, a son and lost an infant son, then the same pattern and loss for her. Much later she lost her husband in an accident using faulty disability equipment that was supposed to keep him safe.

The [inquest] result was "Accidental Death". I rang my youngest daughter (age 46) to try to cheer her a bit. The children had been profoundly moved at losing their dad in such a cruel fashion. She told me that my grandson had voted Labour today for the first time...My son rang to see how I was and I said his dad would have been proud of his children. He said "Mum, I'm shattered and he sobbed and said I'm going to bed now"....

Washed up and made some tea and ate a doughnut (naughty diabetic!). (Barbara, Election, 2015)

Cooked bacon and egg, fried bread and tomato. Washed up made some tea. Phoned my doctor's surgery re blood tests I'd had recently. I was informed that the doctor would call me tomorrow with the results. Watched a bit of the theatrical Judge Rinder then switched off. Read through Review…Its very dull today but not too chilly. Had the heating on earlier. Looked in Balance (diabetic magazine) and did the crossword. I watched "Strictly Take Two" after seeing "Four in a Bed", "The One Show" "Autumn Watch Unsprung 2015". Later saw "Unforgotten" which was harrowing. Saw an episode of Detectorists" sophisticated humour and entertaining. Anyone would think I'm a TV critic as I have seen so much tonight.

Had a cup of Bovril and a slice of bread and syrup. (Barbara, Bonfire 2015)

When life stories are imbued with fate, and bad luck takes loved ones, health advice can be rejected outright. Barbara, like many of the correspondents lists the contents of her meals, and a lot of TV watching, but rather than apologise she identifies as a naughty diabetic. Wendy and Barbara are both expressing agency, one through pragmatic explanation of the 'low fat' focus of her buffet tea, the other with a doughnut.

Richard expresses a more nuanced approach to managing health advice,

From the kitchen cabinet, have brought to my chair a bottle of Harvey's sherry. Not that I am a wine buff but due to my medication of Warfarin my normal evening pleasure, a can of beer and large, very large, whisky - is mostly denied me and can no longer be regarded as my regular evening treat. (Richard, Bonfire, 2015)

He is pragmatic in his switch, having been quite frightened by his brief hospital admission and slow recuperation following an embolism six months earlier. He knows that he has explained to the reader why this is a big compromise; whisky drinking was a shared evening ritual with his wife, from their honeymoon until the time she passed away 57 years later. But this kind of leisure meaning is not considered by the physician; daily 'large' whisky drinking is pathological in medical terms. Nor does warfarin care which kind of alcohol he is drinking. He is aware that the doctor meant for him to stop drinking alcohol, not switch to a bottle of sherry, but when health advice is broadly given (John, 2018), people are desensitised and the advice is easy to ignore. '*Mostly* denied me' tells us that there is agency in the engagement with the advice, there is still whisky some nights, and there is a bottle of sherry for the nights when he is being 'good'.

In the story that follows one of the key aspects of active ageing, 'learning', is the focal point.

I became extremely interested in how financial markets worked. I bought numerous books on a wide variety of financial topics - market analysis, trading systems, charting - and so on. The mathematics of it all fascinated me - though having a bet on, say, a televised football match, certainly increased my enjoyment - and occasional high anxiety.

My sports spread betting was fun. My financial spread betting was serious...

After just 11 months of betting on the financial markets - I had made a profit of £36273. That wasn't just beginners luck - that was the result of careful study of the markets - and a specific strategy... One disastrous week when I had multiple bets open on both the FTSE and Dow Jones Indexes going down - they both continued to rise - and by a considerable amount. On one day I had to write out cheques totalling more than £18000. I was quite calm about it. I was only returning some of the cash I'd won...I was not, nor ever have been, addicted to gambling. Spread betting became an interest to me. Something new that I wanted to understand. The attraction of spread betting was discovering something new about which I knew absolutely nothing. I enjoyed researching what it was all about - and then trying it. My early successes inspired me to continue.

Eventually I probably paid back exactly what I had previously won. So - I had a whole new (and exciting) experience - at no expense. (Charles, Gambling, 2011)

Learning is important to Charles, he was a youth worker until retiring at statutory retirement age, and continued to volunteer with children in retirement;

I became a volunteer with a local 'Riding for the Disabled' group having had no previous experience of working with horses. From nervousness - bordering on real anxiety - I gradually learned to understand these wonderful animals

- and to build trust with them. That made me feel beyond 'happy' - it was satisfying, rewarding and amazing. (Charles, Happy, 2013)

These familiar and not so familiar forms of demonstrating being an active ager add to the earlier themes. People are demonstrating interest in the world, their values line up with those of their peers surveyed ten years earlier (Gabriel & Bowling, 2004). They express wanting sufficient income, staying well or as well as possible, being connected with meaningful participation, and feeling '*in control, happy, secure, at home, valued by others and that life has a purpose*' (Horwitz, 2014, p. 5). But there are times when this active connected identity in a leisurely lifestyle is not so clear for them, and this is discussed in the next three themes.

5.3   His Lordship Goes off to Work

5.3.1   A Balance Is Struck

This theme addresses the way that people interact with ideas around active ageing, and work. William's days are very like a working day, he also reports on the activities of his wife of 12 years. She is out with friends most of the time. There are indications that childhood bronchitis is haunting him, he reports feeling breathless and sweaty after a 20 min walk, in contrast to his wife, who is hyperactive with park runs.

My wife has taken it upon herself to care for hitherto neglected grave stones in a private graveyard nearby. This morning, she placed a simple wooden cross {bought from the same group of people who were selling poppies in Sainsbury's) on one grave... (William, Remembrance 2014)

I spend up to an hour on my latest article, and then have a solo lunch whilst L is at her weekly social-cum-Bible study session with her friends...After lunch L drives to the nearest supermarket. When she returns I help her to pack away the plethora of grocery items she has bought. I fill the recycle bag with cardboard and paper wrapping.

I decide to walk to the post office in the village centre to post material to the editor. The walk there is pleasant in the spring sunshine, but a lot of effort is expended walking back home, uphill whichever way I take. I am outdoors about twenty minutes. I arrive home. L is in a jocular mood. L's sister has arrived: she stays only five minutes. I then have a much- needed shower and resume work on the current article.

L and I have an early cooked meal on account of her evening walk-run walk regime at a park in town. While she is out, I click on You Tube and listen to Ella Fltzgerald singing Rodgers and Hart songs.

The TV is turned on at 8pm. I sit and watch BBC 2's 'Inside the Factory'- a programme about milk, cheese, and butter. L returns in the middle of the programme. After 9pm, we watch an episode of 'Emmerdale'.

We are abed by 10pm. L is particularly tired after her physical activities in the park. (William, Election, 2015)

The exhaustion of a day lived fully is expressed, and the next one is just as interesting,

Read half a chapter of 'The People' by Selina Todd, then make a coffee for myself and my wife. As soon as she prepares to go out, I begin typing captions for an article almost ready to dispatch to the journal. I continue with this until lunch time, circa midday, when my son phones on his mobile phone. We chat for five minutes. Then have a light lunch with a drink of tea.

Empty the dishwasher - always an enjoyable activity. My wife returns from her local visit to see friends. Make her a cup of tea. Decide to go for a walk - this turns out to be a miserable jaunt through wet leaves and a shower before I return home after a period of fifteen minutes.

I continue typing captions for an hour before taking a nap mid afternoon. The typing is still incomplete when my wife returns from her friend. A cooked meal is made ready by 4.30pm owing to my wife going out to run with friends in the local park. After the meal, we watch Channel 4 programmes until 5.30pm. I complete the captions by 5.45pm.

I watch Channel 4 news at 7pm, in my opinion the best news programme on TV. My wife comes home drenched to the skin. After a shower, she joins me watching recordings of Coronation Street and other programmes until 10pm. Glad to retire to bed at this time. (William, Bonfire, 2015)

Work fills William's day, he enjoys writing and emptying the dish-washer, and channel 4 news, but finds a walk miserable. Like Peter in the introducing participants section, he has an active wife, but his work means that she is not the main focus of his story, or indicated in his mini biography. Between them they have the active ageing ideals covered, and are still economically productive. After each busy day they relax with the TV, then fall into bed.

5.3.2   Discord as Work Trumps Leisure

Within self and with others the leisure ethic associated with active ageing can be a source of discord. It appears that people can manage internal conflict relatively well, but the interpersonal is more difficult. There are examples of some relational harm caused by not sharing a similar view of active ageing with others. Home-based leisure lives still require social labour, because home is not a solitary place for most people in later life. Some disruption can occur if people that share space and time do not share the same leisure ethic, thus alienating people from those they could love.

'A former Colleague wrote to tell me that she'd dislocated her shoulder, after a hip op, just in bed. She was feeling very sorry for herself and made me feel very smug. Then my allotment neighbour mentioned she re-tiled the bathroom. It's just your luck – or is it? They have an immaculate productive plot. My husband works a few hours a week, plays golf one morning, and darts one evening. The rest of his life is spent moaning there's "nothing to watch". I have to go out at the third antique/ cookery/ moving house prog. I can't stand it. I beg him to come for a walk, dog or water (allotment). He doesn't "see the need"'. (Brenda, Care, 2011)

Brenda and her husband have differing views on how much control there is over their luck, and what is 'good use of time', and this is a feature of several of the relationships discussed by the correspondents in this study, and it causes conflict. Brenda loved the allotment that she mentions in 2011, in 2013 she tells us.

I took an allotment on my 70th birthday. A fact our girls dine out on. There followed 5 years of bliss, joy, happiness, heaven. I declared I wanted to be buried in it. (Brenda, Happy, 2013)

It enabled active outdoors productive leisure. She held it from age 70–75 and is still angry at the way developers moved in and destroyed her daily routine of working in the allotment in the morning. She considers her husband's non- TV-related activities;

2pm. His lordship has driven off to work. He puts in a couple of hours selling and engraving sporting trophies. It used to be a profitable side line, but kept it on, more as a hobby once he'd retired. It's a sociable occupation and he does well, as he knows all the "sportsmen" from boyhood, V. healthy. (Brenda, Bonfire, 2015)

Brenda is adjusting her views about what is healthy. She is no longer a celebrated allotment holder, through no fault of her own, and her husband's work is now a healthy sign. This active ager occupied in mean-ingful leisure pursuits is no longer making the cut. Now some kind of work is required. Brenda does not like this idea, of her 'TV obsessed' husband being the healthy one, but she is reproducing it. The third and fourth age are not apparent in these stories, but the shift away from telling stories about economically unproductive activity is emerging. When Brenda's husband finally 'drags himself away' from the TV, to go and work, Brenda tells us how delighted she is to turn off the TV, then this is what she does;

In the afternoon, I lock the doors, unplug the phone, and run a bath with everything in it. I do my hair, nails, and rub cream. I dry my hair in the sun (if there is any) and curl up with a book. Some writing. Bliss. Woe betides anyone who comes knocking to sell something. (Happy, 2013)

My husband will go to work at 2pm, and I shall run a bath and wallow, before putting a coq au vin in the oven. That is what is planned. (Brenda, Remembrance, 2014)

The discord in Brenda's home is gently competitive. Initially it seemed she was concerned to get him going for health reasons, then she was developing an idea of his work as health promoting, but there is also the time and space that it affords her to wallow in the bath, with him out of the way.

There are more difficult sides to these time and space politics for other correspondents. Sophie is an Oxbridge graduate, who had the misfortune of having a brain injury in her mid-fifties, which she had been recovering from for about 10 years at the time of the day diaries. Her husband still works full time, and two of her children live at home and also work. She is the only person in the 26 who mentions problems with cognitive skills.

Big row with my older son. He called me in from my bonfire at 5.10pm last night – big row – he refuses to eat with us and messes up when I'm trying to COOK Yorkshires etc, he doesn't put out washing when I ask… Says I upset everyone and cause rows & play the piano when it annoys him. (he's 33, & works at home here & I feel I need a break…)

Very upset.

Saw a Red Admiral in the garden. Sunny. Most of washing got pretty dry.

Went for a Walk Round My "circuit" - up to Xxxxxx Down, to Yyyyyy & Along & Back up Xxxxxx. Typical Sunday Really. (Except I don't Row with People). (Sophie, Remembrance, 2014)

Not all days are this difficult, days where most of her time is spent on the buses are less conflicted. Then we learn more about the busy early starts and her productive focus,

Dumped 4 bags of leaves down my leaf pile next to a local footpath – we live next to a school with large grounds & the only way I can cope with the leaves

from our Oak tree, is to dump as many as I can in a pile in school grounds where they rot down). Dumping leaves? Fly tipping – but they always rot where I put them, whereas they don't in the garden. Put out our rubbish – rubbish, Rubbish, green bin day. This all took until 6.55. breakfast. (porridge; bread and marmalade) went to the local Sainsbury's garage, 5 mins walk to get the Daily Telegraph – If I don't get it early for [husband] to read nothing gets done.

7.25am back. Washed up. Played the piano a bit, have to use earphones, the others complain, found stuff to defrost for Friday tea. (Sophie, Bonfire, 2015)

Sophie is super busy, always on the move, but much of her 'doing' at home causes rows with others, whether playing piano early in the morning, setting bonfires or dumping leaves in the neighbouring school grounds. She has little positive interaction at home, difficult relationships with her sons and her husband. The start of this Bonfire day diary focuses on clearing the way for a day trip, she is ensuring her husband has a quick start to the day by fetching his newspaper. Then the day trip almost happens, her husband, who hates buses, insists on her map reading while he drives. This is something that she finds difficult and very stressful. It rains and he is furious about the bad weather and refuses to go on, stopping the day trip to buy some bacon for his lunch in a discount grocery store instead. He also buys something novel for tea, which worries Sophie. That afternoon she finds refuge and friendly interactions on the buses.

Caught the 12.55 bus to the war memorial (Bus driver I have a crush on? I like him). All the time I was up town I was trying not to cry. Am very upset at not being able to get out by bus [for a day trip]…not a typical day.

2.00-2.30 I did rowing (I hate it – 1km took me 5.4 secs – I have short legs, 6m one stroke, 16 strokes to 100m).

Tea, a near disaster, I hate cooking new things.

All told a very upsetting day…going out with [husband] is so fraught and horrid – I tend to prepare and have sandwiches and drinks, and buses - don't have to map read or find car parks etc…[husband] hates buses). (Sophie, Bonfire, 2015)

'not a typical day' is something that Sophie writes when telling stories about conflict and upset, but the conflict in Sophie's life is apparent in all directives that she writes in. Her confusion is not age related, she is not a confused old lady, she is not even very old, only 64 at the time of the day diary writing. Sophie is someone with a hidden disability who has experienced more than 10 years of compounded relationship deterioration with her husband and sons. She also explains how her sister and mother avoid her. She does not even mention her daughter beyond her birth in the Lifeline directive. She is thankful for the company of strangers on the buses and at bus stops. By measures employed to assess active ageing Sophie is very active. She qualifies for free bus travel but has quite limited access to money. It is Sophie who tells us in the 'meet the participants' section that she has £1/4 million pounds but cannot access it. Bhatti and Church's research on gardening and home-making shows the home is spatialized and gendered in different ways, sometimes leading to discord (2000). This idea of discordant active ageing appears in these two different examples. In Brenda's house different ideas of active ageing cause discord, as she applies her interpretation of active ageing to her husband's sedentary TV watching, and later reveals that his departure gives her some freedom to relax in her own way. In the second example given here it happens that Sophie is doing all the 'right things' and life is not good, so the discord is in being a culturally consonant active ager, which is not valued by her family who are still working.

5.4   Other Old People: 'Active Wife' to 'Intrepid Courageous Lady'

From Summer 2007 until spring 2014 Peter describes himself as 'married'. He enjoyed the Eurovision song contest after some heavy gardening in spring 2014, always in touch, and open to new experiences, there is plenty to say on most directive topics that enable him to express an active ageing identity. Then in Autumn 2014 he adds 'active wife' to his tiny twelve word biography at the top of each directive. Aware that his Remembrance Sunday is a bit quiet, he tells a culturally relevant story incorporating the activity of his wife, and the misfortunes of her friend;

> *Both of us awake by 7.30. Wife dresses. I prepare breakfast (Cereal, Toast, Tea). On this occasion, wife, after breakfast, meets friend X and both go to church. I wash up, water window plants, cut pieces from Saturday papers, make the bed, then dress. TV on for BBC service…Wife takes X home at 12.20. the latter had a stroke five years ago after husband died, three years later a partner died, last year a male friend died. Her two sons have been divorced recently, and she herself has broken with a very old friend …after lunch wife makes military pickle…I do my accounts and two letters… wife says all had poppies in church and she talked to many in the congregation, mostly elderly!! X also talked to many people. One son was at the family home so she was not alone on this day. Near her are very many widows……..now one son has Cancer, so far successful treatment. War is hell and beastly, but to X peace is unforgiving…she works as a volunteer for war charities.* (Peter, Remembrance, 2014)

The story of X, charitable victim of multiple misfortunes, surrounded by other widows, caught in an unforgiving peace-time hell is one of several stories about 'other old people' told by the correspondents, in contrast to their own happier later lives. In this way Peter borrows from his wife's activities, contrasted to her friend's misfortunes to manage the telling of a day that has not got the same potential as some other days to show him at his best. He is delighted to tell us that he enjoys Eurovision, 'get over it', but the remembrance directive does not give him the same opportunity. Another selfless boomer, Brenda, describes how she and others rally around in support of a neighbour:

> *I shall take neighbours dinner between drops [of rain]. I know her tastes by now. Stew and dumplings (2day), shepherd's pie or pasta, and a roastie with all the trimmings. It started when she was discharged from hospital, with only a red button for company. Someone walked her rat of a dog with their own, someone watered the garden and I took round a risotto. After that she had*

wrists strapped up, then cataracts done…She is an intrepid courageous lady and we are all v. fond. (Brenda, Bonfire, 2015)

It is interesting to note how unlucky and courageous the 'other old people' are in the Mass Observation correspondence, in contrast to the 'lazy other old people' in the sports focused leisure constraints research (Gard et al., 2017; Minello & Nixon, 2017). The correspondents do not write themselves in either of these ways, but they are sitting on their couches, in between chores and adventures, watching a lot of television along with the rest of the population.

5.5   A Social Thesis of Leisure in Later Life

The stories are varied throughout the themes, but engagement is what links them, concern for others and the connections are discussed in part one, the importance of the sociable, the adventures and the ordinary, vicarious participation, the role of reminiscence and being honoured. There are pragmatic ideas of active ageing, focusing on an element that they can win with in order to tell a story of a life well lived. Many of them assert themselves, putting active ageing in its place. They share cultural capital in relation to work and leisure, but for some people different approaches to active ageing cause conflict at home. There are no individuals in this study, no independent active agers, because the very idea of an individual is undermined by their stories. Their lives are complex and connected. When we think about the 'active ager' we are thinking about the individual in the liberal sense as a self-determining actor, where the self is defined by the ends which are affirmed by it, where individuals can calculate on whether certain activities or practices are worth pursuing. But I did not find these self-interested individuals, I found deeply connected, concerned unique people.

We are not thinking enough about how these ideas have an impact on how honoured people feel, about how they may have to write themselves as less successful agers than others, or how it may cause discord in homes. Here the examples given were between couples, but there were also reports of patronising children imposing active ageing advice. Active ageing also has forms of encumbrance that are negotiated. People are embedded in or situated in social practices, roles and relationships which can shape their personal deliberations and actions and choices. These social conditions may be required for the effective fulfilment of interests. In this way the culture of active ageing impacts on intrapersonal choice and experiences and influences interpersonal relationships. The next section is the discussion, which will consider these ideas in relation to existing literature.

References

Bhatti, M., & Church, A. (2000). 'I never promised you a rose garden': Gender, leisure and home-making. *Leisure Studies, 19*(3), 183–197.

Carr, N. (2017). Re-thinking the relation between leisure and freedom. *Annals of Leisure Research, 20*(2), 137–151.

Gabriel, Z., & Bowling, A. (2004). Quality of life from the perspectives of older people. *Ageing and Society, 24*(5), 675–691.

Gard, M., Dionigi, R. A., Horton, S., Baker, J., Weir, P., & Dionigi, C. (2017). The normalization of sport for older people? *Annals of Leisure Research, 20*(3), 253–272.

Horwitz, W. (2014). *Looking forward to later life—Taking an early action approach to our ageing society*. London: Community Links. Downloaded from https://transitionsinlaterlife.files.wordpress.com/2014/10/later_life_web.pdf.

John, S. (2018). Should we punish responsible drinkers? Prevention, paternalism and categorization in public health. *Public Health Ethics, 11*(1), 35–44.

Jones, H., Neal, S., Mohan, G., Connell, K., Cochrane, A., & Bennett, K. (2015). Urban multiculture and everyday encounters in semi-public, franchised cafe spaces. *Sociological Review, 63*(3), 644–661.

Kneale, D., Bamford, S.-M., & Sinclair, D. (2013). *Downsizing in later life and appropriate housing size across our lifetime*. Retrieved from https://ilcuk.org.uk/downsizing-in-later-life-and-appropriate-housing-size-across-our-lifetime/.

Kohijoki, A. M., & Marjanen, H. (2013). The effect of age on shopping orientation-choice orientation types of the ageing shoppers. *Journal of Retailing and Consumer Services, 20*(2), 165–172.

Minello, K., & Nixon, D. (2017). 'Hope I never stop': Older men and their two-wheeled love affairs. *Annals of Leisure Research, 20*(1), 75–95.

Neal, S., & Vincent, C. (2013). Multiculture, middle class competencies and friendship practices in super-diverse geographies. *Social & Cultural Geography, 14*(8), 909–929.

Willetts, D. (2010). *The pinch: How the baby boomers took their children's future—And why they should give it back.* Atlantic Books.

6

Freedom and Belonging in Everyday Leisure Lives

This book proposes a new conceptualisation of the relationship between leisure and ageing, one that questions the atomism inherent in the liberal individual, which is a feature of how the literature approaches active agers; from super-grans and heroic individuals, to individuals who make 'good' choices. I set out to find constraints to an active later life, and I found that the idea of 'active ageing' is constraining in complex ways. My study of leisure in later life focuses on exploring leisure lives in deep context, not just the present social environment, but with a long arm view, because context is important (Crouch, 2000, 2012, 2014). I have found the missing voice of the TV watching 'passive' ager, not the sick or frail or vulnerable or transitioning ager, just the ordinary every-day one. The quiet majority.

The findings reveal evidence of how older people are negotiating their leisure lives and how they interact with metanarratives about ageing. They are not just the people that are usually missing, but some people that are usually there in the research, but not telling the whole story, just the things researchers already expect. They are not who they 'should be' according to demographic data and critiques of the mass observation

T. Wiseman, *Leisure in Later Life*, Leisure Studies in a Global Era, https://doi.org/10.1007/978-3-030-71672-1_6

project, they are more diverse. The life story, as understood by the correspondents, and communicated in the Lifeline directive responses creates the context for the stories of day to day life in the day diaries. The days are filled with activities that can be described and explained.

Despite differences in material wealth they write about similar days with connected engaged lifestyles. The stories are illustrations of how people are writing about leisure in later life, elicited by diaries made in 2014–2015, about Bonfire Night, the Eurovision song contest, remembrance Sunday and the general election. These are events and may be considered to have some form of ritual, expected behaviours associated. However, in the world of Mass Observation the impact of this was mixed, because people write about whatever pleases them. Of course, for some there were a highly ritualised multigenerational traditions, but even these accounted only for a portion of the day. For others the event was ignored altogether. Usually the whole day was included, exposing and illustrating stories about the every day and the complexity of leisure within it. There is a telling of the "*dispersed, nuanced happenings in the gentle space and politics of everyday life*" (Crouch, 2016, p. 3), and sometimes the space and politics are not so gentle.

A satisfying leisure lifestyle in later life could be simply explained by increased free time, but given the difficulties that people experience in unemployment, discussed in seminal work by Kay (1987) and Glyptis (1989), it appears unlikely that this is the case. There must be something else in addition to time that begins to explain later life leisure satisfaction. The correspondents talk about things that on one level are culturally consonant, which fit with a view of how they see themselves (Dressler, 2012), but another level of analysis highlights their deeply social experience of 'active ageing', the sometimes subverted nature of their interpretation of the ideas of 'active ageing', and their active resistance to 'health' messages.

Understandings and expressions of metanarratives about ageing were expressed throughout the writings of the correspondents. The dominant ideas that these later lifers engaged with were civic engagement, physical activity and healthy diet, economic engagement, intellectual activity and the caring economy. But there was another level of engagement with these ideas, the way they were used in the negotiation of 'the everyday'. My curators overview considers the interaction of life history with everyday leisure, when people negotiate time use in terms of cultural capital, they personalise it. It is personal but it is rarely individual, it is shared and negotiated with others, past and present, known and unknown.

This study aimed to identify leisure in the every day from the perspective of people in later life. Context is given with a written 'life-line', and opinions on a range of activities from each person. Thematic analysis of narrative of diary entries of 26 socially diverse participants aged 59–93, taken at four points over a two-year period illustrate change and continuity, and the leisurely elements that piece a day together, one thing after another becomes one thing because of another. A nap because of some chores, a sit down with the TV in advance of a social occasion, a glass of whiskey to mark the end of a day. Four themes were constructed; *windows on the world, no great virtue in all this active ageing, work and leisure* and *other old people*. The richness of 'passive' leisure is communicated, and the attractiveness of this leisure lifestyle illuminated for critique. The similarity of life behind closed doors presents a challenge to those who would categorise people as passive or active agers. The similarity of outdoors life is equally challenging. The relative unimportance of material wealth is also apparent, and the importance of love of people and pets, and places or activities is palpable.

They are not individuals, but they are unique and they are hyper-connected, rather than hyper-active. Narrative inquiry helps us see that, and they were not asked to tell us that by the research questions. Very importantly this interconnectedness is not another description for dependency, if anything it is them that are depended upon to support others. In an increasingly individualised culture, with personal responsibility a duty, they did not take that on, did not internalise it, and did not reproduce it in the stories they told in their correspondence about leisure in later life. There are no individuals in this study, no independent active agers, because the very idea of an individual is undermined by their stories.

6.1 The Correspondents

I have constructed a varied group, with differing social and economic situations and different life courses which have led them to living day to day similar lives. Working at the level of the unique person, the background chapter about the long arm is confounded. Richard, at 93 is the oldest person in the sample. He left school at 14 and became a painter decorator, he is still driving to the pub several times a week to socialise, the demographics and health messages tell us he probably should have died 20 years ago (Warren, 2016). Sophie is one of the youngest, has an Oxbridge degree and lives with her family in a big house. She has a very busy leisure life, but due to bad luck in her health she is stressed and lonely. Her demographic markers suggest that she should probably be in the 'healthy, happy' grouping (Pavela & Latham, 2016). There are many studies about the long arm of childhood, and how disadvantage is compounded throughout life (Department of Health, 2010), including early life ill health (Caleyachetty et al., 2018; Pavela & Latham, 2016), early poverty (Hayward & Gorman, 2004; Tampubolon, 2015), limited educational opportunities (Mejía et al., 2017), but when it comes to unique people this information is of limited value, certainly for the unlucky ones, it may be better that they take their chances without this knowledge. Lyotard discusses the postmodern condition, where the enlightenment metanarratives of ultimate knowledge and ultimate control have been discarded (Lyotard, 1984). These large population level studies do not give sufficient attention to the complexity of the immediate social environment, for example, in the context of the last 6 years in the UK the major reason for life expectancy reduction is the death of women over 90 living in austere times, and young men committing suicide (Office for National Statistics, 2018). Each life a person lives has periods of variance. With developments in technology, it must be possible to better situate these studies in the context of the times that they cover. It was also interesting to note that some people flourish in retirement, I illustrate the example of Freda, the daughter of Jewish refugees who retired from being a care worker, and now dines with the Mayor. Over the last century at least, there were social mobility opportunities for people, and the potential for a new opportunity appears to have presented itself again for some people as they retired, shed their work role and took on new opportunities. Both of these points emerged as secondary to the focus of my book and are suggested as areas of further study.

6.2   Windows on the World

This initial theme highlighted important ideas about the multiplicity of connection and the refuge of home. The overarching theme starts by explaining the importance of literal and metaphorical *windows on the world*, creating an image of being secure and outward looking. People in this book, and in other studies mostly spend their free time on screen time of various kinds. There are concerns raised about the impact of this on well-being and happiness, yet people in the town of Bolton, for example, are as happy as their predecessors were before screen time (McHugh, 2017), the well-being literature does not make a case for these forms of leisure (Roberts, 2018). The leisure in later life for well-being literature omits the most prevalent leisure pursuits for most people in later life, and passive leisure is studied as a constraint to other more active leisure, rather than as leisure in its own right (Nimrod, 2017). Connection and education is available through TV viewing. Beyond that there are also stories of time to stand and stare. The Chinese symbol for leisure is 休 Xiu, a person leaning against a tree combined with 闲, Xian, someone at home at peace (Gui et al., 2019). This relates well to this theme, where people take the time to relax, and look out on the world from the refuge of home. A study of leisure meanings in Canada with mainland Chinese students found they mentioned "*outdoor and traveling as leisure, food and drinks as leisure, mass media as leisure and non-leisure, rest and reflection as leisure and non-leisure…*" (Gui et al., 2019, p. 16). The leisure lives of the people in this book closely aligned to the Chinese students in terms of the leisure meanings of outdoors and travelling and food and drink. They share ambivalent views of mass media, which is both entertaining and educational in their stories. This is also the case for older Dutch television viewers, who consider the educational aspects important (Van Der Goot et al., 2012), and Korean viewers who appreciate the immediate social and relaxing aspects of watching sports on TV (Ryu & Heo, 2016).

There is some critique of the developing field of leisure constraints research as driven by a will to increase use of facilities and resources, or out of concern for disadvantaged people, rather than to increase freedom (Kleiber et al., 2008). Rojek and Blackshaw produced theoretical work that considered the place of freedom in studies of leisure (Blackshaw, 2010; Rojek, 2010) which is discussed by Carr (2017). But the freedom to stand and stare in later life may be impinged upon by commercial interests in the commercialisation of mass media, although there is more choice, with new forms it comes with unanticipated costs associated with both subscription and connection services. These additional costs for people on an income that may have been fixed many years earlier, may mean that for some the windows have shutters on them. Many of the participants still read a newspaper and listen to the radio, both of these have maintained a low cost. The familiar routines and habits of media consumption discussed at the beginning of the *windows on the world* theme may mean that people are potentially living in a bubble. This may also apply to interests and political differences, as the majority get their political news from a newspaper. Rather than focus on special examples of rebellion against ageing discourses, involving sport (Gard et al., 2017; Minello & Nixon, 2017), which is a minority pursuit in later life, this book considers that all people in later life negotiate everyday leisure lives, and doing so implies a level of rebellion, because the active ageing metanarrative is powerful, yet people mostly watch television.

The overall focus on traditional media consumption in all of the diaries is similar to the prevalence of synchronous one-to-many media that is reported in a European study (Nimrod, 2017), and this kind of shared timing of watching provides opportunity for the kinds of social interactions illustrated in some of the stories, where families had small parties, or texted each other comments on the show, or commented on Facebook. The idea of connecting to progressive ideas through television viewing is proposed. This has perhaps been highlighted due to the fortuitous focus on the event of the Eurovision Song Contest, which is a culturally broad and inclusive event. I propose that they negotiate their media consumption in relation to its educational and connecting potential. Further to that I attach progressive meanings to 'windows on the world' as a form of connection that seems to be socially beneficial, with opportunities to connect to socially progressive ideas. The television broadcast, and the votes of millions of people across Europe argued with them, changed their minds, showed them some respect, did not leave them behind culturally, in ghettoes, at risk of losing everyone that 'gets them'. TV as a window on the world only works when people watch varied things, and people watch the things that are familiar. Eurovision, always at the forefront of cultural shifts elicited incredulity at the sight of a beautiful, charismatic and talented 'lady with a beard', attitudes that triggered research and re-shaped understanding for some correspondents.

6.3   A Pleasant Couple of Hours in Good Company

Familiar easy company, adventure from the comfort of 'as usual', sociable active ageing is reported widely in the diaries. There are different expressions of sociability, from seeking out spaces away from the home to experience the company of other people such as visiting the pub or a social club, to forms of sharing and connection with family members, to travelling as a couple and experiencing moments together. The importance of freedom on holiday is expressed, free from time constraints, and free to choose what to do, where to eat, what to pay for a drink. Ideas of leisure as freedom are explored in leisure studies (Carr, 2017). Being out and about with a partner in crime is a feature of many of the days in the diaries, but also adventures without a spouse are reported. The concept of conviviality may enrich the study of leisure in later life (Jones et al., 2015; Neal et al., 2018; Neal & Vincent, 2013; Neal & Walters, 2008). Neal's work on conviviality and multiculturalism applies well to cultural aspects of ageing. It looks at coming together and sharing, emphasising the social dimensions of everyday life. It also talks to ideas around communicative rationality in leisure choices (Spracklen, 2011). In contrast to the opportunities offered by observing social difference through media consumption, these embodied adventures are not about reaching across social difference. Rather this grows from the comfort of existing familial relationships and friendships. Engagement across social difference is a key part of how sociologists have conceptualised conviviality as part of social comfort (Jones et al., 2015; Neal & Vincent, 2013), my study highlights a negative finding, a lack of diverse interactions in an otherwise very sociable life, this is suggested as an area for further study. There is some potential in applying the psychological models of socioemotional selectivity theory (Burnett-Wolle & Godbey, 2007), but this idea, like selection, optimization and compensation of leisure activities (Kleiber & Nimrod, 2009) explains what happens when people do not 'age well' the psychological aspect of a person is important but in studying leisure there has to be more than psychological processes explored. Continuity and change are addressed, but in a negative way, driven by reduced ability to participate. That research fails to engage with the studies discussed earlier that suggest that the majority of people in later life do not report reduced ability to participate, like the majority of correspondents in my research who are active and engaged. It is worth pursuing leisure theory, as suggested by McGuire (2000), rather than concepts from other fields. Leisure constraints in-particular engages with the complexity of the whole person, their significant others and the structures around them.

The experience of interacting with other people can be trying, as in Matthews experience where he is treated as a slow old man in the supermarket by strangers. More often sociability offers opportunities to express competencies and does not offer broader socially integrating experiences. There may be something to say here about loneliness and the importance picked up in the background chapter between quantity of socialising and quality (Toepoel, 2013). It may be that familiar acquaintances meet needs for company that cannot be met by unfamiliar others. Richard is at the pub three to four times a week, his daughters visit, he has good friends, and many acquaintances, but he wakes every morning alone in his bed, and starts each day in grief. This is a problem for some proposals for social prescribing in the UK NHS long-term plan (Alderwick & Dixon, 2019). If Richard cannot mend a broken heart in the good company of longstanding friends, then what is the potential of trying to 'fix' loneliness with unfamiliar people in new surroundings, as in befriending schemes (Lester et al., 2012). It may be that we have misunderstood what loneliness is and should look again. There is some evidence that media consumption can fill the void, but contact with loved ones is preferred (Pettigrew & Roberts, 2008). However, people do find new people that they love to spend time with through taking up new pastimes and it is clear quality of time spent with 'good company' is what matters, and new leisure pastimes can lead to new friends (Choi et al., 2018). Grief and bereavement are not age-specific, it is important that we stop conflating being alone with loneliness, and confusing grief with both. Grief is expressed in three stories through acts of remembrance involving previously shared leisure; a pleasant couple of hours in good company brings some respite.

The importance of staying busy and relevant in retirement for older women is discussed by Liechty et al. (2017), the paper presents a critique of 'activity in later life' and the constraints focus. This study carried out in the USA focuses on retirement transition, with a diary-based method of data generation similar to the Mass Observation Archive, followed up with focus groups. They found women's potential reasons for non-participation in exercise,

> *Participants would often forego physical activities, such as going to the gym, when faced with more alluring alternatives, such as reading the newspaper with a cup of coffee, which they had not had time for while working.* (Liechty et al., 2017, p. 29)

It seems that these diary methods are effective in getting behind the anticipated stories that focus on being an active person in later life with a relevant story to tell. These Canadian participants were young transitioning retirees, but the people in my study in the UK, further into retirement, had made these alluring activities the backbone of their days, around which other more active things may be accommodated, or not.

6.4   Other People's Fun

The diary of bonfire night in particular had special qualities that high-lighted intergenerational issues. This Autumn event can be private, or community based, it can be charitable, or commercial, there may not be an event near to someone's home, but it would be unusual for someone to not hear any fireworks around the week of November 5 in England. Due to the focal point of a fireworks display it is intrusive in terms of the noise it makes, so unlike the other 'special' days it cannot pass unnoticed. There are particular foods associated with it, sausages and baked pota-toes, which traditionally would be cooked on a bonfire. There are sweet treats of treacle toffee, toffee apples, parkin. It would be likely that people would have attended bonfire celebrations with their family of origin, and their own children if they had any. There are gendered and age-related roles associated, with men in charge of the explosives, women preparing the food and children with sparklers. There are smells and feelings asso-ciated with the heat and smoke of the fire and the cold autumn night. But this event is usually for families with young children. Many of the correspondents had children and grandchildren, and recounted tales of many past bonfires, but when it came to the diary day only one threw a party, for a new 10-month-old grandchild. There were no invites for everyone else. Some enjoyed the opportunity to participate vicariously, this illustrates the overarching theme of windows on the world as they literally watched through their windows from the warmth and comfort of their home. The participation is not entirely vicarious, they are after all enjoying a fireworks display, just not in the approved manner, outside in the dark and cold in a field or crowded back garden. Perhaps it resonated so much because in many ways I, as a researcher, am vicariously enjoying the stories, as suggested by Allen-Collinson and Leledaki (2015), getting a sense of a relaxed or adventurous, or irritated later life. In the anal-ysis it became a signifier of social exclusion for anyone who did not have children of the right age, this relates to structural constraints where people are excluded from activities by beliefs about appropriate things for 'old people' to do, described as "*reference group attitudes concerning the appropriateness of certain activities*" (Crawford & Godbey, 1987, p. 124), which some negotiated by enjoying firework displays vicariously, but other people resented these celebrations. So this is not a constraint that could be referred to as age induced limitations, such as physical changes, health conditions, finance, mobility and access, weather, moving home, friends and loved ones becoming ill or dying, and ageism (Meisner et al., 2019), but it is life stage related, and family make-up related, it is likely that this impacts on other groups. There is a new perspective emerging in the leisure literature with people reporting they are not embarrassed to do things that are not usually associated with later life, such as skiing or cycle racing (Minello & Nixon, 2017). This sense of rebellion only works if there is an ageist view of vulnerability to work against, however, it is compliant within an active ageing metanarrative, not at all rebellious. So perhaps the transition being noted is from one metanarrative, of decline to another of hyperactivity. But it has not yet extended to including childless people in Bonfire Night celebrations. Perhaps with this group of correspondents in later life, and their intensive sociability with comfortable relationships, the idea of mixing with a crowd of unfamiliar diverse people is not appealing, as Brenda says, '*thank god not been invited anywhere*'. The lifelong experiences of these writers have led them here, to writing/rewriting their relationship to this intrusive family focused event. Some find ways to vicariously participate, others turn up the TV, grit their teeth and hang onto their pets.

6.5   Reminiscence Was a Joy

Leisure time and space—time alone and with others is very important, and leisure can be nested as reminiscence during another activity, as in the daydreaming Brenda describes while ironing. They are busy with chores and the business of looking after themselves and others. They negotiate leisure in relation to work. In general they work then they relax, but here we can start to see that the work can be transformed by reminiscence. How much to tell about how something is enjoyed is complicated, it is suggested that.

"*Much more attention needs to be paid to how women negotiate the conflicting discourses of aging when describing their understandings and experiences of later life*" (Dionigi et al., 2011). This is complicated here, although both are women, reminiscence was also noted in men in the diaries. The reminiscence elicited ideas of freedom from and freedom to in leisure (Carr, 2017).

As leisure researchers we may focus on activity, and well-being, that is observable or reportable and recognisably leisure. This may miss these temporally diffused and imagined spaces of leisure. We may not know enough about how the reminiscence is connected to the body, not an abstract disembodied daydream, but connected in time and space to self and others. This can happen during much louder, more interesting, more visible events, such as a night out in Bangkok, enhancing the day. Or during ordinary everyday chores, such as remembering the joy of imagining a daughter's holiday while ironing on a wet and windy day. Reminiscence is an important area of enquiry in leisure and later life literature (King et al., 2019; Randall, 2013). Reminiscence is used as a therapy in dementia (Woods et al., 2018), and there have been some longitudinal associations found with self-positive reminiscence and both physical and mental health in a healthy population (King et al., 2019). These studies discuss the sharing of reminiscence, in telling of past events, but not the private kind mentioned in my research, although it has been acknowledged for a long time that nostalgia and reminiscence are important to the leisure lives of older women (Scraton & Watson, 1998). It could be argued that this is the site of leisure enjoyment; memory is the source of stories that we tell ourselves about why we like to do what we do, and this may trouble the passive/active time bounded observable leisure activities, that are often the focus of later life leisure constraints studies.

6.6   I Was Honoured

This sub theme engaged with another narrative about people in later life, that of the selfish boomers. It is hinted at in Winifred's story of the middle-aged man on the bus suggesting her pension would be doubled if she voted Tory. It was then engaged with fully by explaining the various forms of civic engagement, with three stories across the social spectrum of civic engagement (Timothy received an MBE, Peggy was invited to a palace garden party and Freda dines with the Mayor). In this sub theme they explained again that they are not atomised, but deeply connected to the past, present and future, and the people they love and the wider community. They talked of being honoured elders. Across the social and political spectrum being an honoured respected elder is clearly illustrated through civic engagement.

Participants in two other studies reported feeling alienated by representations of their 'age group' as a burden, when they are well aware of the contribution they made (Bazalgette et al., 2011; Hubble & Tew, 2013). That research moves away from the problems of confusing getting old with becoming ill and burdensome, and it is also Mass Observation based research. Hubble and Tew strongly argue for a better understanding of the impact of representations of ageing in attitudes and age identities. They particularly cite active ageing as a laudable but 'largely just rhetorical political posturing' stance (Hubble & Tew, 2013, p. 4). Their book comes from a time where the third/fourth age interface looked like it might need to be smoothed, that the third age could offer hopeful and productive ways to engage with the fourth age, gracefully carry forward the best bits of the third age into a fourth age. This process of smoothing, it was felt, could help to reduce an historical fear of old age and infirmity. The empirical data were focused on ageing and reading and were drawn from 1992, 2006 and 2009, written from a time before austerity and increasing protectionism in the UK and US. So that optimism was well placed by the research participants and the researchers in the UK. The opportunity provided by an immigrant workforce that enabled a leisurely time in later life was enhanced by booming property prices, a triple pension lock and the surprise gift of an additional 20–30 years of later life. This combination of good fortune for some has contributed to scrutiny of the third age as a time of leisure and the idea that this generation of people may have it 'too good' at the expense of younger generations (Willetts, 2010). These representations of active ageing relate to a certain period of life in the UK, and a certain portion of the baby Boomer generation, who are very much at the younger end of the age spectrum. This idea of the selfish boomer is at odds with information about the squeezed middle, who are also in this younger demographic (Barnes et al., 2013; Sinclair, 2015).

Later life, as described by the people in my book, has many features of a leisure society, their lives are rich and sociable, and relatively peaceful. They are committed to the future and society. The sociable leisure is not always time bounded, or spatially proscribed, there are reminiscent qualities to many of the preferred activities that connect to past and present others and self, and perhaps create space for future people and selves. This creates problems for those who would measure active leisure as a marker of successful ageing. People cannot manage the active ageing metanarrative with their bodies, because they have little control over them, they must fight fire with fire. Because active ageing is not a state of being, it has no physical form, it is a story we tell ourselves about agency in later life, supported by other stories; in policy and research, in media and biography. The next theme explains how the correspondents managed the active ageing metanarrative.

6.7   No Great Virtue in All This Active Ageing

Even in the Old Testament of the Bible, sloth and gluttony are sins. These ideas persist and shape current research (Sloan, 2011). People have written on the topic of the 'long lived' since at least the sixth century BC, when Sapho lamented her lost youth, and in 44 BC, Cicero, ancient Roman aged 62, divorced and alone, produced 'On Old Age', which affirms old age as a time of life to be enjoyed to the fullest, for those that apply themselves *wisely* (Freeman, 2016). The couplet of doom and gloom and advice on how to age well were there in the earliest texts, recommending that people eat well and exercise (Freeman, 2016). Smoking was not yet a thing in the Roman world and drinking beer was a way to ensure safe drinking water, so these things were not important. So although active ageing has had a recent surge, it is ancient in its provenance. Active ageing varies according to the institution promoting it. The World Health Organisation focuses on quality of later life, the EU on how to pay for it (Lassen, 2014). Age UK tells us it starts at 50, and volunteering for Age UK, or donating to them is a great way to avoid being a tiny, frail and lonely person on one of their leaflets.

There is hyperactive exercise and sports promotion, drumming up business for sports physiotherapists and orthopaedic surgeons. There is travel and self-development and any number of consumptive leisure pastimes. An active later life is a matter of commercial concern. There is a lot of information and advice about active ageing and much of it does not come from a good place. There is intertwining of active ageing and health-based business, and there are huge problems stored up for governments and other pension providers, and insurance businesses. Culture matters, Katz talks about a culture of active ageing (Holland & Katz, 2010). Studies of constraints to leisure in later life write about the need to understand how the inter and intra personal interact with the cultural (Godbey et al., 2010), Active ageing culture values the avoidance of disability; assumes that this is possible, desirable and implies that disability is inevitable with increased age, brought forward by naughty and passive pastimes, but can be held back through good and moral 'active' activities.

Ideas of individual responsibility for successful and active ageing are impacting populations in China, Korea, as well as western nations (Chen et al., 2020; Kusumastuti et al., 2016; Ryu & Heo, 2017), but it seems that the young Chinese students are not reflecting this yet in their leisure meanings (Gui et al., 2019). The financial concerns raised by an ageing population are trans-cultural drivers, so a cause for the focus on well-being in leisure studies could be the commercial concerns created by an ageing population, from welfare providers, insurance companies and a financial system that depends on consumption and the movement of resources to thrive. But it may be that the messages about active ageing are not yet all the way through the life course in China, as they are in western countries. There are the institutional drivers, but then there are the commercial drivers from leisure providers. Emancipatory motivated researchers may be drawn away from commercial concerns by the well-being focused research, leaving the field to overt commercial interests. However, it could be considered that the move towards leisure for well-being still has commercial drivers. Health care is expensive, and the self-help advocated in the drive towards leisure for well-being aims to reduce this, while improving quality of life, this is good not just for the individual and those around them, but also for those that share the costs of the health care. In the case of the UK, the NHS is publicly funded, free at the point of delivery for all. The responsibility to work towards maintaining good health is part of civic responsibility; the care of ill people is a shared endeavour. Healthcare research is well funded in the UK as a result.

Personal responsibility to keep healthy and contribute to society in later life is a matter of public concern (Lassen, 2014). Dionigi and Son state that all forms of leisure in later life, passive or otherwise need further research (Dionigi & Son, 2017). The concept of 'active leisure' is tangled up with the concept of 'instrumental activity'. There is a drive to become hyperactive in later life, this presents a challenge to agency in leisure. Behavioural models of success in later life depend upon the message that is sent being understood in the way it was meant. My research findings show that this is not the case. The message is subject to interpretation, suspicion and subversion; indeed, even having a message risks rebellion. The narratives reveal that active ageing does not work in the way it was intended, to free people from the idea of disengagement; and it certainly does not work for everyone.

There are lots of leisure choices and there is a skill in presenting our choices as culturally acceptable. The ways in which people narrate their leisure lives focuses on activities that are also 'active' in some sense. The people who express satisfaction with their lives have skills in negotiating cultural acceptability for the things they love to do. Some are experienced leisure practitioners managing the moral regulation of leisure, bending it to fit their preferences, which may be age-related, but this is not clear. Some people do a lot of things that are culturally acceptable, but the kinds of pro-social, very active things that they are talking about cannot take up the whole of their time. To write about an entire day, additional things are brought into the culturally consonant, active ageing, fold. TV watching, reading the paper, napping, drinking, gambling all have elements of learning and sociability that can be highlighted to ensure a more comfortable fit with culturally privileged elements of leisure practices, such as physical activity, intellectual activity, learning and sociability.

Some people are better able to focus on specific qualities of the things they love to do, to bring them into culturally acceptable bounds; even the people who 'don't care what others think' make a case for the acceptability of their choices. Some people participate in activities that are 'good for them' even if there is not much enjoyment in them. This is a problem, because enjoyment is good for people (Steptoe & Wardle, 2012). Activities that are carried out for extrinsic instrumental rational reasons may lack subjective intentionality as leisure. Most of the people in this study live with at least one other person, and all of them have frequent interactions with others. Some of these activities can require others, but even if they do not, they will require negotiation with others. Conflict and loneliness can result from a failure of others to share, connect with, or in some cases permit these activities. This adds layers of complex negotiation, not just with the self and the reader of the diaries, but with friends and family too. Failure to share a view of culturally consonant leisure lives can lead to conflict and loneliness.

6.8 Active Ageing

As expected, active ageing was the dominant metanarrative. Value-laden active ageing ideals is a constraint to enjoyment in leisure, it turns active leisure into a chore. But the chores do give meaning to more passive leisure, which is a reward after busy days.

The idea of happiness being important in its own right, touched on earlier in the literature review, complements the original aims of successful ageing strategies, to add life to the years, rather than years to life (Havighurst, 1961). The original proposal for successful ageing was to support "..the greatest good for the greatest number.." of older people (Havighurst, 1961, p. 8). The idea of enjoyment in leisure was overshadowed early in the debate that emerged in support of a better quality of later life, the idea of 'successful ageing' morphed into 'active ageing', with critique of this narrow focus spanning over 50 years (see for example Havighurst, 1961; Katz, 2013). Active ageing amplifies the advantages of an already privileged section of the community (Scherger et al., 2010). This is because old age is heterogeneous in nature so there is a risk that the active ageing discourse can inadvertently emphasise and reproduce social and physical inequalities in later life (Katz, 2000, 2013; Martin, 2011). Active ageing highlights the instrumental reasons for participating in leisure, because it focuses on physical, cultural and economically productive activities, and omits common enjoyable leisure pursuits, such as watching television, that make up the majority of people's leisure in later life and misses what they may offer.

Most correspondents found the time to carry out the work of being active agers, ensuring some exercise, their activity levels are reported, and their leisure as relaxation was clearly earned. Active ageing may bring additional structure, and certainly exercise, but sometimes it was appropriated by the correspondents, and used to justify favoured pastimes. They internalised elements of active ageing that they liked and reproduced it to suit their needs. People focus in on one element, such as Charles who learns about gambling, and explain themselves in this way as active agers.

This can be related to the way that the Canadian cricket spectators described their heavy drinking as medication (Joseph, 2012). The function of alcohol for younger men in this context is not addressed. Although that research is not discussing constraints it is reinforcing a theme that runs through my book of participants appropriating health messages to justify their favoured pastime, this confuses the simple view of neoliberal values bearing down on people and making their leisure lives a chore, as they turn it around.

6.9   Impact of Health Promotion on Health Advice

Most people pragmatically interpret health advice. General health promotion, in the name of active ageing, overshadows specific health advice for two of the correspondents. When health advice is broadly given (John, 2018), people are desensitised and the advice is easy to ignore. Both are people who have more experience of bad luck in relation to grieving for a loved partner. Richard partially takes medical advice, switching from Whisky to sherry most nights. Barbara rejects it outright;

at one point she calls herself a 'naughty diabetic' as she enjoys a doughnut on the day of her husband's inquest. In a later diary she tucks into a fried meal while waiting for the doctor to call with test results relating to diabetes and doing the crossword in the diabetic magazine. Her wilful rejection of health advice is not uncommon. We can start to consider if there is agency in people, to paraphrase Godbey et al. (2010), not doing what is good for them.

Rebellion and subversion are common in leisure practices (Rojek & Blackshaw, 2013) and there are examples of research around leisure rebellion in later life (Jolanki, 2008, 2009; Mitas et al., 2011; van Bohemen et al., 2013) although more often it is resistance that is considered, to dementia (Genoe, 2010), and to ageing (some examples include: Dionigi, 2006, 2011; Dionigi & Lyons, 2010; Mitas et al., 2011; Yarnal et al., 2011), rather than rebellion against an active ageing or health-related message as noted in my findings. Kleiber et al. propose that there is a positive role for some constraints (2008). Initially I could not imagine a positive role of the shush in the garden that took the fun out of active leisure. It appeared that the metanarrative of disengagement was ruining the fun. But now with the context of rejection of health advice by the correspondents, and the potential empowerment that appears to be part of that, it may be that it helps people to feel naughty, perhaps heightening a sense of mild peril or adventure in what is otherwise a socially sanctioned and potentially quite tedious pastime. If those people are used to being judged, and feeling unlucky, as the gardeners were, and as Barbara and Richard appear to be, then perhaps casting themselves as naughty is a more powerful action than other possibilities on offer. To passively accept health advice or admit that the charitable gardening group activity is actually quite good fun, does not offer the same possibility for some control.

Leisure theory is rich and complex, and leisure is a contested concept. A comparatively simple approach to leisure is taken in active ageing research which does not engage fully with the complexity of leisure practices (Clarke & Warren, 2007) or theory (Adams et al., 2011; Fallahpour et al., 2017). The concept of leisure as 'freely chosen activities' that have fortunate instrumental health outcomes is widely used in active ageing research, and this is reasonable; but the idea that a 'freely chosen activity' can be legislated for, that is inherent in active ageing approaches to later life, is contradictory.

6.10 Work and Leisure

My focus on a time of retirement in this research belies a conceptualisation of leisure that depends upon work for definition. Parker's early writing focused on the relationship between work and leisure, valuing both as contributing to a satisfying life (1971). He raised concerns that leisure was becoming more work-like and less equal, and this was conditioned by the sociocultural situation in which people found themselves (Parker, 1971). He later noted a concern that leisure and work were being polarised at a time when people were already retiring early and living longer, potentially as a response to a view of work as burden and leisure as desirable (Parker, 1983). Leisure has historically been an exclusive domain (Ravenscroft & Gilchrist, 2009; Veblen, 2007), as societies become richer more time is free and available for leisure. This free time after work definition; in the case of retirement considerably after work is considered in this book. Leisure in later life can be contextualised by a life time of work and family responsibilities (Gibson et al., 2003).

Here in this book it appears that many people are enjoying a leisurely retirement, but others are managing ideas of retirement that require considerable social or civic labour. It does not obviously serve capitalism to have a large 'unproductive', lightly consumptive population. Some are turning to the idea of paid work.

My research has found an important resource, in the Mass Observation Archive, for confirming ideas of civil labour in leisure studies, where work and leisure are not substantially different, because both can be an expression of meaning and freedom and both can be a chore (Parker, 1971). Rojek discusses civil labour, in all that a person does, he expresses that they choose a suite of activities through which they can express their identity, some paid, some unpaid, none truly free, but leisure has a sense of subjective intentionality (Rojek, 1991, 2010). Rojek's work is often critiqued for lacking an empirical base to support his findings, I believe I have found an important resource for confirming his theory. This enables them to construct an identity that is culturally consonant, if their environment supports them to do so. In the case of 'active wife' … Of men in the USA that retired between 1967 and 1978, a third returned to the workforce, they did so in reduced roles (Beck, 1986). Current retirement is more fluid, perhaps due to more flexible work possibilities due to technology, for example 47% of male Canadians who retired between the ages of 60 and 64 re-entered the workforce within 10 years (Sullivan & Al Ariss, 2019). It is becoming increasingly common for people to work for money in later life. In the UK the Centre for Research into the Older Workforce made its first report in 2004 (Mcnair et al., 2004). There is now a strong return to work agenda for later life (Phillipson, 2013) and the research field is developing with a focus on paid work for those that can, and a general productivity focus for those that cannot (Zaidi, 2015). The story of William's work, and his very active wife illustrates this. The leisure lifestyles of retirement are under scrutiny, with policy, research and financial drivers for an increasingly active and productive later life.

Leisure researchers should critically engage with the concern raised by Roberts that leisure studies is becoming too focused on well-being research (2018). Work is just as capable of making well-being claims as leisure, but with money added, so in the current consumptive culture leisure is weakened in the longer term as the promoter of well-being. Active ageing through leisure could be characterised as forced labour, a spatially diffused workhouse of the project of the self, which is really the project of the financial institutions that do not want to pay for a leisurely later life. So, if we just focus on activity for well-being and do not continue to wrestle with ideas of leisure as freedom we will lose it, and so will the people that we aim to enrich with our knowledge and understanding of leisure. The irony of this is not lost on me, as I engage with leisure constraints theory, which exists to ensure rational instrumental engagement with wholesome activities for well-being. But these are the people that need to read this research and think about and understand constraints in other ways.

Different impacts of work are felt in Brenda's and Sophie's homes. Loneliness is very different from being alone, which here, for both of them brings some freedom to relax, Brenda in the bath, and Sophie on the buses. Bhatti and Church's research on gardening and homemaking shows the home is spatialised and gendered in different ways, sometimes leading to discord and others as spatial fixes as people create or fashion spaces for their own leisure pursuits (2000). Home can provide respite from public attention to the range, frequency and intensity of activity participation in later life. There are ethnographic studies featuring extensive observation of leisure (Joseph, 2012; Lassen, 2014; Mair, 2009; Marhankova, 2011), and autoethnographic studies that are rich in detail about what people do, and how they experience it (Buckley, 2020). There are quantitative studies that explore what people do, the frequency, and the benefits it brings (Arem et al., 2015). There are many activity specific studies (Kim et al., 2015; Richards, 2016; Wang & Glicksman, 2013; Wang & MacMillan, 2013), that enable insights to be drawn about the essential properties that said activities bring. Some of it focuses on age induced constraints, and to do that it finds disadvantaged or disabled people to study, then calls them old (Harley et al., 2010; Milbourne & Doheny, 2012). Or it starts from a problematic stance, how can we keep old people fit and well (Clark et al., 2012; Thurston & Green, 2004). If my participants were the subjects of this kind of research, they would be active agers, at the more exceptional end of the spectrum. However, when lives are shared, but values relating to the balance of instrumental work to leisure are not shared, families can be a source of additional stress, as they channel and reinforce their own interpretation of active ageing ideals. Both of these ladies, Brenda and Sophie, are very active, and identify as such, but it is not sufficient to have cultural consonance as an individual, because like all of the other correspondents they are socially connected in complex ways, and in their homes, work trumps leisure.

6.11   Disengagement and Active Ageing

Disengagement used disrespectfully was also operational, in the way other people's rude behaviour was interpreted and managed by the correspondents, in the way they were driven out of work and in the way people wanted them to get out of their way. It resonated for me with the ageing and care directive, that ended with questions about euthanasia, the idea of the aged as a burden is never far away from the thoughts of researchers, but it is very far away from the thoughts of these correspondents who write with compassion about the difficulties 'other old people' face. There is a mix of admiration and pity in the way they write about other old people. There is gratefulness for their own good luck. Disengagement is not internalised, the one person that applied a label of disability to herself described a home based lifestyle and explained it as externally imposed: 'a fall had me registered as disabled'. The story of withdrawal only makes sense in relation to it following on from an active life, they define each other, like life and death, and they can come to take on those meanings. The idea of an active third age, followed by a disengaged fourth age is operational and people cannot choose which one is applied to them (Gilleard et al., 2005; Higgs & Gilleard, 2014; Lloyd et al., 2014).

Some research into the experience of ageing using the Mass Observation Archive questions the usefulness of the third and fourth age distinctions in the lives of older people (Hubble & Tew, 2013). The participants felt that choice about work, independence, good health care and opportunities for learning and cultural engagement were important whatever their 'stage', and further they did not recognise or relate to the idea of a third then fourth age.

The correspondents in my research use media to safely explore new ideas and tell tales of being mocked and keeping to their own to avoid this. Other old people, particularly unlucky ones appear in the correspondent's stories. Basic attribution theory does not hold so strongly for these less active agers, they are more compassionate and talk much more about luck than the participants in sports research (Gard et al., 2017; Minello & Nixon, 2017). 'Other old people' are described by my correspondents as ill and vulnerable, unless they are exceptional, like Barbara's allotment neighbours who recently tiled their bathroom. Even for these correspondents, with their compassionate views, it is hard to escape the declining ability and ageing couplet when discussing other old people, or the idea of 'exceptional old people' for those that are considerably more productive.

It is interesting to note how unlucky and courageous the 'other old people' are in the Mass Observation correspondence, in contrast to the 'lazy other old people' in the sports focused leisure constraints research (Gard et al., 2017; Minello & Nixon, 2017). The correspondents do not write themselves as lazy, even the ones resisting specific health advice do not consider themselves lazy or ignorant. There is very little about 'other' old people in the way that sports research describes them, the 'other old people' in these stories tend to be 'inspirational survivors' heroic victims of fate. But some of the Mass Observers *are* the other old people that are discussed by hyperactive participants in sport research (Gard et al., 2017; Minello & Nixon, 2017); but they are not lazy, just not very interested in sport, and those that are not trying too hard to be 'active agers' are having a lovely time. They are well aware of the twists and turns of fate, and taking care of themselves and others, living valued, connected, interesting lives, resilient and curious and caring. Everything else represents Veblenesque displays of wealth and luck (Veal, 2016; Veblen, 2007), misattributed to entitlement and hard work. They know that they are lucky, and enjoy something, anything, every day.

In summary a 'culture of active ageing' is not something that gets into these 'individuals'. It is in different places, depending on time, space and company. Its impact on their leisure lives is actively managed through diverse interpretations, wilful forms of resistance and the serendipitous every day. There are many variations on a theme of active ageing. Active ageing is indeed plural and complex, they are active in their negotiation of this complex cultural story, at times the negotiation is intentional and at other time it is non-intentional, but there is negotiation, nevertheless. The active ageing in this book is storied, but within the stories are performances and negotiations, and reproduction of plural, agentic, communal and yielding forms of active ageing. The passive but socially connecting variety of experiences reported show connections to earlier research, and builds on it to recognise that the relationship between leisure and ageing is not between an individual agent and a single dominant culture; but between people as part of a connected system within which they all process, interpret and reproduce their culture in the subtle interactions of everyday life. The findings show a new way of understanding leisure in later life and contribute to research with a 'critical of active ageing' perspective that can be used in further exploration of a more social conceptualisation of 'passive leisure' throughout the life course, without the narrative of decline.

References

Adams, K. B., Leibbrandt, S., & Moon, H. (2011). A critical review of the literature on social and leisure activity and wellbeing in later life. *Ageing and Society, 31*(04), 683–712.

Alderwick, H., & Dixon, J. (2019). The NHS long term plan. *BMJ (Online), 364*, l84. https://doi.org/10.1136/bmj.l84.

Allen-Collinson, J., & Leledaki, A. (2015). Sensing the outdoors: A visual and haptic phenomenology of outdoor exercise embodiment. *Leisure Studies, 34*(4), 457–470.

Arem, H., Moore, S. C., Patel, A., Hartge, P., Berrington de Gonzalez, A., Visvanathan, K., Campbell, P. T., Freedman, M., Weiderpass, E., Adami, H. O., Linet, M. S., Lee I-M., Matthews, C. E. (2015). Leisure time physical activity and mortality. *JAMA Internal Medicine, 175*(6), 959.

Barnes, M., Taylor, D., & Ward, L. (2013). Being well enough in old age. *Critical Social Policy, 33*(3), 473–493.

Bazalgette, L., Holden, J., Tew, P., Hubble, N., & Morrison, J. (2011). *Coming of age*. London. https://dspace.brunel.ac.uk/bitstream/2438/6237/2/Fulltext.pdf.

Beck, S. H. (1986). Mobility from preretirement to postretirement job. *Sociological Quarterly, 27*(4), 515–531.

Bhatti, M., & Church, A. (2000). 'I never promised you a rose garden': Gender, leisure and home-making. *Leisure Studies, 19*(3), 183–197.

Blackshaw, T. (2010). *Leisure*. Routledge.

Buckley, R. (2020). Nature sports, health and ageing: The value of euphoria. *Annals of Leisure Research, 23*(1), 92–109.

Burnett-Wolle, S., & Godbey, G. (2007). Refining research on older aldults' leisure: Implications of selection, optimisation and compensation and socioeconomic selectivity theories. *Journal of Leisure Research, 39*(3), 498–513.

Caleyachetty, R., Hardy, R., Cooper, R., Richards, M., Howe, L. D., Anderson, E., Kuh, D., & Stafford, M. (2018). Modeling exposure to multiple childhood social risk factors and physical capability and common affective symptoms in later life. *Journal of Aging and Health, 30*(3), 386–407.

Carr, N. (2017). Re-thinking the relation between leisure and freedom. *Annals of Leisure Research, 20*(2), 137–151.

Chen, L., Ye, M., & Kahana, E. (2020). A self-reliant umbrella: Defining successful aging among the old-old (80+) in Shanghai. *Journal of Applied Gerontology, 39*(3), 242–249.

Choi, W., Liechty, T., Naar, J. J., West, S., Wong, J. D., & Son, J. (2018). "We're a family and that gives me joy": Exploring interpersonal relationships in older women's softball using socio-emotional selectivity theory. *Leisure Sciences, 0*(0), 1–18. Accessed online at https://www.tandfonline.com/doi/abs/10.1080/01490400.2018.1499056.

Clark, F., Jackson, J., Carlson, M., Chou, C.-P., Cherry, B. J., Jordan-Marsh, M., Knight, B. G., Mandel, D., Blanchard, J., Granger, D. A., Wilcox, R. R., Lai, M. Y., White, B., Hay, J., Lam, C., Marterella, A., & Azen, S. P. (2012). Effectiveness of a lifestyle intervention in promoting the well-being of independently living older people: Results of the Well Elderly 2 Randomised Controlled Trial. *Journal of Epidemiology & Community Health, 66*(9), 782–790.

Clarke, A., & Warren, L. (2007). Hopes, fears and expectations about the future: What do older people's stories tell us about active ageing? *Ageing and Society, 27*(04), 465–488.

Crawford, D. W., & Godbey, G. (1987). Reconceptualizing barriers to family leisure. *Leisure Sciences, 9*(2), 119–127.

Crouch, D. (2000). Places around us: Embodied lay geographies in leisure and tourism. *Leisure Studies, 2012*(December), 37–41.

Crouch, D. (2012). Ordinary lives: Studies in the everyday. *Leisure Studies, 31*(2), 255–256.

Crouch, D. (2014). *The hope of leisure, the leisure of hope*. Retrieved January 3, 2015, from https://leisurestudiesblog.wordpress.com/2014/11/04/the-hope-of-leisure-the-leisure-of-hope/.

Crouch, D. (2016). *Flirting with space*. Taylor and Francis.

Department of Health. (2010). Our health and wellbeing today. *Notes, 3*, 68.

Dionigi, R. (2006). Competitive sport as leisure in later life: Negotiations, discourse, and aging. *Leisure Sciences, 28*, 181–196.

Dionigi, R., & Lyons, K. (2010). Examining layers of community in leisure contexts: A case analysis of older adults in an excercise intervention. *Journal of Leisure Research, 42*(2), 317–338.

Dionigi, R. A., Horton, S., & Bellamy, J. (2011). Meanings of aging among older Canadian women of varying physical activity levels. *Leisure Sciences, 33*(5), 402–419.

Dionigi, R. A., & Son, J. S. (2017). Introduction to critical perspectives on physical activity, sport, play and leisure in later life. *Annals of Leisure Research, 20*(1), 1–6.

Dressler, W. W. (2012). Cultural consonance: Linking culture, the individual and health. *Preventive Medicine, 55*(5), 390–393.

Fallahpour, M., Borell, L., Luborsky, M., & Nygård, L. (2017). Leisure-activity participation to prevent later-life cognitive decline: A systematic review. *Scandinavian Journal of Occupational Therapy, 23*(3), 162–197.

Freeman, P. (2016). *How to grow old: Ancient wisdom for the second half of life.* Princeton University Press.

Gard, M., Dionigi, R. A., Horton, S., Baker, J., Weir, P., & Dionigi, C. (2017). The normalization of sport for older people? *Annals of Leisure Research, 20*(3), 253–272.

Genoe, M. R. (2010). Leisure as resistance within the context of dementia. *Leisure Studies, 29*(3), 303–320.

Gibson, H., Ashton-Shaeffer, C., Green, J., & Autry, C. (2003). Leisure in the lives of retirement-aged women: Conversations about leisure and life. *Leisure/Loisir, 28*(3–4), 203–230.

Gilleard, C., Higgs, P., Hyde, M., Wiggins, R., & Blane, D. (2005). Class, cohort, and consumption: The British experience of the third age. *The Journals of Gerontology. Series B, Psychological Sciences and Social Sciences, 60*(6), S305–S310. https://www.ncbi.nlm.nih.gov/pubmed/16260712.

Glyptis, S. (1989). *Leisure and unemployment.* Open University Press.

Godbey, G., Crawford, D., & Shen, X. S. (2010). Assessing heirachical leisure constraints theory after two decades. *Journal of Leisure Research, 42*(1), 111–134.

Gui, J., Walker, G. J., & Harshaw, H. W. (2019). Meanings of *Xiū Xián* and leisure: Cross-cultural exploration of laypeople's definition of leisure. *Leisure Sciences, 0*(0), 1–19. Accessed online at https://doi.org/10.1080/01490400.2019.1571968.

Harley, D., Fitzpatrick, G., Axelrod, L., White, G., & McAllister, G. (2010). Making the Wii at home: Game play by older people in sheltered housing. *Lecture Notes in Computer Science (Including Subseries Lecture Notes in*

Artificial Intelligence and Lecture Notes in Bioinformatics), 6389 LNCS, 156–176.

Havighurst, R. J. (1961). Successful aging. *The Gerontologist, 1*(1), 8–13.

Hayward, M. D., & Gorman, B. K. (2004). The long arm of childhood: The influence of early-life social conditions on men's mortality. *Source: Demography, 41*(1), 87–107.

Higgs, P., & Gilleard, C. (2014). Frailty, abjection and the 'othering' of the fourth age. *Health Sociology Review, 23*(1), 10–19.

Holland, C. A., & Katz, J. S. (2010). Cultural identity and belonging in later life: Is extra care housing an attractive concept to older Jewish people living in Britain? *Journal of Cross-Cultural Gerontology, 25*(1), 59–69.

Hubble, N., & Tew, P. (2013). *Ageing, narrative and identity: New qualitative social research.* Springer.

John, S. (2018). Should we punish responsible drinkers? Prevention, paternalism and categorization in public health. *Public Health Ethics, 11*(1), 35–44.

Jolanki, O. (2008). Discussing responsibility and ways of influencing health. *International Journal of Ageing and Later Life Introduction, 3*(1), 45–76.

Jolanki, O. (2009). *Fate or choice? Talking about old age and health.*

Jones, H., Neal, S., Mohan, G., Connell, K., Cochrane, A., & Bennett, K. (2015). Urban multiculture and everyday encounters in semi-public, franchised cafe spaces. *Sociological Review, 63*(3), 644–661.

Joseph, J. (2012). Around the boundary: Alcohol and older Caribbean-Canadian men. *Leisure Studies, 31*(2), 147–163.

Katz, S. (2000). Busy bodies: Activity, aging, and the management of everyday life. *Journal of Aging Studies, 14*(2), 135–152.

Katz, S. (2013). Active and successful aging. Lifestyle as a gerontological idea. *Recherches Sociologiques et Anthropologiques [En Ligne], 44*(1). Retrieved January 7, 2014, from https://rsa.revues.or.

Kay, T. (1987). *Leisure in the lifestyles of unemployed people: A case study in leicester.* Loughborough University. https://dspace.lboro.ac.uk/ and was harvested from the British Library's EThOS service. https://www.ethos.bl.uk/.

Kim, H., Woo, E., & Uysal, M. (2015). Tourism experience and quality of life among elderly tourists. *Tourism Management, 46,* 465–476.

King, D. B., Cappeliez, P., Canham, S. L., & O'Rourke, N. (2019). Functions of reminiscence in later life: Predicting change in the physical and mental health of older adults over time. *Aging & Mental Health, 23*(2), 246–254.

Kleiber, D., Mcguire, F., Aybar-Damali, B., & Norman, W. (2008). Having more by doing less: The paradox of leisure constraints in later life. *Journal of Leisure Research, 40*(3), 343–359.

Kleiber, D. A., & Nimrod, G. (2009). 'I can't be very sad': Constraint and adaptation in the leisure of a 'learning in retirement' group. *Leisure Studies, 28*(1), 67–83.

Kusumastuti, S., Derks, M. G. M., Tellier, S., Di Nucci, E., Lund, R., Mortensen, E. L., & Westendorp, R. G. J. (2016). Successful ageing: A study of the literature using citation network analysis. *Maturitas, 93,* 4–12.

Lassen, A. J. (2014). *Active ageing and the unmaking of old age.* University of Copenhagen.

Lester, H., Mead, N., Graham, C. C., Gask, L., & Reilly, S. (2012). An exploration of the value and mechanisms of befriending for older adults in England. *Ageing and Society, 32*(02), 307–328.

Liechty, T., Genoe, M. R., & Marston, H. R. (2017). Physically active leisure and the transition to retirement: The value of context. *Annals of Leisure Research, 20*(1), 23–38.

Lloyd, L., Calnan, M., Cameron, A., Seymour, J., & Smith, R. (2014). Identity in the fourth age: Perseverance, adaptation and maintaining dignity. *Ageing and Society, 34*(01), 1–19.

Lyotard, J.-F. (1984). *The postmodern condition: A report on knowledge.* Manchester University Press.

Mair, H. (2009). Club life: Third place and shared leisure in rural Canada. *Leisure Sciences, 31*(5), 450–465.

Marhankova, J. H. (2011). Leisure in old age: Disciplinary practices surrounding the discourse of active ageing. *International Journal of Ageing and Later Life, 6*(1), 5–32.

Martin, W. (2011). Visualizing risk: Health, gender and the ageing body. *Critical Social Policy, 32*(1), 51–68.

Mcguire, F. (2000). What do we know? Not much: The state of leisure and aging research. *Journal of Leisure Research, 32*(1), 97–100.

McHugh, S. (Ed.). (2017). *The changing nature of happiness.* Springer International Publishing.

Mcnair, S., Flynn, M., Owen, L., Humphreys, C., & Woodfield, S. (2004). Changing work in later life: A study of job transitions. In *Guildford CROW University of Surrey.*

Meisner, B. A., Hutchinson, S. L., Gallant, K. A., Lauckner, H., & Stilwell, C. L. (2019). Taking 'steps to connect' to later life: Exploring leisure program participation among older adults in rural communities. *Loisir Et Société/Society and Leisure, 42*(1), 1–22.

Mejía, S. T., Ryan, L. H., Gonzalez, R., & Smith, J. (2017). Successful aging as the intersection of individual resources, age, environment, and experiences of well-being in daily activities. *Journals of Gerontology—Series B Psychological Sciences and Social Sciences, 72*(2), 279–289.

Milbourne, P., & Doheny, S. (2012). Older people and poverty in rural Britain: Material hardships, cultural denials and social inclusions. *Journal of Rural Studies, 28*(4), 389–397.

Minello, K., & Nixon, D. (2017). 'Hope I never stop': Older men and their two-wheeled love affairs. *Annals of Leisure Research, 20*(1), 75–95.

Mitas, O., Qian, X. L., Yarnal, C., & Kerstetter, D. (2011). "The fun begins now!" Broadening and building processes in red hat society participation. *Journal of Leisure Research, 43*(1), 30–55.

Neal, S., Bennett, K., Cochrane, A., & Mohan, G. (2018). Community *and* conviviality? Informal social life in multicultural places. *Sociology.* https://doi.org/10.1177/003803851876351.

Neal, S., & Vincent, C. (2013). Multiculture, middle class competencies and friendship practices in super-diverse geographies. *Social & Cultural Geography, 14*(8), 909–929.

Neal, S., & Walters, S. (2008). Rural be/longing and rural social organizations: Conviviality and community-making in the English countryside. *Sociology, 42*(2), 279–297.

Nimrod, G. (2017). Older audiences in the digital media environment. *Information, Communication & Society, 20*(2), 233–249.

Office for National Statistics. (2018). National life tables, UK: 2015 to 2017. *Statistical Bulletin.* https://doi.org/10.1016/j.chroma.2004.09.049.

Parker, S. R. (1971). The future of work and leisure. *Annals of Leisure Research, 20*(3), 394–396.

Parker, S. (1983). *Leisure and work.* George Allen & Unwin (publishers) Ltd.

Pavela, G., & Latham, K. (2016). Childhood conditions and multimorbidity among older adults. *Journals of Gerontology—Series B Psychological Sciences and Social Sciences, 71*(5), 889–901.

Pettigrew, S., & Roberts, M. (2008). Addressing loneliness in later life. *Aging & Mental Health, 12*(3), 302–309.

Phillipson, C. (2013). Commentary: The future of work and retirement. *Human Relations, 66*(1), 143–153.

Randall, W. L. (2013). The importance of being ironic: Narrative openness and personal resilience in later life. *Gerontologist, 53*(1), 9–16.

Ravenscroft, N., & Gilchrist, P. (2009). The emergent working society of leisure. *Journal of Leisure Research, 41*(1), 23–39.

Richards, J. A. (2016). *Active older people participating in creative dance—Challenging perceptions.* Middlesex University.

Roberts, K. (2018). A future for UK leisure studies: Back to work. *International Journal of the Sociology of Leisure.*

Rojek, C. (1991). *Ways of escape: Modern transformations of leisure and travel.* Doctoral dissertation, University of Glasgow.

Rojek, C. (2010). The labour of leisure. In *The labour of leisure.* Sage.

Rojek, C., & Blackshaw, T. (2013). The labour of leisure reconsidered. In T. Blackshaw (Ed.), *Routledge handbook of leisure studies* (pp. 544–559). Routledge.

Ryu, J., & Heo, J. (2016). Relaxation and watching televised sports among older adults. *Educational Gerontology, 42*(2), 71–78.

Ryu, J., & Heo, J. (2017). Relationships between leisure activity types and well-being in older adults. *Leisure Studies, 4367*(September), 1–12.

Scherger, S., Nazroo, J., & Higgs, P. (2010). Leisure activities and retirement: Do structures of inequality change in old age? *Ageing and Society, 31*(01), 146–172.

Scraton, S., & Watson, B. (1998). Gendered cities: Women and public leisure space in the 'postmodern city.' *Leisure Studies, 17*(2), 123–137.

Sinclair, D. (2015). *The myth of the baby boomer.* Ready for Ageing Alliance. Retrieved October 28, 2020, from https://ilcuk.org.uk/wp-content/uploads/2018/10/The-Myth-of-the-Baby-Boomer.pdf.

Sloan, R. P. (2011). Virtue and vice in health and illness: The idea that wouldn't die. *The Lancet, 377,* 896–897.

Spracklen, K. (2011). *Constructing leisure: Historical and philosophical debates.* Palgrave Macmillan.

Steptoe, A., & Wardle, J. (2012). Enjoying life and living longer. *Archives of International Medicine, 172*(3), 273–275.

Sullivan, S. E., & Al Ariss, A. (2019). Employment after retirement: A review and framework for future research. *Journal of Management, 45*(1), 262–284.

Tampubolon, G. (2015). Growing up in poverty, growing old in infirmity: The long arm of childhood conditions in Great Britain. *PLoS ONE, 10*(12), 1–16.

Thurston, M., & Green, K. (2004). Adherence to exercise in later life: How can exercise on prescription programmes be made more effective? *Health Promotion International, 19*(3), 379–387.

Toepoel, V. (2013). Ageing, leisure, and social connectedness: How could leisure help reduce social isolation of older people? *Social Indicators Research, 113*(1), 355–372.

van Bohemen, S., van Zoonen, L., & Aupers, S. (2013). Performing the "fun" self: How members of the Red Hat Society negotiate cultural discourses of femininity and ageing. *European Journal of Cultural Studies, 16*(4), 424–439.

Van Der Goot, M., Beentjes, J. W. J., & Van Selm, M. (2012). Meanings of television in older adults' lives: An analysis of change and continuity in television viewing. *Ageing & Society, 32*(1), 147.

Veal, A. J. (2016). Leisure, income inequality and the Veblen effect: Cross-national analysis of leisure time and sport and cultural activity. *Leisure Studies, 35*(2), 215–240.

Veblen, T. (2007). *Theory of the leisure class*. Transaction Publishers.

Wang, D., & Glicksman, A. (2013). "Being grounded": Benefits of gardening for older adults in low income housing. *Journal of Housing for the Elderly, 27*, 89–104.

Wang, D., & MacMillan, T. (2013). The benefits of gardening for older adults: A systematic review of the literature. *Activities, Adaptation & Aging, 37*(2), 153–181.

Warren, J. R. (2016). Does growing childhood socioeconomic inequality mean future inequality in adult health? *The ANNALS of the American Academy of Political and Social Science, 663*(1), 292–330.

Willetts, D. (2010). *The pinch: How the baby boomers took their children's future—And why they should give it back*. Atlantic Books.

Woods, B., O'Philbin, L., Farrell, E. M., Spector, A. E., & Orrell, M. (2018). Reminiscence therapy for dementia. *Cochrane Database of Systematic Reviews*, (3), Art. No.: CD001120. https://doi.org/10.1002/14651858. CD001120.pub3. Accessed 28 April 2021.

Yarnal, C., Son, J., & Liechty, T. (2011). "She was buried in her purple dress and her red hat and all of our members wore full 'Red Hat Regalia' to celebrate her life": Dress, embodiment and older women's leisure: Reconfiguring the ageing process. *Journal of Aging Studies, 25*(1), 52–61.

Zaidi, A. (2015). Creating and using the evidence base: The case of the Active Ageing Index. *Contemporary Social Science, 10*(2), 148–159.

7

A Social Thesis of Leisure

Here I share the conclusions which can justifiably be drawn from my findings. I review them, drawing on the findings and the discussion chapters. This synthesis of the thesis starts by reiterating key points from the early chapters then goes on to support my claim to have made an original contribution to knowledge.

My curiosity about later life sparked this enquiry. The action of one of the people that I worked with in a gardening project 'shushing' us while we laughed symbolised that they could not admit to, or encourage, empowered views of themselves at leisure. They could not be frivolous in their leisure, they had a responsibility to participate in health and community promoting activities, so long as they were not fun. This made me realise that there is a huge gap in our understanding of leisure in later life. Academic and professional experiences reinforced this concern, as I presented the work at conferences; audiences were astonished that the visibly aged participants in the pictures had created the gardens in the pictures; the gardener's capacities and my academic peers' perceptions of their capacities were unrelated. It was apparent in the gardens, in the conference rooms, in the written research and the media; that what we think is a suitable way to see leisure in later life, and the empirical day

© The Author(s), under exclusive license to Springer Nature
Switzerland AG 2021
T. Wiseman, *Leisure in Later Life*, Leisure Studies in a Global Era,
https://doi.org/10.1007/978-3-030-71672-1_7

to day leisure lives of older adults, are very far apart. It is a problem that we may be applying ill and vulnerable roles to people, and they to themselves, because they are older. This may be constraining leisure in later life, causing inhibitions, and taking the fun out of leisure. So I set out to undertake an in-depth qualitative study to expose and illustrate alternative stories about leisure in later life, in order to present a counter narrative to challenge the current ideas of leisure in later life being useful only for instrumental purposes.

The background chapter introduced us to a new healthy, happy population of people in later life. They do not really plan for their later life but anticipate participating in generally 'active' leisure. However, what they actually do is engage in enjoyable passive pastimes. Despite this inactivity they are enjoying continued good health and high levels of life satisfaction. There are two paradoxes in later life leisure studies. The big one is that these 'old people' that 'need help' to be 'more active', report feeling happier than the majority of younger people in many countries (Kusumastuti et al., 2016). The second one is that despite more and more research evidence about 'what is good for them', active leisure; people do more and more of what is 'bad for them', passive leisure (Phoenix & Bell, 2018), and yet they are living longer and healthier lives than ever. The focus on health and well-being means that there is a knowledge gap in research and theory for more leisurely pastimes in later life for those that are ageing well. My research asks what happens if we disconnect declining ability and later life and look instead at what people are reporting about their leisure lives. In order to better understand the 'shush in the garden' that triggered the enquiry, we first need to know what older people are doing in their private leisure lives, then we can ask if and how they negotiate the impact of metanarratives about ageing that the 'shush in the garden' represented.

Leisure constraints theory offers ways of understanding why people do not do what is good for them, but it has not yet looked at the more 'passive' yet healthy ager. Many studies of later life presuppose decline and disability as people age, including active ageing and leisure constraints research. The focus on health and well-being means that there is a knowledge gap in research and theory for more leisurely pastimes in later life for those that are ageing well. My research asks how people negotiate leisure in the context of everyday later life, and how they interact with metanarratives about ageing.

If we wish to understand how lives are lived, then one way of investigating this is through narrative inquiry. Narratives require context, stories are designed, told and interpreted for many functions and are historically situated (Riessman, 2008). Negotiation is a concept that is most often used in leisure studies in relation to how people manage particular constraints to leisure participation, in order to do particular activities (Jun & Kyle, 2011). Here it is more widely understood in a constructivist paradigm. A person lives a life, and that life involves understanding and applying the rules and regulations and norms of the culture within which a person finds themselves (Goffman, 1959; Lyotard, 1984).

Constructing candid accounts of later life leisure is problematic because it requires generation of data about people's leisure lives, and this area of life is private. People are constrained in their disclosures about leisure, but a research resource, The Mass Observation Archive allows a level of openness that enables a richer story to be told (Sheridan, 2000). With no connection between respondent and researcher the anonymity is stronger, and storied accounts are more candid (Pollen, 2013; Smart, 2011). I had a choice of many directives that would give rich detailed information about leisure in later life, and chose to focus on five, including a lifeline, and four day diaries. I selected 26 people that were retired in 2008, and analysed diaries from 2014 to 2015. I carried out a thematic analysis of narrative in order to address the research questions: How do people negotiate leisure in the context of everyday later life, and how do they interact with metanarratives about ageing.

7.1   Findings

I introduced some demographic information about the correspondents to give some context to their stories. Four themes were constructed, they were 'windows on the world', 'no great virtue in all this active ageing', 'His Lordship goes off to work', and 'other old people'. People negotiate leisure in the context of everyday lives from the refuge of home.

They interact with a range of metanarratives about ageing, resisting with-drawal for themselves, casting 'active ageing' as 'work', and introducing ideas about being selfless, and honoured agers. They are compassionate about 'other old people' who are less fortunate than them. The themes are reprised here:

7.1.1 Windows on the World

They are not neoliberal individuals; they are stewarding from the prospect and refuge of their homes. They are sociable with selected people. They are subjected to a withdrawal metanarrative, and manage it through expressing competencies, such as Wendy singing in the choir; subtle assertion like Matthews shopping trip; externalisation as when Marjorie explains a fall had her registered as disabled, and vicarious participation in other people's fun with Peters good seat in his lounge for a fireworks display. They have large reminiscence resources to enhance leisure, where freedom can be expressed. They engage with intergenera-tional distrust, and the ideas of selfish boomers, as illustrated in the story of changing £20 on the bus, through stories of selfless behaviours and being honoured. They are negotiating the metanarratives about ageing whether they know it or not. These narratives of the selfless ager and the honoured ager provide nuanced alternatives to the active ager and with-drawn ager narratives that dominate their stories and the literature. They all identify as connected agers.

7.1.2 No Great Virtue…

Active ageing was engaged with and dominated some correspondents' stories. But it was a chore, and not considered virtuous or leisurely. The active ageing messages were simple but subject to writerly interpretation, for example when gambling is cast as learning. The same happened to health advice, with drinking sherry a noble compromise. Resistance was linked to bad luck, with a 'naughty diabetic' taking some control. Active ageing was pragmatically engaged with, but it also offered something to resist.

7.1.3 His Lordship Goes Off to Work

A balance within a household is illustrated where both people in a couple are busy, one with work who is not so fit, the other with hyper-active leisure. This contrasts to Peters day that focuses on his active wife. Work provides an alternative to being a hyperactive ager. There are households where the work and leisure ethic clash and cause discord. Brenda wants her husband to be busy, so she can relax. A shift towards telling stories about being economically productive is noted, and the time and space politics are gently negotiated. In Sophies household, where she is an active ager but there are three family members in paid employment who do not value her hyperactivity, the politics are not so gentle.

7.1.4 Other Old People

They engage with ideas of luck and chance and courage that explain the situations that unfortunate 'other old people' find themselves in.

A secondary finding that emerged suggested that the demographic research in the background chapter would not predict these correspondents' situations, so I did not use demographic markers in the conclusions I drew. In addition to this there is potential for social mobility in retirement, related to volunteering, that is picked up in the recommendations for further research.

7.2   Analytical Findings

The leisure lives of this group are endangered by financial drivers, and the idea that they have had it too good. I advocate for an appreciation and re-evaluation of passive leisure in later life as a valid choice. Now I have gone native and been behind closed doors, I realise that people are never free to do as they please unless they are alone. But in being alone they are judged as failures. Perhaps because leisure is so private, us at our most free, perhaps that is why we consider it so important. Leisure participation and consumption is almost a window on the soul, and we always want to better know the 'other'. But for researchers there is an ethical dilemma, the very act of publicising private leisure lives risks exposing people to instrumental purposes, to know the other to better control them. I am left questioning whether true leisure, like "*true grief, is a private affair*" (Richard, remembrance 2014).

So, the great crisis facing our age is not a tsunami of centenarians, it is the struggle to balance freedom and belonging, winning and love, doing and being, performing and relaxing, producing and consuming, greed and generosity. I aimed to tell stories that persuade people of the value of 'passive' leisure in later life, for the fun, sociability and connection, including reminiscence, with self and others. Because the 'active' is such a small part of life. The term has been appropriated to include anything valued by the observer or researcher, and so instrumentally overtaken that it is hard by any definition to call it leisure.

The findings from this study illustrate that leisure in later life is not a poor or diminished version of a lost youthful leisure life. It is important to understand the impact of life stage and the constitution of families, and also consider the importance of ritualised events or moments that make later life leisure vibrant in its own way, active, passive and connected, and it should be judged, if at all, on its own terms. This private domain of life should be allowed to flourish, because even if the devil does make work for hands that are a little aged, they have managed this far, and will continue to do so. They may humour our intervention, if it's a bit of a laugh, but they know that life's a lottery, and find a good balance for themselves. Primitive human creatures like high energy food and sensuous pastimes; like our literature with all the books laying open in all their different times; our bodies are also all that they have ever been. Primitive human bodies need to be strong and alert, and to do this we need to be well fed and connected. So, when we are greedy, lazy and sensuous, we are in many ways doing the right thing.

The majority of the correspondents' time is spent in 'passive' enjoyable activities. There were many 'active' activities but these were reported with little elaboration, as chores, or with reference to appropriation of potential leisure. The social benefits of media consumption and relaxing and socialising, and the 'naughty' activities such as drinking, eating 'bad' food are explained and celebrated, creating agentic views of people at play. Subjective freedom appears to be part of leisure's reward. People are acutely aware of active ageing pressures and explain their lives in this way, but with creative twists, and negotiations such as gambling as learning. Leisure is good for people, but not always in the way that it is conceived by leisure scholars, it relates much more to the early successful ageing ideas that supported sociability and agency in later life, than the hyperactive rational instrumentality of current active ageing.

Engagement across social difference is a key part of how sociologists have conceptualised conviviality as part of social comfort (Jones et al., 2015; Neal & Vincent, 2013), my study highlights a negative finding, a lack of diverse interactions in an otherwise very sociable life, this is suggested as an area for further study. Condescending attitudes, different interpretations of what is culturally required of an active ager within close and distant relationships, and the privileging of working families with children all diminished pleasure in the day to day lives of these writers.

If we shift to a more plural perspective we could move forward faster in our thinking about leisure in later life. We could locate/recognise power within ourselves and our communities to protect the leisure of the people around us from the machinery of growth and consumption. We should recognise the rational instrumental drivers behind the enquiries we make, and when we use up our own lifetime trying to control the lifetimes of others, we should not pretend it is emancipatory. We should know that it is economic production functioning ever more effectively that we are contributing to (Lyotard, 1984). We can take comfort from those that ignore, rebel, re-purpose or twist the messages that they receive. We researchers have found a way to make a very comfortable life from talking to people we like about things we are interested in, and in doing so, we talk mainly about 'other old people' and how to make their lives cost less.

I am developing a social thesis of leisure and ageing, one that questions the atomism inherent in the liberal individual, which is a feature of how the literature approaches active agers; from super-grans and heroic individuals, to individuals who make 'good' choices. I set out to find constraints to an active later life, and I found that the idea of 'active ageing' is constraining in complex ways. My study of leisure in later life focuses on exploring leisure lives in deep context, not just the present social environment, but with a long arm view, because context is important (Crouch, 2000, 2012, 2014). I have found the missing voice of the TV watching 'passive' ager, not the sick or frail or vulnerable or transitioning ager, just the ordinary every-day one. The quiet majority.

7.3   Contribution to Knowledge

I would characterise my original contribution as a modest development in Leisure Constraints Theory, developing understanding of the complexity of disapproval (interpersonal constraint) and "*attitudes concerning the appropriateness of certain activities*" (Crawford & Godbey, 1987, p. 124) (structural constraint) on later leisure lives, thus troubling ideas of separate levels of interpersonal and structural constraints. I have also made a small methodological contribution in demonstrating that Mass Observation Archive offer additional voices for the study of leisure in the context of everyday life, and demonstrated that it is possible to conduct a study of later life leisure that gets beyond the noisy concepts of death and disability and 'age induced constraints' that direct much leisure in later life research.

I made research choices based on what spoke more to the questions, and helped to better explain the data, and thematic analysis of narrative did that. I was very concerned to demonstrate impartiality in the way that I selected correspondents. The result was a diverse group, and the development of a method of sampling from the Mass Observation Project. I am conscious that in focusing on the sampling I may look like I am taking some elements of a realist stance. But the research I produce has an audience, who have already asked me about selection of my correspondents at conferences, they work in different ways, and apply those standards broadly. So, I am not just speaking to the questions, I am also speaking to other researchers.

The work the preface was based upon was disseminated in a journal article (York & Wiseman, 2012) and a book chapter (Wiseman & Sadlo, 2015). Work from the early stages of the Ph.D. includes a journal article about garden visiting and book chapter about rambling (Finnie et al.,

2017; Leaver & Wiseman, 2016). This early work certainly has an instrumental health focus, so the critical active ageing perspective truly was grounded in the stories from the archive, and developed through conference presentations in both leisure studies and the Mass Observation Archive communities of practice.

During the development of this research the research questions were answered, though as outlined in the following section, further work would support the development of this research area to its full potential, and secondary findings unveiled another research agenda. I found that the demographic research in the background chapter would not predict the situations of the correspondents. This is an area for further research, the narrative slopes of decline, the long arm influence, which are all lovely and clear in the demographic research are not so clear here, I am troubled by the impact of an individual's history and inequality and cultural capital being used in predictions. I am not sure that we are using good enough measures to be able to accurately speak about socioeconomic status across a long life, or healthy life expectancy, partly because these are individualised, and that is not how people live their lives. In addition, there is potential for social mobility in retirement through volunteering, which will be lost if people return to work, and this warrants further investigation. Grief and bereavement are not age-specific, like many of the experiences shared by the correspondents it is important that we stop conflating being alone with loneliness, and confusing grief with both. Grief is expressed in three stories through acts of remembrance involving previously shared leisure, a pleasant couple of hours in good company brings some respite.

This research has profoundly affected me, both in the process of managing the complexity of the ideas, and in the writing and sharing of those ideas. The implications have unfolded, and I anticipate more to come. The findings have impact for my family's leisure life, they have initiated a paradigm shift from I to us. I no longer have a leisure life of my own to write about, I have acknowledged it as shared. I have gone native at the archive and native in narrative, and social in my understanding of leisure lives. The process of transcription brought me close to the stories and raised unanticipated ethical issues. During the process of transcription, I became sad and anxious, and fell a little bit in love with the correspondents and their 26 unique lives. There were 26 lifetimes of joy, love, death, loss and triumph. There were surprises from the first to the last; they appeared to be oblivious to the demographic studies that would have them passed away 30 years earlier. They did not know that their early life of privilege should have given them extra years of health. No one told them that being a sick child should have limited their adventures. They were just doing their thing. The overwhelming unpredictability of life was alarming, and it made me realise why I love a good story. In reading and writing we can defy gravity, centuries of oppression and even time. The wonderful thing about stories is no matter how hard we wish it to be different, the star crossed lovers always die and Jurassic park always ends in 'the running and the screaming'. The certainty of a written narrative soothes the savage heart, takes the unpredictability of life away briefly. In our consumption of fiction, we queue up to defy chance and exchange it for a bitter certainty. In the creation of our own stories we are constrained by the days we expect and the stories that we know. Accessing this different range of stories during this research process has shown my family different plots, more fun, connected and unpredictable ways to grow old together, and we plan to try some of them.

If time allowed I would start again with the analysis, I would take a genealogical Foucauldian approach following Tamboukou (2013, 2017). Having done the research forwards, I now find looking backwards that there is a more coherent story to tell about my research. I started at an emancipatory level, I did not know how powerful the correspondents were, how they played with power, made space to resist and exercise freedom and pursue their interests (Tamboukou, 2013). If I had taken this approach, I could have traced the idea of active ageing to see how it evolved. Now I know, that this would have been a rich approach, so this would be a good thing to recommend for further research, taking this position from the start that I have only just come to.

7.4   Plans for Further Research

The correspondence in this dissertation did not highlight transitions over the two years of diaries, but further following of these correspondents is underway to extend the study to a longitudinal view. I intend to analyse leisure practices and meanings in these contemporaneous day diaries for as long as I can. I see already how Brenda's attitude to active ageing has become more cynical in 2018, as virtuous friends pass away, and her TV watching husband continues to thrive.

The participants all indicate identifying as heterosexual, and that is skewed. I plan to purposively sample and co-opt some more diverse participants, starting with Dennis from my initial study, who has recently found a new love.

Sex was mentioned once by the 26 in all of their correspondence, by Sophie, after a fractious day, and it was '*No sex!*'. However, there is a directive in the archive that asks about sex, and many of the correspondents in my research group have answered it, they have a lot to say about sex, but only when directly asked. I am not sure it is a truly social theory of leisure in later life with no sex.

7.5   Further Research Suggestions

Now the individual neoliberal active ager is a troubled idea, and the intrapersonal, interpersonal and structural constraints are less distinct, it is time to think again about a Leisure Constraints Model that can deal with more than measuring behaviours.

Further research is indicated to explore more 'passive' later leisure lives, specific to other times and places. The Mass Observation Archive spreads from 1936 to 1960s and 1981–present. Comparative studies would help trace the genealogy and interpretation of these ideas of passive and active leisure and competing metanarratives about ageing in the UK.

There is a case for a follow-up study 15–20 years on from Gibson et al. (2003), what is now known, what has changed in relation to the dominance of leisure in retirement and how that relates to an active ageing and return to work agenda. Asking what has changed and what has stayed the same in the permanent retirement holiday in Florida, has it become snowbirding, or does it still exist?

Engagement across social difference is a key part of how sociologists have conceptualised conviviality as part of social comfort (Jones et al., 2015; Neal & Vincent, 2013), my study highlights a lack of diverse interactions in an otherwise very sociable life this is suggested as an area for further study.

Differing work and leisure ethics in later life has implications for intergenerational family cohesion and later life divorce. There is a powerful longitudinal research project on later life estrangement and divorce waiting in the Mass Observation Archive for someone with the patience to find the stories.

References

Crawford, D. W., & Godbey, G. (1987). Reconceptualizing barriers to family leisure. *Leisure Sciences, 9*(2), 119–127.

Crouch, D. (2000). Places around us: Embodied lay geographies in leisure and tourism. *Leisure Studies* (December 2012), 37–41.

Crouch, D. (2012). Ordinary lives: Studies in the everyday. *Leisure Studies, 31*(2), 255–256.

Crouch, D. (2014). *The hope of leisure, the leisure of hope*. Retrieved January 3, 2015, from https://leisurestudiesblog.wordpress.com/2014/11/04/the-hope-of-leisure-the-leisure-of-hope.

Finnie, K., Wiseman, T., & Ravenscroft, N. (2017). Rambling on: Exploring the complexity of walking as a meaningful activity. In M. C. Hall, R. Yael, & N. Shoval (Eds.), *The Routledge international handbook of walking* (pp. 253–263). Routledge.

Gibson, H., Ashton-Shaeffer, C., Green, J., & Autry, C. (2003). Leisure in the lives of retirement-aged women: Conversations about leisure and life. *Leisure/Loisir, 28*(3–4), 203–230.

Goffman, E. (1959). *The presentaion of self in everyday life*. Penguin Books Ltd.

Jones, H., Neal, S., Mohan, G., Connell, K., Cochrane, A., & Bennett, K. (2015). Urban multiculture and everyday encounters in semi-public, franchised cafe spaces. *Sociological Review, 63*(3), 644–661.

Jun, J., & Kyle, G. (2011). The effect of identity conflict/facilitation on the experience of constraints to leisure and constraint negotiation. *Journal of Leisure Research, 43*(2), 176–204.

Kusumastuti, S., Derks, M. G. M., Tellier, S., Di Nucci, E., Lund, R., Mortensen, E. L., & Westendorp, R. G. J. (2016). Successful ageing: A study of the literature using citation network analysis. *Maturitas, 93*, 4–12.

Leaver, R., & Wiseman, T. (2016). Garden visiting as a meaningful occupation for people in later life. *British Journal of Occupational Therapy, 79*(12), 768–775.

Lyotard, J.-F. (1984). *The postmodern condition: A report on knowledge*. Manchester University Press.

Neal, S., & Vincent, C. (2013). Multiculture, middle class competencies and friendship practices in super-diverse geographies. *Social and Cultural Geography, 14*(8), 909–929.

Phoenix, C., & Bell, S. L. (2018, March). Beyond "Move More": Feeling the Rhythms of physical activity in mid and later-life. *Social Science and Medicine, 231*, 47–54.

Pollen, A. (2013). Research methodology in mass observation past and present: 'Scientifically, about as valuable as a chimpanzee's tea party at the zoo'?. *History Workshop Journal, 75*(1), 213–235.

Riessman, C. K. (2008). *Narrative methods for the human sciences* (2nd ed.). Sage.

Sheridan, D. (2000, December). Reviewing mass-observation: The archive and its researchers thirty years on. *Forum Qualitative Social Research, 1*(3), Article 26.

Smart, C. (2011). Families, secrets and memories. *Sociology, 45*(4), 539–553.

Tamboukou, M. (2013). A Foucauldian approach to narratives. In M. Andrews, C. Squire, & M. Tamboukou (Eds.), *Doing narrative research* (2nd ed., pp. 103–121). Sage.

Tamboukou, M. (2017, April). Reassembling documents of life in the archive. *European Journal of Life Writing, 6*, 1–19. https://doi.org/10.5463/ejlw.6.215.

Wiseman, T., & Sadlo, G. (2015). Gardening: An occupation for recovery and wellness. In *International handbook of occupational therapy interventions* (2nd ed.).

York, M., & Wiseman, T. (2012). Gardening as an occupation: A critical review. *British Journal of Occupational Therapy, 75*(2), 76–84.

Index